Rescue by breeches buoy.

The U.S. Life-Saving Service

Heroes, Rescues and Architecture of the Early Coast Guard

Ralph Shanks

Wick York

Lisa Woo Shanks, editor

Rescue by surfboat.

Costaño Books
P.O. Box 355
Petaluma, CA 95953

email: CostanoBooks@att.net

Books by Ralph and Lisa Shanks

Guardians of the Golden Gate: Lighthouses & Lifeboat Stations of San Francisco Bay

North American Indian Travel Guide

Library of Congress Catalog Card Number: 95-092424

ISBN: 0-930268-16-4 (softcover edition)

ISBN: 0-930268-15-6 (hardcover edition)

Publisher's Catalog in Publication
(Prepared by Quality Books, Inc.)

Shanks, Ralph C.
        U.S. Life-Saving Service : Heroes, Rescues & Architecture of the
Early Coast Guard / Ralph Shanks, Wick York; Lisa Woo Shanks,
editor. — Petaluma, CA: Costaño Books, 1996.
p. cm.
Includes biographical references.
ISBN 0-930268-16-4 (softcover)
ISBN 0-930268-15-6 (hardcover)

1. United States. Life-Saving Service—History. 2. United
States. Coast Guard—History. 3. Life-Saving—United States—History. 4.
Life-saving stations—United States—History. I. York, Wick. II. Shanks, Lisa
Woo, ed. III Title

VK 1323.S43 1996 363.12'381'0973

QBI95-20340

A MESSAGE from J. REVELL CARR,
DIRECTOR and PRESIDENT of MYSTIC SEAPORT MUSEUM

The sea and the stories of those who venture out upon it create extraordinary drama and capture our imagination. Within the history of maritime endeavors few elements are more stirring than the heroics and pathos of disasters at sea and daring rescues. This book, for the first time, chronicles the history of the U.S. Life-Saving Service and examines the remarkable architecture that was a part of the service. The authors have brought together in one volume a comprehensive study of this fascinating organization which served this nation and the mariners along its shore so well.

Maritime historian Ralph Shanks has focused his study of over a quarter century on both lighthouses and life-saving activity and has published books and articles on these subjects. Best known for his work on the Coast Guard in California, he now addresses the national spectrum of activity of the Life-Saving Service. The reader can see all aspects of the profession from moments of crisis and courage to days and months of routine training. The organization and its antecedents are documented as a way of life of the men and women associated with the Service. The boats and equipment developed for the rescue operations are also thoroughly covered.

The exceptional architectural heritage of the Life-Saving Service is studied through the professional eye of Wick York who began his investigations while working on the restoration of the New Shoreham Life-Saving Station. This structure had been moved from Block Island, Rhode Island, where it had been threatened, to Mystic Seaport. He pursued this study through graduate school and beyond and here documents the range of architecture found in stations around the country as well as the architects who created these designs.

These two authorities have combined their talents to produce a work that will not only be an important academic contribution to the field of maritime history but also a book that will be intriguing to anyone with an interest in the sea or in American architecture.

Surfmen wearing cork life jackets pose proudly with their lifecar, surfboat and beach carts. Long Branch Life-Saving Station, New Jersey station number five, an 1875-type station. (U.S. Coast Guard Academy)

The 1876 Philadelphia Centennial Exposition Life-Saving Station. After the exposition, it became the Cape May Life-Saving Station guarding the New Jersey entrance to Delaware Bay. (U.S. Coast Guard Academy)

U.S. Life-Saving Service

Heroes, Rescues and Architecture of the Early Coast Guard

Table of Contents

Shipwreck at night. A fire lights up the night and gives hope to those on board that help is on the way. 1871. (Shanks collection)

Chapter 1
Introduction

THE LIFE-SAVING SERVICE

They were the greatest heroes of the American coast, routinely risking their lives in the grand maritime rescues. Their work was respected and honored by America's most prestigious leaders, celebrated in the most popular publications of their time and of deep interest to medical, educational, religious and political leaders. The Wright Brothers knew them well, poet Walt Whitman wrote of them, and the artist Winslow Homer painted them. But somehow America forgot these peaceful heroes. Yet anyone reading of their bravery today will always remember them. The Life-Saving Service answered that most basic of human questions, "Who will help in our hour of greatest need?"

The heritage of American life-saving is linked to China where the world's first organized life-saving service began.[1] China's Chinkiang Association for the Saving of Life was established in 1708 and was the first life-saving institution in the world.[2] The Chinese developed a complex and advanced series of manned life-saving stations using specially built boats and conventional junks with distinctively colored sails and special markings.

There were many other early life-saving organizations in China. Chinese benevolent societies sponsored privately owned lifeboats and paid volunteers on a per rescue basis. The Yangztse River region was the center for early life-saving development, particularly upstream from Shanghai at Chinkiang.[3]

Besides the work of the benevolent societies, there were Chinese life-saving services sponsored by the Imperial Chinese government and paid for through rice and land taxation. These life-saving stations were established by 1737 on the Min River and its tributaries and had at least five lifeboats in operation. Thus, the Chinese founded the two major forms of life-saving organization: government funded services and privately sponsored services.[4]

Chinese life-saving organizations were not an isolated development and they certainly influenced later rescue organizations. Major features incorporated in early European and American life-saving operations seem to have Chinese roots. The Dutch and English began limited life-saving in 1767 and 1774 respectively, although the British did not begin actual lifeboat operations until 1824. It is significant that both the British and the Dutch were deeply involved in Asia and had ample opportunity to observe Chinese lifeboat organizations. The British, at least, studied and recorded some of the history of Chinese life-saving. Early British organizations shared many traits with the Chinese services: volunteer crews paid on a per rescue basis, emphasis on restoring to life the apparently drowned, awards for heroism, specially designed and marked boats, and the role of benevolent societies in sponsorship. It seems hardly coincidental that all these features had been part of the Chinese life-saving system. Chinese practices were incorporated into British and early American systems, particularly into the Massachusetts Humane Society.[5]

The Imperial Chinese concept of government support for organized rescue operations paid for by taxation was the principle later adopted to fund both the U.S. Life-Saving Service and the U.S. Coast Guard. It seems likely that in an era of European imperialism and racism that the Chinese inventors were systematically denied the recognition due them. The significant fact is that the Chinese were the first to act responsibly and humanely by establishing the world's first sea rescue organizations.

Establishing rescue organizations for those in peril of the sea was one of the great humanitarian achievements of humankind. In China, Europe and America, the founding of life-saving organizations came to involve many of the most important and often most thoughtful people of the time. Emperors, kings, queens, presidents, educators, physicians, ship owners, social workers, clergy, authors, business leaders and scientists were all prominent in supporting, founding or operating early life-saving organizations. When England's famed maritime life-saving organization, the Royal National Lifeboat Institution (RNLI), was begun in 1824, humanitarian Sir William Hilary was the prime mover. The institution's founding meeting was presided over by the Archbishop of Canterbury (at that time Dr. Manners Sutton). His Majesty King George IV was the first patron and Prince Leopold and various dukes became vice-patrons. The Earl of Liverpool served as the first president and the great humanitarian and anti-slavery pioneer, William Wilberforce, was one of the opening speakers. In later years Queen Victoria added her support

to the RNLI.

The Duke of Northumberland especially must be credited for his interest in and sponsorship of early lifeboat development. Partly as a result of his early support, brilliant inventors and boat builders were drawn to the British institution and self-righting, self-bailing lifeboats with buoyancy compartments were perfected by the English. From England the life-saving values spread to America, especially to Boston.[6]

In May 1784 Dr. Mayes, a British physician, had arrived in Boston. He met with a number of distinguished Boston citizens and interested them in developing a society for restoring the apparently drowned to life. Dr. Mayes suggested that an American organization could be modeled after the existing British Royal Humane Society which was dedicated to life-saving. The result of these meetings was the founding in Boston of America's pioneering life-saving organization, the Massachusetts Humane Society

(more formally called, the Humane Society of the Commonwealth of Massachusetts). Its goal was saving not animal lives, but human lives.

The Massachusetts Humane Society evoked "a new realization of the necessity to become your brother's keeper." Its membership "represented the humanitarian, scientific and public-spirited interests of their community." Originally founded in 1785, it could soon count many of the most distinguished people of the time among its members or supporters. James Bowdoin, governor of Massachusetts and esteemed philosopher, was the Society's first president. Second Vice-President was Dr. John Warren, a founder of Harvard Medical School. Dr. Benjamin Waterhouse, another founder of Harvard Medical School was a Trustee. Paul Revere was a member, as was Dr. Samuel Adams. John Hancock endorsed the Society. Thomas Jefferson became quite interested in the Society's efforts to develop a suitable lifeboat and corresponded with

A line-carrying rocket is fired to a shipwreck, a lifecar rides on a wagon and a surfboat is about to be launched. Scene captures drama of the rescue. (Shanks collection)

the organization. President George Washington was an admirer of the Society and wrote the Massachusetts Humane Society that their "provision made for the shipwrecked mariners was highly estimable." The Society's publications were in Washington's personal library. Others active in the Society included prominent clergy, scientists, business leaders and humanitarians.[7]

The foundation of American maritime rescue work would be laid by the Massachusetts Humane Society. In 1787 the Society began constructing small huts as houses of refuge to provide shelter for shipwrecked mariners along the Massachusetts shore. If sailors or passengers could struggle ashore alive, they would find the little huts stocked with food, candles, tinderbox for making fire, kindling and fuel. These buildings could be a godsend for mariners cast upon isolated shores during harsh New England winters. The house of refuge on Lovell's Island off Boston had the distinction of being the first life-saving structure

in American history.

The huts, also called Humane Houses or Charity Houses, did save lives but they were largely unattended and theft and vandalism became major problems. Provisions were often stolen or eaten by mice and maintenance was a problem. Responsible local people were delegated to watch over the huts but the lonely little houses were vulnerable. Mariners sometimes arrived only to find them gutted of all supplies. Worst, the huts had no boat to aid those trying to reach the shore.

In 1803 the Society began investigating the possibility of using lifeboats for life-saving. The British had been developing lifeboats and their potential value was obvious. William Raymond of Nantucket was commissioned to build a lifeboat and in October 1807 the vessel was completed. The first American lifeboat was a 30-foot long whaleboat rowed by ten men and guided by steering oars. The Humane Society both launched America's first life-

Breeches buoy rescue of the steamship Pliny *at Deal Beach, New Jersey in 1882. Among those saved by breeches buoy were ten children, one of whom is shown coming ashore in the charming illustration at lower left. Surfmen from Deal, Shark River and Long Branch Life-Saving Stations saved everyone on board. (Shanks collection)*

Rare photo believed to be a Massachusetts Humane Society House of Refuge. Also called Humane Houses or Charity Houses, these unmanned structures pre-dated true life-saving stations. Mariners had to struggle ashore unassisted, but once at a house of refuge found food and shelter. This building was similar to a House of Refuge shown on an 1852 Massachusetts Humane Society trustee's medal.

In later years this House of Refuge seems to have served as a Halfway House for surfmen on beach patrol. Halfway Houses were placed halfway between two stations so the USLSS surfmen could meet at the far end of their respective patrols to exchange "checks" (small badges) which proved they had completed their patrol. This structure looks like a typical Halfway House but has a chimney of the type used in the Massachusetts Humane Society Houses of Refuge. Halfway Houses did not normally have chimneys. (Richard Boonisar)

The Massachusetts Humane Society established the first life-saving stations in America. In front of the station is the surfboat and beach cart with line throwing Hunt gun. (Richard Boonisar)

boat and established America's first lifeboat station in 1807 at Cohasset, Massachusetts southeast of Boston.

Additional lifeboat stations and boats were placed along the Massachusetts coast. From 1807 through 1871, the Massachusetts Humane Society experienced its "golden age." Little lifeboat houses, typically twenty feet long, eight feet wide, shingled on top and battened on the sides were built to shelter the boats and equipment. The lifeboat stations were typically supplied with boats, rafts, line throwing mortars and other equipment. By 1872 the system had grown to comprise 76 lifeboat stations plus eight of the old huts of refuge which were then still in use. Volunteer lifeboat crews manned the boats, a person was placed in charge of the station, crews were paid for rescues, medals were awarded and some additional financial assistance was provided sporadically by the state of Massachusetts and by the Federal government.

Many daring rescues were conducted by the Massachusetts Humane Society's surfmen and numerous lives were saved. The Society was a leader in life-saving boat development and, after its invention by Edward S. Hunt of Weymouth, Massachusetts in 1879, also pioneered the use of the Hunt gun for throwing lines to shipwrecks. The lifeboat houses gradually replaced the houses of refuge; the last hut in use was at Tom Never's Hill, Nantucket Island. Even after the U.S. Life-Saving Service was established, the Massachusetts Humane Society crews continued their rescues, often in cooperation with the Life-Saving Service crews.[8]

Despite its admirable achievements, the Massachusetts Humane Society's stations were confined to a single state. Thus, by 1848 Congressman William A. Newell of New Jersey, a physician, was strongly advocating government involvement in life-saving. Congressman Newell, as with so many advocates of improved life-saving, had witnessed at least one terrible shipwreck and was horrified by the nation's lack of preparedness outside Massachusetts. His appeals prevailed and appropriation passed into law on August 14, 1848 providing $10,000 for "surfboats, rockets, carronades (line throwing mortars), and other necessary apparatus for the better preservation of life and property from shipwrecks on the coast of New Jersey lying between Sandy Hook and Little Egg Harbor." All this was to be placed under the supervision of an officer of the Revenue Marine Corps (later called the Revenue Cutter Service and still later the U.S. Coast Guard).[9]

Revenue Marine Captain Douglass Ottinger was placed in charge of establishing the stations and equipment. Ottinger was hard working and keenly interested in life-saving. Captain Ottinger began by establishing eight stations extending from Sandy Hook south along the New Jersey shore. They were little wooden boathouses supplied with a metal surfboat, a lifecar, a mortar for firing lines, rockets, lanterns and support equipment. The boat-house key and a set of instructions were left with as trust-worthy a person as Ottinger could find.[10]

Dramatic events during the next year, 1850, demonstrated both the need for and the benefits of a formal Life-Saving Service. In January, the New Jersey coast was devastated by a great storm which wrecked many vessels. Among them was the *Ayrshire*. Thanks to the new government life-saving stations, the lifecar rescued 201 people, including many children. It was a good start for the new stations.[11]

But that same year the *Elizabeth* was wrecked on Long Island which as yet had no life-saving stations. Ten people were lost in the wreck, including the renowned author, scholar and feminist Margaret Fuller. Authors such as Ralph Waldo Emerson and the Alcott family were among the voices raised in calling for more and better life-saving services.[12]

Along with the growing number of Americans expressing moral outrage at the inadequate Congressional support for rescue work was an increasing economic voice expressing interest as well. Insurance underwriters and shipping companies were paying for losses of both vessels and valuable cargoes. Given the time-consuming transportation and communication systems of the day, there often was no responsible person on hand to look after the cargo after a wreck. This helped fuel the demand for responsible government representatives to be present after wrecks occurred. An expanded government life-saving system of paid employees would answer both the humanitarian and the economic problems.

During the period of 1849-55 more new stations were opened, nearly two-thirds in New Jersey and New York. The life-saving stations were small, garage-like structures manned by volunteers who were often unavailable when needed. The volunteers' stations soon fell into disrepair through neglect or even "by wanton destruction." Boats were taken for private use, repairs went undone and supplies were stolen. Despite praises sung about volunteerism, the results were a disaster.[13]

The problems were easy to identify. First, there were no paid crews. As a result, there was little or no training, drill or practice working together. No regulations were written to guide employees or set minimum standards. No reports or records were mandated so no one knew what was going on. Most of the stations remained in this defective and unorganized condition.[14]

The winter of 1870-71 was an infamous one. There were spectacular, well publicized fatal shipwrecks along the Atlantic coast and on the Great Lakes.[15] The terrible disasters once again outraged the public and forced Congress to take more realistic steps to address the problem of marine transportation safety. On April 20, 1871 Congress finally appropriated $200,000 to create a real life-saving system. The authorization included provisions allowing the Secretary of the Treasury to employ crews of paid surfmen at such stations as he deemed necessary and to build new stations where needed.[16]

The Treasury Department immediately detailed Revenue Marine Captain John Faunce to visit the stations. When Faunce submitted his report in August 1871 it showed that the deplorable condition of American life-saving had not been exaggerated. Captain Faunce "found that most of the stations were too remote from each other, and that many of the houses were much dilapidated, many being so far gone as to be worthless, and the remainder in need of extensive repairs and enlargement. With but few exceptions, (the stations) were in a filthy condition and gave every evidence of neglect and misuse. The (life-saving) apparatus was rusty for want of care, and some of it ruined by the depredations of vermin and malicious persons. Many of the most necessary (life-saving) articles were wanting…(and) such indispensable articles as powder, rockets, shot-lines, shovels, etc. were not to be found. At other stations not a portable item was to be found." Faunce also found many unfit volunteer keepers and crews. A highly skilled, dangerous occupation such as life-saving would require paid, professional crews in the United States.[17]

The man in charge of straightening out this mess was Sumner Increase Kimball and there was no finer choice for the job. Kimball was a Maine man, born September 2, 1834 in the town of Lebanon. He entered Bowdoin College at age sixteen and during his college years taught school in Maine and at Orleans, Massachusetts. He graduated from college and followed his father's career as a lawyer. Kimball entered politics by 1859 and was elected to the Maine state legislature as that body's youngest member. A year later, he moved to Boston and practiced law there until 1861. Then at the outbreak of the Civil War, he was appointed to a position in the Treasury Department by President Abraham Lincoln. Sumner Kimball found his most worthwhile work in government service. As a government worker, he was well-organized, efficient, honest, opposed to special interest manipulation of government agencies, highly intelligent, and deeply caring—the ideal government employee.

In 1871 the Revenue Marine Bureau was reestablished by Secretary of the Treasury George S. Boutwell and Kimball became head of both life-saving stations and revenue cutters (later called Coast Guard cutters). As chief of the Revenue Marine Bureau, Kimball was head of what would later be the modern Coast Guard. In a few short years, he would distinguish himself by laying the foundation for what would become the U.S. Coast Guard Academy. He had the rare ability to generate political support for his improvements and yet remain above partisanship. He became one of the most respected government administrators in U.S. history.[18]

Kimball's deepest interest and lasting contribution was in life-saving. Sumner Kimball understood the sociological fact that dynamic beliefs can motivate people. He be-

Surfboats were hand launched into often treacherous surf. (U.S. Coast Guard)

The challenge of the surf is evident as the Life-Saving Service sets out for the stranded Atlantic liner Prinzess Irene *off Long Island, New York. April 1911. (Fire Island National Seashore)*

Surfmen braving a series of breakers as they face the sea in their lifeboat. Coquille River Life-Saving Station, Oregon. (National Maritime Museum)

lieved there was a vital message to spread—that saving lives and property at sea was right and good and that to do so required a first class, paid professional organization of well managed life-savers. These were controversial concepts at the time.

Kimball would dedicate the rest of his long and active life to his goal of a model government life-saving service. He was concerned with acquiring quality personnel, building new stations nationwide and improving rescue equipment. Kimball understood public relations skills and the need for human decency in an era dominated by "robber baron" business leaders. He would become the first and only head of the U.S. Life-Saving Service, serving as head of all government life-saving stations beginning in 1871. In 1878, President Rutherford B. Hayes officially nominated Kimball to be General Superintendent of the newly formalized U.S. Life-Saving Service and, in a rare action, the U.S. Senate unanimously approved him.

When Kimball assumed responsibility for life-saving stations he found that "before 1871 there was probably no other arm of the public service so little held in esteem, as there was none more withered and feeble…(and) its existence a thin line of weather-broken huts upon the

Classic scene of surfmen setting out to the rescue. This is the ship Alice, *wrecked at Ocean Park, Washington in January 1909. Klipsan Beach Life-Saving crew mans the surfboat. (San Francisco National Maritime Museum)*

Keeper Joshua James (in dark uniform) and his surfmen at Point Allerton Life-Saving Station at Hull, Massachusetts. Joshua James served as keeper until age seventy-four. Note that three surfmen hold Coston signals in their hands.

beaches of Long Island and New Jersey—huts scantily furnished with poor equipment and only one of every two provided with men."[19] Historian Stephen H. Evans added that "between 1854 and 1871 the life-saving system turned out to be no system at all." By the mid-1870s Kimball began to show what he could achieve.[20]

One of Kimball's first actions was to hire William D. O'Conner as assistant to the General Superintendent. O'Conner was an exceptionally talented journalist of high moral standards and superb credentials. O'Conner cared about people, having once been fired by a national magazine for writing in support of John Brown's actions toward the abolition of slavery. The poet Walt Whitman was among his literary friends. William O'Conner's lasting contribution was to write vividly and eloquently about the Life-Saving Service's rescues. Without his writing skills, winning the support of elected officials and the public would have been much more difficult. O'Conner was followed by other writers, but his style of filling each *Annual Report of the U.S. Life-Saving Service* with thrilling shipwreck accounts permanently set the style of the USLSS's bid for public support. The *Annual Report's* were distributed to selected individuals and institutions and they and the press were effective in spreading information about Sumner Kimball's remarkable Life-Saving Service.

In Kimball the nation had the right person for the job and finally the political will to spend the necessary tax money to deal with the deficiencies. His initial steps showed that he was quite serious about improving the American life-saving system. He ordered incompetent station keepers fired and replaced with qualified men. New crews were required at nearly all the stations and these were selected. Written regulations were provided to guide employees. Stations were repaired and new equipment brought in. New and larger stations were built with room for paid live-in crews. Not all stations would have paid crews yet, but all would have a full time paid keeper.

The new stations were immediately effective. The best demonstration of success was to compare the life-saving rates of the old, disorganized volunteer system and the new, well managed organization with paid crews. There was an astounding 87.5% decrease in shipwreck deaths within the areas covered by the Life-Saving Service.[21]

Kimball served as head of the Life-Saving Service from the day it was formed until the day it ended in 1915. For the five succeeding years he was head of the board which investigated and selected new life-saving equipment. He contributed 59 years of dedicated public service and lived until 1923, dying just short of age ninety.[22] The story of Sumner Kimball's life-saving crews is one of the most exciting in American history.

An early Life-Saving Service crew in New Jersey with surfboat and beach cart. Surfmen had to harness themselves to their beach cart and pull its heavy load of equipment to wrecks. (Richard Boonisar)

Surfmen were generally men of good character and courage. They risked their lives to save strangers of all nationalities. Young surfman at Umpqua River Life-Saving Station, Oregon. (Coast Guard Museum Northwest)

Chapter 2
Launching the Life-Saving Service

"Remarkable agitation" in favor of the bill to establish the Life-Saving Service swept along the coasts and the Great Lakes by 1878. There had been an upwelling of public support among intellectuals, coastal citizens, merchants and shipping interests. It was a broad coalition of Americans tired of tragic shipwrecks going unassisted. On June 18, 1878 the Act to Organize the Life-Saving Service became a reality.[1] The bill establishing the Life-Saving Service was passed by a unanimous Congressional vote and signed into law.[2]

The Life-Saving Service was now an agency of the Treasury Department. Sumner Kimball, the head of the Revenue Marine, had chosen to lead the life-saving stations rather than the revenue cutters. Best of all, the Life-Saving Service was to be designed and managed by the most capable civilian leader in Coast Guard history.[3] Only George R. Putnam of the Lighthouse Service would achieve a long term stature rivaling that of Kimball.

Kimball began by organizing the new United States Life-Saving Service (USLSS) into districts. Although the numbers and boundaries of districts varied over the years, ultimately there would be thirteen districts. Station lists in this book are based on the 1914 *Register of the United States Life-Saving Service*, the final official station list.[4] The districts ultimately were as follows:

Sumner Increase Kimball was General Superintendent of the Life-Saving Service during its entire existence. He is shown at his desk in Washington. (U.S. Coast Guard Academy)

First District	Maine and New Hampshire, 15 stations
Second District	Massachusetts, 32 stations
Third District	Rhode Island & Fishers Island, NY, 10 stations
Fourth District	Long Island, New York, 30 stations
Fifth District	New Jersey, 41 stations
Sixth District	Delaware, Maryland and Virginia north of Chesapeake Bay, 19 stations
Seventh District	North Carolina and Virginia south of Chesapeake Bay, 34 stations
Eighth District	South Carolina and Eastern Florida, 1 station and 8 houses of refuge
Ninth District	Gulf Coast, 8 stations
Tenth District	Lakes Erie & Ontario and Louisville, KY, 12 stations
Eleventh District	Lakes Huron and Superior, 19 stations
Twelfth District	Lake Michigan, 31 stations
Thirteenth District	Pacific Coast, 19 stations

Classic 1870s era life-saving station. Lifecar is in front of the entrance, surfmen man the beach cart at center and surfboat at right. Surfside Life-Saving Station, Nantucket Island, Massachusetts, an 1874-type station. A replica of this station serves as the Nantucket Life-Saving Museum, an outstanding place to visit. (Nantucket Historical Association)

Lifeboat Station with surfmen and lifeboat. By early 1880s the lifeboat stations became fully equipped and manned and from then on were classified as life-saving stations. Manistee Life-Saving Station, Michigan. (Manistee County Historical Museum)

Florida's Houses of Refuge were unique in the Life-Saving Service. Unlike other stations, they had no surfmen and no rescue boats. A keeper and his family did all the rescue work at a House of Refuge. Fort Lauderdale House of Refuge, Florida. (U.S. Coast Guard)

THE PEOPLE

All personnel were under Sumner Kimball, the **General Superintendent** of the Life-Saving Service. Kimball's office was in Washington, D.C. where he was aided by an assistant general superintendent, an inspector of life-saving stations, clerks, an engineer, a topographer-hydrographer and a draftsman. A Board of Life-Saving Appliances worked under Kimball to investigate and test new equipment for possible use by the USLSS. The Board was the vital research and development arm of the USLSS.[5]

The **Assistant General Superintendent** filled in whenever the general superintendent was away, wrote the annual reports, assisted in public relations and acted somewhat as vice-president of the organization. Unlike the Washington based USLSS officials, the **Inspector of Life-Saving Stations** was stationed in New York City. He was a Revenue Cutter officer whose major tasks were to periodically inspect life-saving stations and arrange for contracts, repair work, purchases and deliveries. Nearly all the Service's self-righting and self-bailing lifeboats were built in New York state and many items purchased by the USLSS were obtained in New York City. The inspector and his assistants also oversaw USLSS storehouses at New York City, San Francisco and Grand Haven, Michigan.[6]

Every life-saving district had both a district superintendent and an assistant inspector.[7] Thus, the Life-Saving Service had two chains of command reporting directly to Sumner Kimball. The district superintendents were a civilian line while the assistant inspectors were a military line.

The civilian **District Superintendents** had awesome responsibilities. When possible they would go to wreck scenes even in terrible weather and help direct the rescue work, a dangerous task.[8] Additionally they served as paymasters and disbursing officers. They were inspectors of customs who made certain that salvaged property was properly handled and duties collected. They conducted the business of the stations, requisitioned supplies, oversaw repairs and the like. They visited all stations at least quarterly and some more often. Visits were conducted even during terrible weather and the trips were often difficult and exhausting. There were only thirteen district superintendents active at any one time, yet in the course of the USLSS's history one district superintendent drowned while making a tour of stations and seven more died "from disease contracted in the line of duty." Because of their endless travel to remote stations, the district superintendents' job was second only to that of keepers and surfmen for its hazards.[9]

The **Assistant Inspectors** were all military officers detailed from the Revenue Cutter Service. Each was assigned to a district. At first these officers made monthly visits to stations, but as the USLSS grew in size their visits became quarterly. On his first tour after the seasonal opening of the stations, the assistant inspector examined the keeper and crew and dismissed any physically, mentally or morally unqualified personnel. Upon each succeeding visit he would similarly exam any new employees. When shipwrecks occurred with loss of life he went to the sta-

The 1855-type Long Branch Life-Saving station in New Jersey. Note the simple design and lack of windows. Inside doorway is a surfboat and mortar. (Photographic Archives of the Monmouth County Historical Association)

tion to investigate and determine if the rescue had been properly conducted.[10]

Keepers were the commanding officers of the individual stations. **Surfmen** were the crew members at the stations.

THE STATIONS

For a brief time keepers commanded three types of stations, but these quickly evolved into two basic station types. In 1873, the Secretary of the Treasury had designated a commission to study establishing stations. With savings in mind, the commission had recommended that three types of stations be built: life-saving stations, houses of refuge and lifeboat stations.[11] Life-saving stations and houses of refuge became the standard station types.

Life-saving stations were designed to house paid crews with surfboats, a classic American life-saving approach. Life-saving stations initially were built primarily on the Atlantic Coast, but were soon standard everywhere except the Florida east coast. Some life-saving stations eventually were equipped with lifeboats as well as surfboats.[12]

Houses of refuge were built solely along Florida's east coast where mariners generally could reach shore without aid. The concept was a specially designed house where mariners, once ashore, could find water, food, cots and shelter. The idea was obviously borrowed from the Massachusetts Humane Society, but the Life-Saving Service improved upon the concept by employing a year-round keeper to supervise the facility. At houses of refuge only a keeper and his family were in residence and no surfmen or rescue boats were provided. Signposts were

placed along the then lonely Florida beaches directing mariners to the nearest House of Refuge.[13]

Lifeboat stations were to be built on the British system of using volunteer crews and large lifeboats. The lifeboat stations were to be built on the Great Lakes, Pacific Coast and on the Atlantic Coast between Cape Henlopen, Delaware, and Cape Charles, Virginia. Volunteer-manned lifeboat stations proved unrealistic on the sparsely populated American coast and these stations were soon converted to life-saving stations. The distinction between life-saving stations and lifeboat stations completely broke down in a few years since lifeboat stations were found to need paid crews, too. Some life-saving stations also received lifeboats in addition to the usual surfboat, further blurring the distinctions. Most importantly, the lifeboat stations got both paid crews and surfboats which ended any real difference between lifeboat stations and life-saving stations in the USLSS.[14]

For the rest of the history of the Life-Saving Service, life-saving stations and houses of refuge were the only station types.[15] The concept of a lifeboat station, in a new sense of a motor lifeboat station, would be revived by the Coast Guard after 1915.[16]

Both life-saving stations and houses of refuge were repeatedly threatened by the wind and sea. The Life-Saving Service was constantly experiencing sea encroachment on the Atlantic Coast forcing stations to be moved back from the beach. Sometimes the ocean would then reverse itself and build up the beach, leaving a station far inland. The Life-Saving Service realized it could never withstand the sea so it made its stations moveable. If the beach went one way, the station could be moved along with it. Build-

District Superintendent Thomas J. Blakeney was responsible for the entire Pacific Coast, the largest Life-Saving Service District in America. (Shanks collection)

ing wooden structures gave the Life-Saving Service a freedom of movement that its sister agency, the Lighthouse Service, lacked. While the Lighthouse Service lost some of its finest lighthouses to the sea, in contrast the Life-Saving Service could usually save its stations by moving them. Some stations were even barged to new locations, although one station was lost at sea. Far Rockaway station in New York was "destroyed by sudden gale while being moved across the water to a new site" about 1891.[17]

Life-saving stations were constantly challenged by the sea. In 1877 Jones Beach station on Long Island was hit by a storm that forced abandonment of the building and sent the crew fleeing. The sea tore the station from its foundations and began to carry it away. Surfmen literally had to anchor their station like a ship so it wouldn't float away. In October 1886 a hurricane produced the highest Atlantic tide in a quarter century, flattened telephone lines and damaged a dozen stations between Cape Hatteras, North Carolina and New Jersey. At Oregon Inlet, North Carolina, "no person could safely venture outside the buildings" and the life-saving crew fled in their boat, rowing inland to safety. At Virginia's Cobb Island Station, almost the entire island was submerged and local inhabitants crowded into the station for safety. Sometimes crews remained in their station until the hurricane floods almost covered the building, then the surfmen would row out through their station doors at the last possible moment, ducking their heads as they barely cleared the portal. Such

situations were among "the most annoying difficulties which beset" the Service.[18]

There were other station problems as well. Arson occurred at stations at such diverse places as Virginia, North Carolina, upstate New York and at Bolinas Bay, California. The Bolinas Bay incident was particularly disturbing because the accused arsonist was a former station keeper.[19]

Even getting appropriations from a Congress often blindly opposed to public services was an ordeal. The Life-Saving Service fought an endless battle to convince Congress to spend the money needed to establish new life-saving stations. Members of Congress were forever blocking needed funding. When the money finally arrived, usually only after some dramatic shipwreck had occurred to arouse the public, the Life-Saving Service then faced the task of acquiring the land.[20]

Most commonly the government simply purchased the desired property. But land acquisition for stations ranged from wonderfully easy to a nightmare. Life-saving stations were usually welcomed as a great humanitarian improvement. In the best case, compassionate citizens, local governments or businesses donated land to the federal government to build a station. Some Atlantic Coast and Great Lakes communities seemed especially generous in donating station sites. In contrast, perhaps the worst case of private greed occurred in southern California. The Point Conception station, authorized in 1874, was listed in the *Annual Reports* as "not yet built" for years.[21] The Life-Saving Service repeatedly attempted to buy land for Point Conception Life-Saving Station. Negotiations with the large landowners failed and finally the USLSS gave up. Shipwrecks continued in the Point Conception area with no help available other than a distant U.S. revenue cutter and southern California never received a U.S. Life-Saving Station. The continued loss of lives and vessels illustrated what happened when establishment of a life-saving station was blocked. The most dramatic incident occurred one night in 1923 when seven U.S. Navy destroyers ran aground at nearby Point Arguello and even then the station still was not built. It would not be until 1936 that the Coast Guard finally was able to build its Point Arguello Lifeboat Station and protect the Point Conception area.[22]

Despite all, by the end of the Life-Saving Service in 1914-15 there were 279 life-saving stations in the United States, an all time high for the USLSS. They ranged from the northeast at Quoddy Head Life-Saving Station at Lubec, Maine to the southwest at Southside Life-Saving Station in San Francisco. They stretched from the southeast at Biscayne Bay House of Refuge at Miami Beach, northwest to Alaska's Nome Life-Saving Station. What the station crews endured is one of the most amazing and inspiring stories in American history.[23]

White Head Life-Saving Station was built on "Maine's stern and rockbound coast." The crew of this 1874-type station stand beside their surfboat. Note the X-shaped braces on end walls, a distinctive feature of the 1874-type. (Richard Boonisar)

Classic Maine scene. Cape Elizabeth Life-Saving Station with lobster traps and surfboats. Built in 1887 this station was one-of-a-kind. (U.S. Coast Guard)

Chapter 3

Maine and New Hampshire

THE LIFE-SAVING STATIONS IN MAINE AND NEW HAMPSHIRE

The First District of the Life-Saving Service covered a coastline of 241 miles and by 1914 had 12 stations in Maine and three in New Hampshire. The stations were "located at the most dangerous points on the coast of Maine and New Hampshire (which abounds) with rugged headlands, islets, rocks, reefs, and intricate channels."[1] The *Atlantic Coast Pilot* warned that, "wrecks have occurred on practically all of the off lying islands and rocks between Portland and Machias Bay, most of them in thick weather, either fog or snow."[2]

Maine's coast is unusually jagged with long, narrow glacially formed valleys and numerous narrow bays. Maine and New Hampshire's life-saving stations were built at the extremities of these coastal headlands or islands.[3]

Maine and New Hampshire surfmen were generally employed during the annual "active season" from August 1 to May 31. As at other northeastern U.S. life-saving stations, an additional surfman called "the winter man" was typically added to the crew from December 1 to April 30 (dates varied slightly over the years). A winter man meant there was an extra person to replace off duty or ill crew members, stand extra patrols during the longer nights of increased darkness and to be at the station when surfmen returned with survivors.[4] Most First District stations had a keeper, six regular surfmen plus a winter man.[5] Yet when the active season ended, shipwrecks continued. Even June and July could bring foul weather and danger.

The *Edward W. Schmidt* was a three masted schooner built at Bath, Maine, in 1881. She cleared Saco, Maine, on Monday, July 12, 1897 with a crew of seven on board, bound for the Kennebec River port of Richmond, Maine to take on a cargo of ice. In the days before refrigeration it was common to ship ice from northern states south to provide cold storage. Shortly after midnight the *Schmidt* came to anchor on the inside of Pond Island Bar, off Popham Beach at the Kennebec River mouth. A light breeze was then blowing, but a heavy fog had set in and the *Schmidt's* captain decided to wait until morning for a tug to tow his vessel upstream.[6]

When morning broke, the wind was blowing shoreward with increased intensity. Then the fog lifted and those on shore could see that the bar at the harbor entrance was already breaking. The *Edward W. Schmidt's* captain had anchored close to the jagged rocks off Pond Island.

Hunniwells Beach Life-Saving Station Keeper Z. H. Spinney anxiously watched the *Schmidt*. He could also see another schooner at anchor, the *Horace G. Morse*, but she had chosen a much safer location than the *Schmidt*. The active season was over and Keeper Spinney had no crew on hand. He seemed especially worried today.

F.H. Hodgkins, Hunniwells Beach station's Number One surfman, could also see that the weather was turning worse. Although off duty since the active season was over, Surfman Hodgkins rowed out in a small boat to offer to help the *Horace G. Morse* by piloting her to safety. The captain of the *Horace G. Morse* declined his offer. While the captains of both schooners apparently were not yet worried, the surfman knew that the ships could not remain in their present positions. Surfman Hodgkins could not get near the *Schmidt* because the breakers in her vicinity had become so large. No signal for assistance was given by the *Schmidt* and the surfman returned to shore.

Two tugs now arrived, having steamed down from Bath. They, too, saw no signal displayed for assistance. Consequently, the tugs both came about and proceeded homeward. The schooners kept their places all day, vainly expecting conditions to improve. The *Schmidt* labored heavily and had to drop a second anchor to hold its position. Additional heavy anchor chain was also let out, in the hope that it would help hold her but this only moved the *Schmidt* closer to the rocks. The ships remained in this perilous position throughout that night. Again, no signal for help was given.

The next morning broke with a full gale blowing from the south. The conditions "revealed to all observers the fact that the *Schmidt* was in the midst of extreme peril from which there was hardly a reasonable hope that she could escape. The bar was white with breaking seas, while the schooner plunged and rolled with such force that it seemed impossible for her anchors to hold, or her chains not to give way under the terrible strain upon them."[7]

As the sun rose, Keeper Spinney stood watching.

Breakers higher than a surfman's head do not stop a Life-Saving Service crew from launching their surfboat.

Surfmen bringing survivors ashore from a sinking sailing vessel, in their surfboat . (U.S. Coast Guard)

Quoddy Head Life-Saving Station at Lubec, Maine, was the eastern-most station in the Service. An 1874-style station. (Shanks collection)

Neither vessel had made any signal for aid, indicating that both masters felt they would have no trouble riding out the gale. Spinney knew better, but was powerless to assist the ships unless they asked for help. Both were taking a pounding, but were still afloat and the keeper couldn't force either captain to accept help. The local people on the beach commented that even if the tugs returned, the *Schmidt* was now in such a position that even they would "have found it extremely hazardous, if not impossible, to reach" her.

A little before noon Keeper Spinney suspected that the *Schmidt* might be starting to drag anchor. Spinney left the station and went to a hotel located on a point that would give him a cross view. Sure enough, the schooner was being blown toward Pound Island rocks.

That was it. Signal or no signal, the *Schmidt* was in trouble. Crew or no crew, Spinney was going to the rescue. He ran from the hotel back to Hunniwells Beach Life-Saving Station and raised the customary flag signal calling his off duty crew. Some of his men would be around and see he needed help. Spinney's two daughters also went off in the storm in search of surfmen.

Surfman Hodgkins was already on hand. Together the keeper and surfman placed their Lyle gun and faking box into the surfboat in case the *Schmidt* hit the rocks where a shore rescue would be necessary. Number Seven Surfman G.A. Oliver soon arrived and the three ran the surfboat down to the edge of the sea. They were still too shorthanded to man the surfboat.

As the Life-Saving Service men were putting on their cork life jackets, four volunteers arrived, two of them relatives of Surfman Oliver. A sufficient crew was now on hand and, although a vital twenty minutes had been lost rounding up a crew, the surfboat could finally be launched. Into the water she went and the rescuers began rowing down the stormy Kennebec River.

As they rowed through "heavy wind and sea," Keeper Spinney could see the *Schmidt* about a mile ahead. To make headway, Spinney steered his surfboat close to the beach to take advantage of an ebb tide to ease the task of rowing and make better speed. Time was running out for the schooner.

Then, looking ahead, Keeper Spinney saw the *Schmidt* suddenly roll over on her side. He urged his crew ahead. "Bending to their oars with all the energy at their command they reached the wreck in fifteen or twenty minutes."[8]

It was standard Life-Saving Service practice to try to approach a shipwreck on its lee side so the wreck would give the surfboat some protection from sea and wind. But in the case of the *Schmidt* there "were the spars, tangled rigging, and confused mass of drift stuff that precluded the possibility of getting near the hull that way. To approach on the weather side (from windward) was extremely difficult and perilous, requiring great skill and courage, but there was no other possibility of effecting a rescue." Keeper Spinney commanded his crew to pull windward.[9]

A lifecar drill was being conducted the day this photo was taken at Fletchers Neck Life-Saving Station at Biddeford Pool, Maine. A Duluth-type station built in 1904. (U.S. Coast Guard)

Hunniwells Beach Life-Saving Station guarded the entrance to Maine's Kennebec River. An 1882-type station. Station is now Popham Beach Bed and Breakfast. (U.S. Coast Guard)

Cranberry Islands Life-Saving Station watched over the waters around Mount Desert Island and Bar Harbor, Maine. An expanded 1876-type station. (Richard Boonisar)

Damiscove Island crew with surfboat on launchway. 1912. (U.S. Coast Guard)

Damiscove Island Life-Saving Station near Boothbay Harbor, Maine had a prominent lookout tower reminiscent of a lighthouse. It was a Port Huron-type station. (U.S. Coast Guard)

The sea was still too rough and dangerous to get along side the schooner. A sailor could be seen in the rigging and he looked as if he could not last much longer. A line was thrown, but the sailor made no movement to secure it. Without warning, the wreck swung around to the south making the water momentarily a bit less rough. Seizing this opportunity, the surfboat was worked in closer and a line again thrown to the sailor. This time the seaman, probably suffering from hypothermia, roused himself from his stupor, tied himself to the line and literally dropped into the sea. The rescuers pulled him safely to the surfboat.

Keeper Spinney and crew next went after four men clinging to the ship's rail. The tide, however, was now working against the Life-Saving Service. The *Schmidt* was being carried out over the bar "into more boisterous water" and quick and effective work was necessary if there was to be hope of saving anyone else on board. "The keeper, therefore, casting aside all thought of danger, speedily ran his boat close against the hull of the schooner." This action put everyone's life on the line since the ship was rising and falling, and masts, lines and wreckage were all about the surfboat. "The slightest mismanage-

ment was likely to crush or capsize her, and then not a man of them could have escaped with his life. The keeper risked everything when he put the bow of his surfboat against the wreck."[10]

In those terrible moments the surfmen "took the four sailors one by one over a line and into their outstretched arms." Another sailor was picked out of the rigging and now six were safely on board the surfboat. The surfboat was backed away from the wreck.

Keeper Spinney asked the first mate if anyone else was on board. The mate reported that the ship's captain had drowned just ten minutes before the surfboat arrived. The captain's delay in calling the Life-Saving Service had cost his life. All others on board were saved by the Hunniwells Beach surfboat.

Keeper Z. H. Spinney, surfmen Hodgkins and Oliver and the four volunteers had taken great risk, but they had succeeded. In the wreck report, the action was described as "one of the most notable and praise worthy" in the First U.S. Life-Saving District.[11]

A rocky shore and dark conifer trees frame Cross Island Life-Saving Station off Machiasport, Maine. The second farthest east of stations, Cross Island guarded a stormy "Down East" coast. An expanded 1874-type station. (U.S. Coast Guard)

Portsmouth Harbor Life-Saving Station on Wood Island, Maine, oversaw the entrance to New Hampshire's most important seaport. A modified Duluth-type station. (Richard Boonisar)

Great Wass Island Life-Saving Station stood proudly a top a rock-ribbed island off Jonesport, Maine. The station symbolizes Maine's maritime heritage. A modified Port Huron-type station. (U.S. Coast Guard)

Burnt Island Life-Saving Station off Port Clyde, Maine served a wild coast on the sea lanes between Penobscot Bay and Portland. A windblown Marquette-style station. (Wick York)

New Hampshire's Wallis Sands Life-Saving Station overlooked a sandy beach. This is a Bibb #2-type station. (U.S. Coast Guard)

New Hampshire had three life-saving stations in only thirteen miles of coastline. Rye Beach Life-Saving Station was a Bibb #2-type station built in 1890. (Shanks collection)

Hampton Beach Life-Saving Station guarded the southern New Hampshire coast. It was the only Jersey Pattern station in New England. (Shanks collection)

Life-Saving Stations of Maine and New Hampshire

Life-Saving Stations of Maine

(Stations are listed from north to south)

Station	Location
Quoddy Head	Carrying Point Cove near Lubec, Maine
Cross Island	Off Machiasport at east entrance to Machias Bay
Great Wass Island	Off Jonesport
Cranberry Islands	On Little Cranberry Island off Mount Desert
White Head	Whitehead Island off Spruce Head
Burnt Island	About 7 miles off Port Clyde on Burnt Island
Damiscove Island	Damiscove Harbor, near Boothbay Harbor
Hunniwells Beach	Kennebec River mouth near Popham Beach
Cape Elizabeth	On cove near Cape Elizabeth lighthouses
Fletchers Neck	Biddeford Pool
Portsmouth Harbor	Wood Island, Maine, off Portsmouth, NH
Isles of Shoals	Appledore Island, Maine, off Rye Harbor, NH

Life-Saving Stations of New Hampshire

Wallis Sands	South side entrance to Portsmouth Harbor
Rye Beach	North end of Rye Beach
Hampton Beach	1½ miles north of Great Boars Head, Hampton Beach

NAME CHANGES: Stations occasionally changed names as they were moved short distances or simply renamed for clarity. In other cases, a newer station replaced an older one. Thus, in MAINE Great Wass Island replaced Crumple Island and Browneys Island; Fletchers Neck was once Biddeford Pool; Cranberry Islands was Little Cranberry Island. NEW HAMPSHIRE: Rye Beach was Locke's Point; Hampton Beach was Great Boar's Head.[12]

NEW HAMPSHIRE STATION DISCONTINUED. In 1887 New Hampshire's Jerrys Point Life-Saving Station was built on Great Island, Portsmouth Harbor, NH. The station property was under the control of the War Department and in 1907 was reclaimed by the military. Forced to move, the Life-Saving Service's operations were conducted for a time in rented buildings until the new Portsmouth Harbor Life-Saving Station was completed nearby on Wood Island, Maine. Thus, New Hampshire once had four life-saving stations in 13 miles, one of the most densely protected coastlines in America.[13]

Isles of Shoals Life-Saving Station was located amidst a famed art colony on Appledore Island off the New Hampshire coast. Note square lookout tower and dormer windows of this an Isles of Shoals-type station. (U.S. Coast Guard)

Surfmen row toward a wreck in their lifeboat. Many rescues were extremely dangerous. (Shanks collection)

LIFE-SAVERS BURYING A SHIPWRECKED SAILOR

The sea exacted a high price in the lives of sailors, passengers and surfmen. Surfmen often conducted burials on the beach. (National Archives)

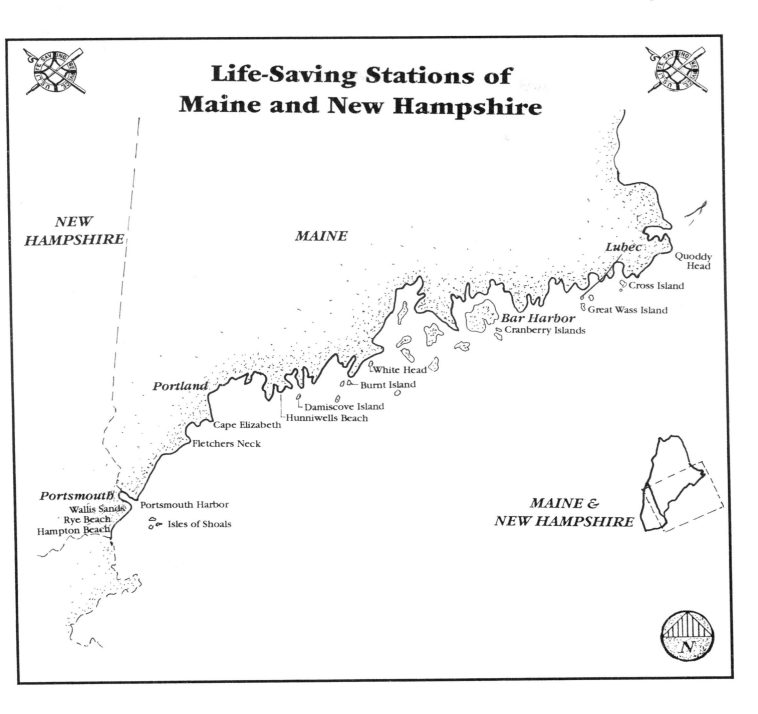

Life-Saving Stations of Maine and New Hampshire

NEW HAMPSHIRE

MAINE

Lubec

Quoddy Head

Cross Island

Great Wass Island

Bar Harbor

Cranberry Islands

White Head

Burnt Island

Damiscove Island

Hunniwells Beach

Portland

Cape Elizabeth

Fletchers Neck

Portsmouth

Wallis Sands

Rye Beach

Hampton Beach

Portsmouth Harbor

Isles of Shoals

MAINE & NEW HAMPSHIRE

N

FEBRUARY 18, 1922 · "News That Makes Us Think" · PRICE 10 CENTS

The Storm Veteran

The image of the brave keeper at the steering oar was an accurate one. Leslie's Weekly *featured a front page painting of a keeper wearing a life preserver. (Richard Boonisar)*

IN THIS ISSUE
Heroes of the Coast Patrol

Surfmen were heroes of their day featured in many publications. The Boston Sunday Herald illustrated a breeches buoy rescue during a snow storm. (Richard Boonisar)

Greatest heroes were often the keepers. Keeper Benjamin Truedell of Grand Marais Life-Saving Station on Lake Superior was one of best. (Pictured Rocks National Lakeshore)

Chapter 4
Surfmen and Keepers

SURFMEN'S LIVES

At night you could see the surfmen's lanterns as they walked the lonely beach patrols. Time and again during the night the surfmen would pass by. They were always alone except when they reached the extremity of their patrol. There, often at a little shed called a half-way house, the surfmen would meet the patrolman from an adjacent life-saving station and exchange small metal badges called "checks." Each check had the number of the surfman's rank and the number of his station on it. The surfman would carry his counterpart's check back to his station with him to prove that the patrol had been completed.[1]

Some stations were so isolated that there was no one else to meet and the surfman had to carry a patrol clock (punch clock). At the most distant point on his patrol was a key and the surfman would insert it in his patrol clock to prove he had gone the distance. Either way, the patrol was always completed, no matter what the weather.[2]

Sometimes when surfmen were on night patrol you could see them burn a Coston flare. It was a vivid red flare inserted in a wooden holder which a surfman would hold high in the air. Then you knew something was wrong. The burning signal might only be warning a ship to turn away from the shore. But at other times the Coston signal was burned because the surfman had seen a shipwreck and the flare told survivors that the Life-Saving Service was coming. Whatever the reason, the Coston flares were always a symbol of help.[3]

Life followed a pattern prescribed by the Service. Day watch was kept from sunrise to sunset, usually by a surfman stationed in the lookout tower. Lookout towers were most commonly atop the station, although detached towers were built at some stations. Lookouts literally stood watch since the Life-Saving Service felt a man standing watch was more alert than one sitting. If the lookout could not see the patrol limits from the tower, then he would walk the beaches at least three times to a point as far as necessary to see the limits of the area covered by the station.

Beach patrols were always walked during thick weather and at night. Patrols commonly ranged from about a mile to four miles in length, with about two miles being typical. For the night patrol, the night was divided into four watches—one from sunset to 8 o'clock, one from 8

to 12, one from 12 to 4, and one from 4 to sunrise. Two surfmen were designated for each watch. When the hour of their patrol arrived, they set out in opposite directions along the beach.[4]

Weekly routine began with Sunday as a day of rest and sometimes worship. Even on Sundays, however, beach patrol and lookout duty watches were stood, just as on every other day. Drills followed a fixed routine. Every Monday and Thursday crews practiced with the beach apparatus, pulling the beach cart, firing the line throwing Lyle gun and rigging a breeches buoy to the mast-like wreck pole. Occasionally drills with the lifecar would also be done with a boat anchored offshore to simulate a wreck. On Tuesdays it was boat drill, involving launching, landing and rowing the pulling boats. At the discretion of the keeper, "capsize drills" could be performed which involved purposely capsizing and righting the surfboat or Dobbins lifeboat. Crews had to be prepared for accidental capsizing because surfboats and Dobbins lifeboats, although typically self-bailing, were not self-righting (the larger English-type lifeboats were self-righting). Capsize drill was by far the most dangerous drill and surfmen were known to be killed when hit by the surfboat in heavy breakers. Capsize drills were usually done during warm, calm weather because they took such a toll on crews and equipment. Wednesdays were signal practice days with two types of flag codes. The International Code for signals was used with flags arranged to represent letters of the alphabet to send a message. Wig-wag signal flags were also practiced with two three-foot-square flags, one red and one white. The red flag symbolized a dash and the white flag stood for a dot, as in Morse code, so that by raising the flags in a pattern a message could be sent. Typically, one surfman held the red flag, another the white flag and in the distance yet another surfman looked through a telescope and dictated the message to a fourth surfman who transcribed it. Thursday repeated the beach apparatus drill with the Lyle gun. Fridays saw practice in methods of restoring the apparently drowned. Techniques for restoring breathing and counteracting hypothermia were taught, as was basic medical aid using the Service's medicine chest. On Saturdays the station was thoroughly cleaned and repair work done. Maintenance and repairs of buildings and boats was

Proud surfmen in a Dobbins lifeboat on boat carriage. (Shanks collection)

spread out during the week.[5]

Actual rescues often began with a surfman rushing into the station from patrol. If a patrolling surfman had seen a wreck, he hurried back to the station to tell the keeper. Sometimes he came bursting in the door breathless and excited. At other times he staggered in exhausted from the cold and stunned by what must lie ahead. The surfman might have heard the cries of shipwreck victims or the flapping of torn sails. If it was a moonlit night, he may have seen people clinging to the ship's rigging. Sometimes patrolmen entered the station bringing a survivor with him. The surfman might also report that bodies were washing ashore.

Upon hearing of the wreck, the keeper might dash up the lookout tower to try to see the wreck. The keeper had to decide whether to use the beach apparatus with Lyle gun and beach cart or to roll out a surfboat. At some stations he might be fortunate enough to have a lifeboat too. But whatever was to be done it was the keeper's responsibility to decide how to respond. People's lives, including those of his crew, depended upon his decisions. His career also rode on his decisions.[6]

The story is told that once a keeper and young surfman stood looking at ominous breakers just before launching their surfboat. The young surfman asked the keeper if he thought they would come back alive. The old keeper turned to him and responded, "The regulations only say we have to go out. They don't say anything about coming back."

From this was born the eventual surfmen's motto, "You have to go out, but you don't have to come back." The USLSS *Regulations* did indeed say you have to go out. The keeper "will not desist from his efforts until by actual trial the impossibility effecting a rescue is demonstrated." A keeper must test the surf by launching his boat. He did have to go out.[7]

And so they went out no matter what the weather, even if they were sick or exhausted from a previous wreck. They went out no matter what the nationality of the ship in distress. There was no hesitation. People were in need of help and it was their job to save them. If lives were lost the keeper would have to explain why. If even one life was lost it would be written up in detail in the Life-Saving Service *Annual Report* for Congress and all the people on the coast to read.

"In attempting a rescue the keeper will select either the boat, breeches buoy, or lifecar," and if one fails "he will resort to one of the others, and if that fails, then to the remaining one. He will not desist," the *Regulations* commanded. Whether the keeper decided to use Lyle gun or boat was often a difficult choice. If he chose to use the Lyle gun, then the beach cart had to be hauled out to the wreck. The surfmen actually harnessed themselves to the heavy beach cart like horses and pulled it to rescues. It wasn't too hard pulling the cart on firm, level ground in fair weather, but then shipwrecks rarely happened under those circumstances. Most often the beach cart had to be pulled through soft sand or along the beach with the break-

"They had to go out, but they did not have to come in" was the legendary motto of the surfmen. Regulations required that life-saving crews had to go out no matter what the weather and there was no guarantee they would make it back. The Coquille River Life-Saving Station crew in Oregon is shown here. (Coast Guard Museum Northwest)

ers clawing at your feet. Wrecks happened in the foulest weather with snow, hail or rain beating down on the struggling surfmen. Sand blown by hurricane force winds tore at their faces and threatened their eyes. Some people felt sorry for the surfmen and said they looked like "beasts of burden" pulling the beach cart. Many people admired them and called them "heroes of the surf," "storm warriors" and other noble names.[8]

When the surfmen finally got the beach cart to the wreck, they had to set up the beach apparatus. The Lyle gun was loaded with black powder and a 17-pound projectile with its attached line. The Lyle gun would be fired until a line reached the ship and the breeches buoy or lifecar could be rigged to bring survivors ashore.[9]

Often the shipwreck was too far offshore to use the Lyle gun. Then the surfmen had to use a surfboat or lifeboat. Sometimes a surfboat could be launched in front of the station by moving it along rollers arranged in a frame

much like a horizontal ladder. Sometimes logs substituted for rollers. But more often a heavy boat carriage was used to arduously haul the boat some distance closer to the wreck before launching. Launching had to be timed just right or a breaker could hurl the boat back upon the surfman, crushing a man. The keeper watched for a brief flattening of the breakers and then ordered his men to rush the surfboat into the water. With split second timing everyone got the boat launched, climbed in and manned the oars. Each action was carefully rehearsed in drills and everyone knew his exact role.

The lifeboats (except for the lighter Dobbins type) were so big and heavy they were launched down a launchway on a railroad track running into the sea. For decades, until motors were installed in some of the boats, both the surfboats and the lifeboats were rowed to wrecks. That is why they were called "pulling boats," because you just pulled and pulled on those oars. After launching only

Surfman Fred Marsh with the Life-Saving Service logo on one arm and the number four on the other indicating his mid-level rank as a surfman. North Manitou Island Life-Saving Station, Michigan. (Sleeping Bear Dunes National Lakeshore)

A young surfman at the beginning of his career. Hilman Persson rose to become a keeper and to win the gold life-saving medal during the Coast Guard years. Grays Harbor Life-Saving Station, Washington. (U.S. Coast Guard)

the keeper could look ahead, as all the surfmen were seated facing the stern rowing in unison. One keeper said he would fire any man who took his mind off rowing long enough to look forward.[10] Both lifeboats and surfboats went out when no other boat would dare to go.

Sometimes the surfmen would be at sea for hours rowing, enduring cold, hunger and exhaustion. The keeper had no easy job either. The big steering oar was heavy and the keeper had to fight the sea to steer his boat. In stormy seas, the steering oar could yank him about and knock him overboard. If waves swept the boat, the keeper standing at the steering oar was vulnerable to being washed overboard.[11]

When the Life-Saving crews finally got to the wreck they might be exhausted from rowing, but their most difficult task was just beginning. The people they were saving were sometimes a help, but often not. Sailors and passengers were commonly in poor condition, hardly able to help even themselves. Sometimes the surfmen had to board a ship and carry the people off the vessel.

Worst were the times when the sailors were panicked. When they saw the life-savers arrive they might all jump simultaneously into the surfboat or lifeboat. This could spill everyone into the sea and loss of life was probable. This happened on a number of occasions resulting in some of the Service's most terrible losses.

But usually, no matter how high the seas ran or how hard the wind blew or how cold it was or how crazed the sailors were, the surfmen managed to rescue all or most of those on board. The surfmen had a remarkably high success rate and once they were on scene the odds of mariners' survival approached ninety-nine percent. If the Life-Saving Service couldn't rescue someone, and at times they couldn't, that person was either in a very horrible situation or had been incredibly foolish.[12]

As the survivors were brought ashore by boat, breeches buoy or lifecar, they were cared for by the surfmen. Survivors were brought back to the station and clothed and fed and often put to bed in one of the spare cots kept for that purpose. Each station had a medicine chest and surfmen or the keeper's wife nursed the ill or injured as best they could.

Often, survivors had no usable clothing. In the early years of the Service the survivors were given clothes by

A veteran at the peak of his career. Keeper Alanson C. Penny of Shinnecock Life-Saving Station, New York. The Penny family was a distinguished one in Long Island life-saving. (U.S. Coast Guard)

read by survivors and surfmen alike. Little cabinet-like portable USLSS libraries housed the books which were rotated among stations. While survivors were at a station, their food was provided from the station mess using funds from the keeper. If they could afford it, the survivors were asked to pay. If not, then the government later paid the costs.[13]

Except for the tremendous reward of saving lives, it was a wonder that anyone ever became a surfman. The job was extremely dangerous, poor health too often resulted from the long hours and there was no health care program or long term disability coverage. On top of that the pay was low and pensions lacking.[14] Yet the quality of most USLSS men was high.[15]

In some locations coastal people were so poor and the seafaring tradition so deep that even a surfman's meager pay seemed appealing. But in other areas, particularly the Great Lakes, it was inadequate and high turnover and loss of many of his best qualified employees was a frequent worry of General Superintendent Kimball.[16] The typical $65 a month pay ($40 a month in earlier years) did not allow a surfman to save money for his retirement or to care for his family should he become disabled. If he was disabled or killed, he or his survivors could receive his full pay for up to two years, but after that time the family was left destitute.[17]

The toll of disease, disability and accident continued to fall heavily on the surfmen as the years passed. Kimball wrote: "The majority of these men enter the vocation of life-saving at the most vigorous period of their lives. They know that if they continue in the Service—and its efficiency depends upon their retention—they will sooner or later incur disability and be compelled to stand aside. Their incapacity may be the result of injury sustained in the performance of wreck duty, such as broken bones, sprains, hernia, etc., or it may be due to heart trouble, rheumatism, tuberculosis, or a complication of these afflictions or several of a dozen others traceable to overstrain or exposure."[18]

Work related disease killed more surfmen than all the shipwrecks combined. In 1914 Sumner Kimball updated and issued a "List of Persons Who Have Died By Reason of Injury or Disease contracted in the Line of Duty in the Life-Saving Service." Despite the relatively small size of the Service, the list was six pages in length. It included all jobs, from surfmen to superintendents. No one in the USLSS was immune. There were many who drowned attempting to save the lives of others, but there were far more who "died from disease contracted in the line of duty." The public was always aware of the noble surfmen who drowned trying to rescue others. But the countless men who died by diseases from long months in cold, damp climates with little health care remained largely unsung. Most were lost from diseases contracted after exposure

the life-saving crews and fed at the surfmen's expense. But American women stepped into this unfair situation and did something about it. They formed the Women's National Relief Organization which supplied clothing to donate to shipwreck victims at the stations. Sometimes people were stranded at stations for days and the Seaman's Friend Society and other charities donated books to be

A surfman and his bride. They would face a challenging future of long hours, no health care and dangerous rescues. In many ways the wives were as courageous as the husbands. Coquille River Life-Saving Station, Oregon. (Shanks collection)

Even stations as remote as Vermilion in upper Michigan had many wives and children who played important roles in station life. (Lake Superior State University)

Surfmen with their children. Ilwaco Beach (Klipsan Beach) Life-Saving Station, Washington. (U.S. Coast Guard)

Keepers had the pleasure of being able to have their family live with them in the station. Keeper Christopher Hunt gives his daughter Stella a ride in a wheelbarrow at Point Reyes Life-Saving Station, California. (Point Reyes National Seashore)

Since the Life-Saving Service only provided housing for the keeper's family, surfmen often built their own homes. Many stations came to be surrounded by cottages built by surfmen for their families. Point Reyes Life-Saving Station, California. (Howard Underhill photo in Shanks collection)

On a rare day of liberty a keeper takes in a movie on the Titanic *sinking, a film of more than passing interest to a life-saver. (Sleeping Bear Dunes National Lakeshore)*

Many notable people were drawn to the excitement of the Life-Saving Service. Among them was the famous Apache chief Geronimo (front center in dark hat) who enjoyed watching capsize drills and breeches buoy demonstrations. To the left of Geronimo is Keeper Henry Cleary of Marquette (Michigan) Life-Saving Station, holder of the record for fastest capsize drill at thirteen seconds. (Michigan State Archives)

during beach patrols and rescues and from the high stress nature of the work.[19]

Just as risking their lives was almost routine, at over ninety percent of the stations layoffs were also regular occurrences. The period when stations were open was called the "active season." Atlantic Coast surfmen were laid off during the summer months, generally June and July, when wrecks were few. On the Great Lakes, navigation closed for the winter and surfmen were out of work. For these surfmen, pay stopped during the inactive season. Because wrecks could occur at any season on the Pacific Coast, West Coast stations remained open and provided surfmen with year round employment. The Louisville, Kentucky, floating station was also manned year round.[20]

Family life was difficult under Life-Saving Service rules. Although the keeper's family could live in the station, there was no provision for housing the surfmen's families. While some stations were located in or near cities or towns, most were built on lonely, remote coasts, completely isolated from other human associations. Some places were so isolated that the life-savers were the only winter residents of their section of coast. Even on the Great Lakes where stations closed during winter, surfmen might stay on at their stations because they had nowhere else to go.

Since no family housing was provided, surfmen and their wives often built little cottages near the station.[21] "The arrangement has been a happy one all around; the men are contented to stay close to the station, and the women and children make the place quite a bright, cheerful little settlement." Wives and children brought much to a station and vastly improved morale.[22]

But in some cases the nearest housing remained miles away and the husbands were cut off from their families for long periods of time. Life-Saving Service rules for liberty were harsh. Surfmen were allowed time off only from sunrise to sunset one day a week as liberty was rotated through the crew. Only by acquiring a cottage and having his family close to the station could a surfman participate properly in family life.[23]

Many surfmen supplemented their income by other work. Fishing, hunting, logging, whaling, raising livestock and gardening could frequently be done in the vicinity of the station.[24] Fresh seafood, game and vegetables were always welcome. Although some stations had a full time cook, at others surfmen took turns cooking, even baking their own bread. District Superintendent David Dobbins also noted that crews took pride in their stations. Dobbins admired "the handiwork of keepers and crews in the construction of boat and store sheds, pier breakwaters, launching ways, roads and walks about the station, lookouts in prominent points, house decoration and furniture."[25]

In between wrecks, during good weather the pace at the stations was fairly relaxed. Some surfmen played instruments such as the banjo or violin and the whole crew would sing. If families lived nearby they would join in, too, and dances could be held. Through all the pleasant hours, however, watches and patrols were still maintained and a dramatic image of the Service was a beach patrolman bursting into a station during a dance with news of a wreck. Surfmen then ran for their storm clothes and to get the boat or beach cart. The women rushed to gather warm clothing and prepare hot food for survivors. Sometimes the women built a bonfire on the beach and they often prayed while awaiting the return of their husbands.[26]

During the early days of the Service the arrival of surfmen at a wreck could actually frighten survivors since surfmen did not get uniforms until 1889. A number of foreign ships, upon seeing a band of rugged, roughly dressed men rowing rapidly toward their disabled ship thought the surfmen must be pirates. It didn't help when the roughly dressed men were seen to possess a small cannon. When surfmen used their Lyle gun to fire a life line toward a stranded vessel, one crew promptly offered to surrender.[27]

With such confusion and fear about, the good-hearted surfmen sometimes tried to create their own uniforms. Lacking an official uniform, these surfmen decided to clothe themselves in a uniform of their own design. Unfortunately, fashion design was not their strong point and some bizarre

The loneliest stations were those where families could not live near by. A New England surfman plays his banjo in an empty station sleeping room. (Richard Boonisar)

One type of signaling practiced on Wednesdays was with the International Code for signals where each flag represented a letter of the alphabet. All flags are flying in this scene at Fishers Island Life-Saving Station, Long Island Sound, New York. (U.S. Coast Guard)

uniforms resulted. To overcome such problems, the USLSS had a standardized uniform designed for its surfmen and keepers and required that they be worn. It is said that there was elation at stations at finally having a fine uniform. The joy quickly ended, however, when headquarters announced that "no appropriation is available to defray the cost (of the uniform) and therefore the men will be obliged to purchase their own outfits." Such was the life of a surfman.[28]

Actually, there were two sets of uniforms. For the keeper there was a formal dark blue uniform of woolen cloth or flannel with a double-breasted coat and two vertical rows of gilt buttons. There was a vest and pea-jacket type overcoat for heavy weather. The hat was also dark blue with a black leather bill. Some hats had the logo with a life-ring crossed by an oar and a boathook, while on other hats "USLSS" appeared. The surfmen wore a similar coat, but it was single-breasted with plain buttons. On the surfmen's right sleeve just below the shoulder was the Service emblem and on the left sleeve just below the shoulder was the surfman's rank number. A turtleneck pullover sweater with the station name was sometimes worn by keeper and surfmen alike. The surfman's cap was the same as the keeper's except that the wording "U.S. Life-Saving Service" appeared alone. Surfmen also had a work uniform consisting of a sailor-style jumper and overalls, sometimes called "summer whites." The work uniform appears most frequently in old photos of drills and was worn regularly. The work uniform included a white hat with a short,

usually upturned brim encircling the hat (the hat was a standard Spanish-American War era U.S. Navy sailor's hat). In foul weather, both keepers and surfmen wore a "storm suit." The storm suit was of brown rubber cloth or duck cotton, with the station name on the breast. The southwester hat was black, typically with the station name and "LSS" on it. Long black, southwester type foul weather coats were worn as part of the storm suit. Hip boots and life jackets were worn when appropriate.[29]

As the uniforms emphasized, the surfmen were always ranked according to their experience and ability. The number one surfman was the highest ranked, the number two surfman was second ranked and so on. Depending on the size of the station's crew, the numbers extended to number eight surfman. The numbers were worn on the shoulders of the uniforms so everyone knew each other's rank and duties. Being number one surfman was often the step before moving up to keeper. To be a keeper brought both new challenges and privileges.

KEEPERS' LIVES

Keepers were important, highly respected members of the maritime community and were selected from among the very best of the surfmen. They were generally men of intelligence, leadership, responsibility and courage. They were required to handle all paperwork, including wreck reports and personnel matters. A keeper supervised sometimes rough surfmen with no other officer on station.

The number one surfmen was usually the keeper's

Surfmen practiced two types of signaling every Wednesday. Wigwag signals involved two flags, one red and one white. The red flag symbolized a dash and the white flag a dot, as in Morse code. By raising flags in a pattern messages could be sent. (Richard Boonisar)

right-hand man. He took over in the keeper's absence and was often essentially a keeper in training. Generally, the keeper and his number one surfman seem to have been the station's management team. Turnover was high at many life-saving stations in the lower ranks and teaching and drilling was unending, both to stay in practice and to train new men. The keeper hired his own surfmen and had to be an excellent judge of character. A new man in the boat could endanger everyone if he panicked or refused to obey orders.[30]

But rank did have its privileges. Keepers' families could live in the station. The keeper's pay was generally acceptable during most of his era and he was highly valued by the Life-Saving Service and the community. He did not have to go out on the endless beach patrols. During surfboat capsize drills, if he was quick he would no more than get his feet wet before stepping over the stern into the righting boat. By comparison his men would get thoroughly wet in a capsize drill and then spend the rest of day cleaning up the boat and equipment.[31]

The keeper's weekly round followed the same schedule as his crew. He had to have his men trained to be ready for anything. Besides shipwrecks, the Life-Saving Service frequently acted as physicians and nurses, policemen of the sea, fire fighters, life guards and more. They thwarted suicides, aided imperiled swimmers, sheltered the homeless and the lost. They captured runaway boys, outlaws, teams of horses and lost pets. They recovered lost horses, bicycles, buoys, loads of hay,

cows, pigs, sacks of mail, fish nets and eventually even automobiles.[32] The Life-Saving Service was perhaps best described by the Coast Guard motto, Semper Paratus, "Always ready."

SCIENCE AND THE SURFMEN

A little known but important contribution of the Life-Saving Service was the role of keepers and surfmen in scientific projects. The Smithsonian Institution, famous scientists and great inventors all crossed paths with the Life-Saving Service.

Keepers aided Smithsonian Institution scientists by collecting rare marine specimens for them. No one was in a better position to know what existed along American shores than the patrolling surfman, and the best scientists recognized this fact. In 1884 the Smithsonian's Commission of Fish and Fisheries entered into agreement with the Life-Saving Service to have keepers ask their surfmen to watch for unusual marine life coming ashore. As a result, species previously unknown on our coasts were found and other species had their known range extended. Unusual sharks excited the scientists, but when the keeper at New Jersey's Barnegat Station caught a rare marine mammal related to "a bottle nose whale" the Smithsonian scientists were ecstatic.[33]

There was also the mysterious case of the "singing sands" in 1884. "Another service to a curious scientific inquiry has engaged the life-saving crews. At many points on our sea-coast and on the shores of the Great Lakes, the

A row of surfmen's "checks" ready for use on future patrols. These small badges were exchanged with surfmen from adjoining stations to prove a patrol had been completed. Below the checks are Coston flares and their holders. (U.S. Coast Guard Academy)

A fully equiped surfman wearing storm clothes on beach patrol. From left to right he carries a walking staff, patrol clock and punch key, a case containing Coston signals, and a patrol latern. (U.S. Coast Guard)

Keepers were managers and as such responsible for the station log, wreck reports, record keeping, correspondence and the like. Keeper of the Deal Life-Saving Station in New Jersey types at his desk. (U.S. Coast Guard)

beach sand has, in small tracts, very curious properties. In certain places the dry sand between the water-line and extreme high tide marks yields a peculiar sound when struck obliquely by the foot, or even when stroked by the hand; at the same time a tingling sensation can sometimes be felt in the toes or in the fingers. The sounds produced by friction, as described, somewhat resemble the distant barking of a dog, and may be represented by the syllable 'groosh.' They are unlike and louder than the ordinary noise caused by wagon wheels on sand, and when once heard may be easily recognized. Under favorable circumstances they may be heard one hundred feet. Only dry sand has this property and...sands having this peculiarity are called 'singing sands.'" The Life-Saving Service directed keepers to locate "singing sands" and send samples to Professor H. Carrington Bolter of Trinity College.[34]

Yet another scientist who crossed the path of the Life-Saving Service was inventor Guglielmo Marconi, the father of radio communication. Marconi built wireless stations and conducted experiments at various coastal locations, all of which had life-saving stations. Having Marconi as a neighbor was an experience since his transmitters, at least on Cape Cod, could be heard up to five miles away. Worse, Marconi had discovered that the best time for transmission was between ten p.m. and two a.m. The poor surfmen patrolling Cape Cod's beaches had to walk right by the Marconi transmitting facility. One night in 1903 a patrolling surfmen was near the Marconi facility when he suddenly saw "frightful sights and heard terrible sounds" as huge blue sparks flew out atop the soaring Marconi antenna. The surfman rushed back to the life-saving station to report the disaster. But no fear, it was just the great inventor at work and no rescue work was needed. Marconi had just made his historic first transatlantic radio transmission to England.[35]

Surfmen were more than just witnesses to scientific history. Surfmen were always there to help and two inventors down on North Carolina's Outer Banks obviously clearly needed assistance. The inventors, Orville and Wilbur Wright, befriended the surfmen from Kill Devil Hills Life-Saving Station. Wilbur Wright lived at the Kill Devil Hills station for a time and he and Surfman Bob Wescott had discussed Wescott's ideas for building a perpetual motion machine. It was an era where all things seemed possible and Wilbur Wright was impressed with the surfman's concepts and said so in his diary.[36] But instead of attempting a perpetual motion machine, Wright stuck with his plan to build another seemingly improbable invention, an airplane. As friendship grew, the surfmen started bringing the Wright brothers needed lumber and supplies. Mail for the Wrights arrived by way of the beach patrol from Kitty Hawk station and surfmen dropped the mail off daily. On slow days the surfmen would spend time watching the

The painting and cleaning required at all stations was seldom photographed. Surfman Gustave Christensen painting at Southside Life-Saving Station, San Francisco. (Carl Christiansen photo in Shanks collection)

Wrights' first experimental gliders fly among the dunes.[37]

On the night of December 16, 1903 a strong winter wind was blowing along North Carolina's sandy Outer Banks. The next morning it was cold, icy and gusty, but the Wright brothers hoisted a red flag which was the signal for the Kill Devil Hills surfmen to come to their camp. Despite winds up to 27 miles per hour, the Wright brothers had decided to attempt the world's first airplane flight. A coin was tossed and Orville won the right to be the pilot. The Wright brothers gave their camera to Surfman John T.

The only photograph of the Wright Brothers' historic first flight was taken by Surfman John T. Daniels of Kill Devil Hills Life-Saving Station. Surfmen helped the Wright Brothers with their secret project to build the world's first successful airplane. (U.S. Coast Guard)

Surfmen from Kill Devil Hills Life-Saving Station on North Carolina's Outer Banks worked with the Wright Brothers to make the world's first airplane flight a success. Wilbur Wright lived at Kill Devil Hills Life-Saving Station during his stay on the Outer Banks. (U.S. Coast Guard Academy)

Daniels, the only photographer present. In short order, the motor roared, Orville Wright gunned it ahead and off the plane flew for twelve historic seconds. Surfman Daniels took the only picture of the world's first airplane flight.[38]

All were elated after the flight, but then suddenly strong winds struck the plane and began to turn it over. Everybody rushed to save the plane and two surfmen got there first and grabbed it. The plane turned over and over and one surfman let go, but Surfman John Daniels refused to give up and hung on. Daniels was tossed head over heels inside the plane and battered against the motor. Finally, Daniels got the plane stopped but was badly bruised. Perhaps his pain was lessened by being hit by a piece of history.[39]

Except for Daniels' unfortunate bruising, the Wright brothers were very satisfied with what they had accomplished. The Wrights later removed the plane and took it back with them. Before they left the North Carolina dunes the Wright brothers sent a message via Life-Saving Service lines to Miss Katherine Wright in Dayton, Ohio. It read: "Flight Successful. Don't Tell Anybody Anything. Home for Christmas, (signed) Orville." The confidential nature of this message and the subsequent gift of a 1905 plane's wings to another surfman demonstrates how much the Wright brothers trusted and appreciated the vital support of the surfmen.[40] Whatever happened along America's beaches, the surfmen were there always doing their best to help.

Surfmen and their families often enjoyed having pets at the station. Pete Clark (left) and Tom Gunerson of Fort Point Life-Saving Station in San Francisco with station dogs. (Fort Point National Historic Site)

Lake Superior's Marquette Life-Saving station crew with pet bear they raised from a cub. (Pictured Rocks National Lakeshore)

Old Harbor Life-Saving Station had a prominent lookout tower to survey Cape Cod shipping. Duluth-type station. Station is preserved at Cape Cod National Seashore and execllent breeches buoy drills are presented by the Park Service. (U.S. Coast Guard)

Peaked Hill Bars Life-Saving Station lost Keeper David H. Atkins and Surfmen Elisha M. Taylor and Stephen F. Mayo during the 1880 rescue attempt of the C.E. Trumbull on Cape Cod. This was an expanded Red House-type station. After the station was closed it became the home of playwright Eugene O'Neill. (Shanks collection)

Chapter 5

Massachusetts and Rhode Island

THE LIFE-SAVING SERVICE IN
MASSACHUSETTS AND RHODE ISLAND

The very first *Annual Report* of the U.S. Life-Saving Service warned of the dangers on the Massachusetts coast. "The coast of Massachusetts embraces Cape Ann and Cape Cod, Massachusetts Bay, extending seventy miles in length between them, and Nantucket and Vineyard Sounds, and Buzzards Bay and the several islands which separate them." The coastline is "bordered by dangerous small islands, rocks and ledges. Massachusetts Bay contains the important port of Boston, and being open and exposed to the sweep of the easterly and northeasterly winds, many inward-bound vessels have struck upon its islands and unsheltered shores. Nantucket and Vineyard Sounds embrace a collection of hidden dangers in a network of shoals, rips, and ledges." But it is Cape Cod which "most fiercely menaces" commerce.[1] Nearly every point in the seaward side of the cape has been the scene of a shipwreck. There were sound reasons why Massachusetts had thirty-two and Rhode Island had nine U.S. government life-saving stations to watch over such dangerous shores.[2]

The most renowned surfman in Massachusetts was Joshua James and the terrible hurricane of 1888 would put him to an amazing test. He was at the time a keeper for the Massachusetts Humane Society. On the afternoon of November 25, 1888 Keeper Joshua James observed several vessels dragging anchor southeast of Boston off Nantasket. He called together the sturdy commercial fishermen who served as Massachusetts Humane Society (MHS) surfmen. With his crew on hand, Keeper James got the MHS's surfboat ready for action. No sooner had this been done when the schooner *Cox and Green* stranded a short distance away, off Toddy Rocks. The sea was so high that the keeper thought it was best to fire a line to her and land the crew by means of a breeches buoy. Joshua James successfully used the Humane Society's Hunt gun to fire a line, then rigged a breeches buoy and saved the schooner's entire crew.[3]

Meanwhile, the coal-laden schooner *Gertrude Abbott* had struck the rocks about an eighth of a mile eastward and hoisted a signal of distress in the rigging. She was so far off shore that a breeches buoy rescue was impossible. It was growing dark, the tide was high, and the storm was

raging with increased fury. These conditions prompted Joshua James and his men to wait for low tide before attempting a launch. A fire was set ablaze on a bluff so the vessel could be kept in view and to serve as a symbol of encouragement to those on board the ship. Due to the increasing violence of the gale that night the surfmen felt they could delay no longer and decided to board the schooner. Captain James warned his crew that they would probably never return alive from this desperate rescue. Only volunteers would be allowed to go. All the men stepped forward to volunteer.[4]

Keeper James and his crew managed to launch the surfboat through the furious breakers and bent to the oars. Two of the Massachusetts Humane Society surfmen had to bail constantly to keep the surfboat from swamping. After a desperate pull, the rescuers got near enough to pass a line to the wreck. The eight sailors on board then swung themselves by means of ropes into the rescue boat and a start was made for the beach. The wind and sea were sweeping wildly along the coast, which made the return trip hazardous. When within two hundred yards of the beach the surfboat struck a rock, filled, and nearly capsized. The occupants quickly shifted to windward and righted the boat, although one man fell overboard. Miraculously, he was pulled back into the boat before the sea could sweep him out of reach. The surfboat again struck the rocks a number of times and was buffeted along at the mercy of the waves. The surfmen barely managed with the few oars that were left to keep it headed for the shore so that the sea might carry them in. As shore was approached, Keeper James admonished everyone to stick to the boat as long as possible. The boat was finally thrown upon rocks in shoal water and all hands jumped out and scrambled safely ashore. With everyone safely on land, the *Gertrude Abbott's* crew was taken to a neighboring house and cared for.[5]

The storm raged on. By now it was nine p.m. and despite hours of work and the extremely cold storm, Captain James ordered volunteers to maintain a beach patrol to continue throughout the night. Surfmen on patrol had to wade deep gullies and dodge wreckage that was thrash-

Massachusetts was surfboat country and the Salisbury Beach crew stood ready to man their surfboats. (U.S. Coast Guard)

Rugged crew at Massachusetts' Orleans Life-Saving Station with silver pitcher, a gift from grateful survivors of the steamer Horatio Hall *which collided with the* J.F. Dimock *and sunk in 1909. Keeper James H. Charles is at lower right in photo. (Cape Cod National Seashore)*

ing about in the surf.

Conditions continued to worsen. At three o'clock in the morning Joshua James was called out again. The sunken schooner *Bertha F. Walker* was wrecked offshore and seven men were clinging to her rigging.[6] The wind was blowing with unusual violence, accompanied by rain and sleet. Since their first surfboat had been wrecked, the volunteers, aided by horses, dragged another surfboat four miles overland to the wreck site. Using a partly new crew, Joshua James launched the surfboat at dawn. Out Captain James and his surfmen went and saved all seven sailors from the *Bertha F. Walker*.[7]

Just as Joshua James was landing the seven sailors, a horseman arrived with the stunning news that two more shipwrecks had occurred. Everyone now hurried off to the wreck of the schooner *H.C. Higginson*. Both the North Scituate Life-Saving Station crew (at this time the nearest USLSS station) and Massachusetts Humane Society volunteers had reached the *H.C. Higginson* wreck scene. The North Scituate crew had pulled their heavy beach cart across nine miles of snow, slush and rough terrain in a gale to reach the site. Both rescue crews simultaneously fired lines from their guns out to the wreck. The ship's crew grabbed the Humane Society line, but it soon fouled.

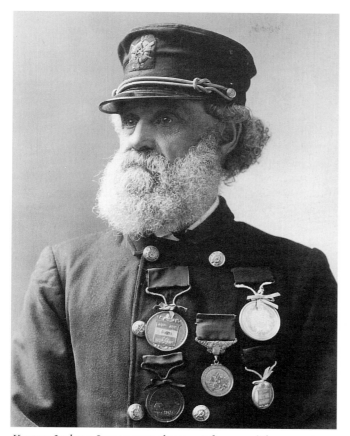

Keeper Joshua James was the most famous life-saver in American history. He wears both Congressional and Massachusetts Humane Society life-saving medals. He served as keeper into his seventies. (U.S. Coast Guard)

A breeches buoy rescue was now unlikely.

Joshua James arrived with the surfboat. Despite the hurricane, he launched the surfboat and rowed toward the schooner. A surfboat rescue seemed almost impossible since the sea was breaking heavily about the stranded vessel. Keeper James' boat was rowed for forty-five minutes, hitting rocks and sustaining two holes in its side and still failed to reach the schooner. James returned to shore, the surfboat was patched and then Joshua James and his men went out again. This time he rescued the five living half-frozen survivors.[8]

A fifth wreck occurred, the schooner *Mattie E. Eaton,* but the vessel came ashore so high the ship's crew got ashore on their own. But as Joshua James and his surfmen headed home, they found a sixth wreck, the abandoned brigantine *Alice.* Two would-be salvors had boarded the *Alice* and become trapped on the vessel. So Joshua James saved them and then finally went home.[9]

With six wrecks and twenty-nine lives saved, it had

been a remarkable storm. Gold medals were awarded to Captain Joshua James by both the U.S. Life-Saving Service and the Massachusetts Humane Society.[10]

A year later, in 1889, the U.S. Life-Saving Service opened its Point Allerton Life-Saving Station at Hull, southeast of Boston. There was no question that Joshua James would be the best choice for keeper. He was, however, sixty-two years of age by then, well past the maximum entry age of forty-five to join the USLSS as keeper. The USLSS waived the initial hiring age limit and he became Point Allerton's station keeper. At age 62, Joshua James was still in his prime.[11]

One of the most terrible storms in American history was to occur during Joshua James' years at Point Allerton. "The Great Storm of November 1898" hit Massachusetts on the evening of Saturday, the 26th. Two thirds of all the lives lost within the scope of the U.S. Life-Saving Service that year died in this single storm. "Forty-four persons perished...(along) the coast of Massachusetts, and one-half of this number were on vessels which were destroyed on islands and outlying rocks in the night when they could not be seen from the mainland, and the first knowledge of which was gained from wreckage coming ashore. (This) overwhelming loss of life on a coast long noted for frightful disasters was the result of a single stroke inflicted in the dark, which was so sudden that it could not be parried, and so powerful that its awful effects could not be mitigated. The almost unprecedented tempest wrought its direst effects between Gay Head (on Martha's Vineyard) and Point Allerton (southeast of Boston)."[12]

There had been warning that the storm was coming. Lt. Worth G. Ross, assistant inspector of life-saving stations, reported at sunset "marked indications of approaching bad weather." By seven p.m. scores of vessels were seeking shelter from Gay Head to Cape Ann. "Many found refuge in Provincetown and Gloucester while others were crowding every stitch (of sail) they could bear to reach port." Once in port, extra lines and additional anchors were run out.[13]

"Snow began falling early, and the wind increased. By 10 o'clock, Keeper Joshua James reported 'it was blowing a gale from the northeast with sleet and snow so thick that we could not see one hundred yards at most. At midnight it was a hurricane.'"[14]

When this storm hit, Joshua James was ready at Point Allerton. Keeper James' crew had struggled through a wearisome night of patrol. In the early morning, a wreck was sighted and they went to the rescue of the schooner *Henry R. Tilton,* a mile and a half northwest of their station. They dragged the beach cart out and took the Lyle gun to the scene. Despite the hurricane, Joshua James successfully fired a line to the ship. A breeches buoy was then rigged and all on board were brought ashore safely.

Arriving back at the life-saving station at Hull, the weary life-savers were informed that *Coal Barge Number 4* was wrecked on outlying rocks. Since Massachusetts Humane Society life-savers were working with the U.S. government surfmen, Keeper James used the Humane Society's Hunt gun to fire a line so a breeches buoy could be rigged. All five crewmen were saved, but they were in terrible condition. The keeper felt they wouldn't survive the trip back to the station and needed warmth immediately. The nearest house was unoccupied so Joshua James broke in, built a fire and clothed the frozen sailors.[15]

Returning to Point Allerton Life-Saving Station, Joshua James climbed the lookout tower atop his station and saw masts on the far side of Little Brewster Island, site of Boston Light. Keeper James "apprehended that there might be trouble there, but aside from the sheer impossibility of reaching the point in the night and against the wind and sea then raging, he had standing agreement with the keeper of the lighthouse that in case assistance should ever be needed there the latter would set a flag signal to that effect. Therefore, as the next morning approached, James was alert to find out the situation, and at the first suggestion of daylight he turned his spyglass toward 'the Brewsters.' The signal flag was flying."[16]

The surfboat was launched and Keeper James arranged for the tug *Ariel* to tow his surfboat to the island. The sea was so high that the tug could get no closer than a quarter of a mile from the island. It was almost routine for the men of the Life-Saving Service to go where virtually no other vessel dared go and, amidst the fury, the surfboat with its crew was cast loose from the tug. The breaking bar on the island's shoal was ahead and Joshua James steered right for it. The crests of the waves began "flying over and completely enveloping" the surfboat. The surfboat was rowed among the huge breakers and along side the schooner, which proved to be the *Baker*. The surfmen found the *Baker* was a nightmare scene with survivors in pitiable condition and three sailors already lost. "The scene was one no eyes could wish to dwell upon, and the life-savers hastened to flee the place. The living—but half alive—and the dead were quickly handed over into the surfboat, which was promptly pulled away to the tug that stood by to tow her home." Joshua James and his surfmen saved all those still alive on the schooner.[17]

When Keeper James and his surfmen returned to Point Allerton Life-Saving Station, they encountered a messenger bearing word that three men were stranded on Black Rock, a quarter mile offshore and six miles southward. The barge *Lucy Nichols*, a former sailing ship, had been under tow by the tug *Underwriter*. The tug could not hold both herself and her tow against the storm and she was forced to cut the *Lucy Nichols* towline, leaving her crew helplessly adrift. The *Lucy Nichols* went ashore about nine o'clock Sunday morning. The three survivors clung to Black Rock hoping for rescue.[18]

The Cohasset crew of the Massachusetts Humane Society got to the wreck scene first. It was very rough, but the Cohasset surfmen had launched lifeboat *Number 23* in a brave attempt. The Massachusetts Humane Society crew began rowing out to the *Lucy Nichols* when disaster struck, capsizing their boat and throwing all the surfmen into the ocean. With storm clothing still on, the rescuers struggled for their own survival. They and their boat drifted toward shore where the unfortunate surfmen attempted to swim toward the rocky coast. Other Massachusetts Human Society volunteers, using oars and wearing life belts, went into the water and reached the struggling surfmen. Miraculously, all were pulled ashore safely.[19]

At Point Allerton, Joshua James obtained four horses to pull the boat carriage and then he and his crew set out for Black Rock. Once there "we succeeded in launching," Joshua James recalled "rowing one mile to the rock. As it was very difficult to land with the heavy sea breaking around the rock, we had to wait an hour or more, watching a favorable opportunity to make a landing. When the chance presented itself, made a strong pull and landing safely on the rock. Got the men three in number on board and again waited for a favorable chance to launch." That opportunity to escape the rock did not come until just before sundown. With the sea running high, it was a hard mile long row against a strong wind to reach shore, but the three survivors were landed safely. As the terrible storm continued, other vessels went down, some with all hands lost, but wherever Joshua James and his crew managed to go they "succeeded in getting every man that was alive at the time we started for him, and we started at the earliest moment in each case."[20]

The same hurricane was battering Brant Rock Life-Saving Station on Massachusetts Bay's south shore. "Such a violent outburst of the elements had not occurred in this vicinity within the memory of the oldest inhabitant. (The) storm caused the rushing seas to take possession of the beaches, break through the banks, flatten the sand hills, and flood the highways, marshes and fields beyond. The sea walls were demolished and the summer resorts of Brant Rock, Ocean View, and Duxbury Beach laid in ruins, more than half the cottages damaged and a large number completely destroyed."[21]

When the storm hit, Brant Rock Life-Saving Station surfmen promptly began their work of rescue and assistance. Conditions were so bad that three surfmen on patrol were unable to return to the station and only the keeper and three other surfmen remained at Brant Rock Life-Saving Station. These four life-savers were to face huge challenges.

The storm drove many of the people, half-clad, from their cottages into the open, and they were in great peril

Breeches buoy rescue of the Hannah E. Shubert *in March 1886 by Peaked Hill Bars and High Head surfmen. (U.S. Coast Guard Academy)*

Rare photo of the dark day when Cohasset's Massachusetts Humane Society surfmen struggled to reach shore after the capsizing of their lifeboat while attempting to rescue the crew of the Lucy Nichols, *November 28, 1898. (Cohasset Historical Society)*

Orleans Life-Saving Station and crew. This was an expanded red house-type station in Massachusetts. (U.S. Coast Guard)

Famous Race Point Life-Saving Station, an expanded red house-type, watched over the tip of Cape Cod. (Shanks collection)

Highland Life-Saving Station served the Truro area of Cape Cod to the north of Highland lighthouse. An expanded red house-type station. (Shanks collection)

During the 1902 Wadena *rescue attempt off Cape Cod all of the Monomoy Life-Saving Station crew except one man were lost. The lone survivor was heroic surfman Seth Ellis. Mr. Ellis recovered and became keeper at Monomoy. He is shown here with a new crew ready to test the Atlantic.*

Crews usually pulled surfboats along the beach before launching. (Shanks collection)

Keeper Seth Ellis of Monomoy Life-Saving Station was the only survivor from his station in the rescue attempt of the Wadena. *(Shanks collection)*

Plum Island Life-Saving Station near Newburyport, Massachusetts was an 1874-type station. Note lookout platform atop the station and the surfboat and crew at the entrance. (Richard Boonisar)

High Head Life-Saving Station was a busy station on Cape Cod. Surfmen at this 1882-type station have the surfboat on their boat wagon. (Cape Cod National Seashore)

Fourth Cliff Life-Saving Station on Massachusetts Bay's south shore was an 1876-type station. (Richard Boonisar)

from the sea and the cold. Survivors fleeing homes were brought to the life-saving station and to the Union Church, a substantial stone building 75 yards from the station. Conditions were so bad that the area between the church and the station, a normally pleasant ground often used for breeches buoy and signal drills, was "inundated with surging waters." More people, particularly women and children, continued to arrive at the life-saving station seeking help and shelter. By now "the storm was at its height, a howling, terrific hurricane, with blinding snow, spray and sand." The surf spread out and around the buildings "sweeping rocks and wreckage in its path."[22]

The terrified people inside the station were "almost in a frenzy of fear and despair." With a "thundering crash the sea burst in the (Brant Rock Life-Saving Station) boatroom doors and dining room windows and made a clean sweep through the lower part of the building. Tons of stone were hurled upon the floors, the stoves were thrust aside and the fires drowned out. Life belts were immediately put on the women and children, and they were hurried upstairs. The serious question was, would the building stand the onslaught of the sea?"[23]

Using a technique that had worked at other life-saving stations during hurricanes, the surfmen "opened the rear doors, which permitted the waves to run through, and this expedient saved" the Brant Rock Life-Saving Station. The surfmen then dragged the boat carriage with the surfboat on it outside to allow the sea to run freely through the lower portion of the station.[24]

Seas continued to sweep the station. The Brant Rock surfmen decided that they had to get everyone from the wooden life-saving station to the stone church where chances of survival would be best. In an act of great bravery, Surfman Harris awaited a favorable moment and "ran with a lifeline to the church, but in doing so he was carried off his feet by the waters, and barely saved from the sea by two other surfmen. Finally, after perilous but careful effort, all those at the station were taken to the church. There was no fuel there, but the life-saving men carried some coal over and started fires." The church "had become a blessed sanctuary for these thirty or more disconsolate souls, whose homes had been desolated by the wild fury of the elements."[25] All those in the church survived.

There were many more stories during those terrible thirty-six hours of the great 1898 hurricane. Heroism was displayed at Wood End, Peaked Hill Bars, Gay Head, High Head and other stations. The Life-Saving Service could be defeated, but only rarely.

Four years later, in 1902, the Life-Saving Service experienced a grievous defeat. The Monomoy Life-Saving Station crew on Cape Cod suffered "by far the worst calamity to the Life-Saving Service during many years, one unequaled by more than two or three in its history." On March 17, 1902 Monomoy Keeper Marshall N. Eldridge and six of his surfmen drowned while attempting the rescue of five seamen from the coal barge *Wadena*. A northeast gale was blowing and after a difficult pull the barge was reached and her crew were taken into the surfboat. Then as the barge's captain was coming aboard he fell from a rope and into the surfboat, breaking a thwart. The loss of a thwart, where surfmen sat and rowed, left the surfmen at a disadvantage in handling the boat. A second later, a big sea came up and swept into the surfboat. Even worse, at that moment the men from the barge "went into a considerable panic, which neither injunction or command could quell. They stood up, clung to the surfmen, crowded them out of their places at the thwarts...(and made) the situation impossible." Despite this madness, the Monomoy crew remained the professionals they were. They stayed calm and manfully rowed toward the station. But too many things were going wrong and when a huge wave hit, the surfboat capsized. The Monomy life-savers righted the surfboat but it capsized again. The surfmen righted it yet again and again it capsized. "The water was bitter cold, and the foam of the breakers nearly suffocating." The merciless grey sea rolled the surfboat over and over. One by one, the surfmen and sailors "lost their hold and disappeared." Finally only one person remained alive, Seth L. Ellis, number one surfman at Monomoy station.[26]

Surfman Ellis was miraculously saved by Captain Elmer Mayo of Chatham.[27] Ellis was awarded the Congressional gold life-saving medal for his heroic part in the rescue attempt. He never forgot Keeper Eldridge's words when the barge was first seen. Despite the horrible weather conditions, the keeper had turned to his men and said simply "we must go, there is a distress flag in the rigging." They had to go out, but they did not come in.[28]

Two days later, on March 19, 1902, Captain Joshua James, now 74 years of age and still keeper of the Point Allerton Life-Saving Station, was returning to the station from a surfboat drill. As they beached the surfboat, Joshua James observed, "The tide is ebbing." He then stepped from the surfboat "and fell dead at his post of duty." He was buried a short distance beyond the Point Allerton Station, not far up the hill from the sea.[29]

Life-Saving Service General Superintendent Sumner Kimball wrote, "Captain Joshua James was probably the most celebrated life-saver in the world, having spent all the years of his manhood in the service of the Massachusetts Humane Society and the United States Life-Saving Service... He was a man of the highest moral character and frugal habits, yet at the time of his death was practically without means. He left an invalid wife and several children."[30]

Point Allerton Life-Saving Station at Hull, Massachusetts was Joshua James' station. Today the station is the Hull Life-Saving Museum, an outstanding place to visit. This is Bibb #2 type station. (Shanks collection)

Gurnet Life-Saving Station off Plymouth, Massachusetts is a fine example of a Bibb #2 type station. Today it has been beautifully restored as a private residence by USLSS expert Richard Boonisar. (U.S. Coast Guard)

Newburyport Life-Saving Station at the mouth of Massachusetts' Merrimac River was a Bibb #2 type station. (Shanks collection)

North Scituate Life-Saving Station near Scituate, Massachusetts worked some of the same rescues as Joshua James' crews. This was a Bibb #2 type station. (Richard Boonisar)

Monomoy Point Life-Saving Station stood at the south end of Monomoy Island off Cape Cod. Note small lookout tower typical of Quonochontaug-type stations. (U.S. Coast Guard)

Cahoons Hollow Life-Saving Station with surfboat and beach cart visible. Located near Wellfleet, Massachusetts today it is the Beachcomber Restaurant surrounded by the lands of Cape Cod National Seashore. A Quonochontaug-type station. (Cape Cod National Seashore)

Brant Rock Life-Saving Station near Marshfield, Massachusetts, had waves sweep through station during the great storm of November 1898. A Quonochontaug-type station. (Shanks collection)

Muskeget Life-Saving Station had a lonely existence on a small island off Nantucket Island, Massachusetts. Quonochontaug-type. (U.S. Coast Guard)

Rockport, Massachusetts was guarded by Straitsmouth Life-Saving Station. A wreck pole for the beach apparatus drill stands in the foreground. This Duluth-type station had a prominent square lookout tower and hipped roof. Today it is a private residence. (U.S. Coast Guard)

Salisbury Beach Life-Saving Station was the northern-most station in Massachusetts. There were twenty-nine of these Duluth-type stations built nationally and they were a popular subject for early postcards. (Shanks collection)

Gloucester Life-Saving Station watched over the famed Massachusetts fishing port. Duluth-type station. (Shanks collection)

Manomet Point Life-Saving Station east of Plymouth, Massachusetts. During Coast Guard years, Manomet Point's surfboat was tossed end over end in the March 10, 1928 Robert E. Lee rescue attempt. Acting keeper William Cashman, and surfmen Griswold and Stark were lost. A monument marks the loss at Manomet Point. (Shanks collection)

Life-Saving Stations of Massachusetts and Rhode Island

Life-Saving Stations of Massachusetts

Station	Location
Salisbury Beach	⅔ miles south of state line
Newburyport	North end of Plum Island
Plum Island	About 2 miles from south end Plum Island
Straitsmouth	On mainland near Rockport
Gloucester	West side harbor at Old House cove
Nahant	On the neck, close to Nahant
City Point	Floating station on Dorchester Bay, Boston
Point Allerton	At Hull, 1 mile west of Point Allerton
North Scituate	Near Minot, 2½ miles south Minots Ledge Lighthouse
Fourth Cliff	South end of Fourth Cliff, North Scituate
Brant Rock	On Green Harbor Point, Brant Rock
Gurnet	Gurnet Point 4½ miles NE Plymouth
Manomet Point	6½ miles SE Plymouth
Wood End	Near Wood End Lighthouse, Provincetown
Race Point	1⁹⁄₁₀ miles NE Race Point Lighthouse, Provincetown
Peaked Hill Bar	2½ miles NE of Provincetown
High Head	3½ miles NW Cape Cod Lighthouse, near Provincetown
Highland	About a mile NW Cape Cod Lighthouse, North Truro
Pamet River	3½ miles south Cape Cod Lighthouse, North Truro
Cahoons Hollow	2½ miles east of Wellfleet
Nauset	NE of Eastham 1³⁄₁₀ miles south of Nauset Lighthouse
Orleans	Abreast Ponchet Island, East Orleans
Old Harbor	NE of Chatham
Chatham	1¼ miles SSW Chatham Lighthouse
Monomoy	2¼ miles north Monomoy Lighthouse, south of Chatham
Monomoy Point	¾ miles SW Monomoy Lighthouse, Chatham
Coskata	2¼ miles south Great Point Lighthouse, Nantucket Island
Surfside	2½ miles south town of Nantucket at Surfside
Maddaket	6 miles west of Surfside, Nantucket Island
Muskeget	Near west end Muskeget Island off Nantucket
Gay Head	Near Gay Head Lighthouse, Martha's Vineyard
Cuttyhunk	Near east end Cuttyhunk Island

Life-Saving Stations of Rhode Island

Station	Location
Brenton Point	Prices Neck, Newport
Narragansett Pier	In the town of Narragansett Pier
Point Judith	Adjacent to Point Judith Lighthouse
Green Hill	6 miles west of Point Judith Lighthouse
Quonochontaug	7½ miles east of Watch Hill Lighthouse
Watch Hill	Near Watch Hill Lighthouse
Sandy Point	North side Block Island near lighthouaw
New Shoreham	East side Block Island near landing
Block Island	West side Block Island near Dickens Point

NAME CHANGES: Straitsmouth was Davis Neck and Gap Cove; Maddaket was Great Neck. The original Plum Island station at the north end of Plum Island was renamed Newburyport while Knobbs Beach station at south end of Plum Island was renamed Plum Island station.

Upholding the dignity of his office, this keeper presented a commanding appearance in his uniform. His crew were in the more casual "summer white" uniforms. Quonochontaug Life-Saving Station in Rhode Island. (Shanks collection)

The unique Narragansett Pier Life-Saving Station had an old world look with its stonework. Today it is a restaurant called Coast Guard House in the community of Narragansett Pier, Rhode Island. (U.S. Coast Guard)

Sandy Point Life-Saving Station on Block Island was where victims of the infamous Larchmont *sinking were brought ashore. Keeper of this Quonochontaug-style station stands at right. (U.S. Coast Guard)*

Newport, Rhode Island could boast architecturally impressive Brenton Point Life-Saving Station. Upscale summer resort communities often received fancier stations. This was an 1884 Deal-type station designed by Paul J. Pelz. (U.S. Coast Guard)

Quonochontaug Life-Saving Station in Rhode Island was the prototype of the Quonochontaug-style stations. Station design types were usually named after first station built in the series. Twenty-one Quonochongtaug-type stations were built. (Richard Boonisar)

Watch Hill Life-Saving Station with entire crew including cook. This Port Huron-style station cared for the Rhode Island and Connecticut coast. (Shanks collection)

Cuttyhunk Life-Saving Station stood on the southern Massachusetts island of the same name. It was a unique design by the architect Albert Bibb. (Shanks collection)

Nahant Life-Saving Station northeast of Boston was one of George Mendleheff's finest designs. A unique design, today this historic building is used by the Coast Guard as a recreational facility. (Shanks collection)

Changing times at Point Judith Life-Saving Station. This Rhode Island station had both an 1875-type (at left) and a Bibb #2-type building at right. Sometimes old and new station houses were used side by side for years. (Shanks collection)

Gay Head Life-Saving Station on Martha's Vineyard had a rich heritage dating to the days of the Wampanoag Indian surfmen. This station was the single example of the Gay Head-style. (Richard Boonisar)

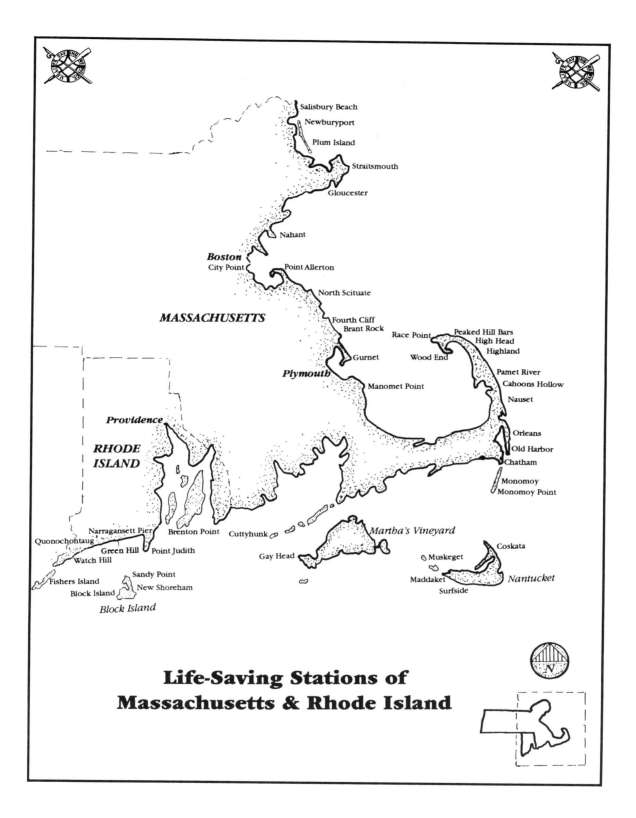

Salisbury Beach
Newburyport
Plum Island
Straitsmouth
Gloucester
Nahant
Boston
City Point
Point Allerton
North Scituate
MASSACHUSETTS
Fourth Cliff
Brant Rock
Race Point
Peaked Hill Bars
High Head
Highland
Gurnet
Wood End
Plymouth
Pamet River
Cahoons Hollow
Manomet Point
Nauset
Orleans
Providence
Old Harbor
*RHODE
ISLAND*
Chatham
Monomoy
Monomoy Point
Narragansett Pier
Brenton Point
Cuttyhunk
Martha's Vineyard
Coskata
Quonochontaug
Green Hill
Point Judith
Watch Hill
Gay Head
Muskeget
Maddaket
Nantucket
Fishers Island
Sandy Point
New Shoreham
Surfside
Block Island
Block Island

Life-Saving Stations of
Massachusetts & Rhode Island

A sailor is brought ashore high in the air in a dramatic breeches buoy from a stranded steamer. (U.S. Coast Guard)

Violent seas dramatically demonstrate the need for breeches buoys in rescue work. Note survivors in ship's rigging awaiting their turn in the breeches buoy. (Richard Boonisar)

Chapter 6
Equipment: Rockets, Mortars, Lifecars and More

LIFE-SAVING SERVICE EQUIPMENT

Life-Saving Service equipment had the overriding goal of bringing survivors safely ashore. To be sure, there was some preventive work in warning ships away from shore. Coston signals were regularly burned to turn ships away and in foggy weather a Lyle gun minus projectile was occasionally fired as a warning. But transporting survivors safely from ship to shore was the most important and most dangerous duty of the Life-Saving Service. There were two basic methods of bringing survivors to land—by boat or by life line. In this chapter we will describe the life line techniques.

HEAVING-STICK & LINE

The simplest rescue technique was to use a heaving-stick and attached line. Heaving-sticks were short sticks with an oval weight at one end. The surfman grasped the heaving-stick and swung it around vertically and then threw the stick. The stick's momentum pulled the line along with it through air at distances up to about fifty yards. This was a good method of passing a line from shore to ship or between vessels if a relatively short distance was involved. Heaving-sticks were carried in the beach cart to all wrecks. After a wreck, surfmen might be dispatched to search the beach for survivors and heaving sticks would be carried during the search.

MORTARS

With the Chinese inventions of gun powder and rockets, the way was paved for propelling lines with something more powerful than the human arm. It was Captain George William Manby, an English army officer born in 1765, who perfected the use of the mortar as a line throwing device. By age fifteen he had already shown an interest in mortars. This interest was most clearly demonstrated when, to the horror of his mother and the church rector, Manby used a homemade mortar to fire a line over the local church, breaking a window in the process. After this incident, Manby's interest in mortars seems to have been put aside some years until he witnessed a terrible shipwreck in 1807. Manby saw a ship grounded just 100 yards off shore, yet 67 men, women and children died before his eyes because they could not get ashore through the surf.

Stunned by what he had seen, Manby dedicated himself to saving lives and within a year had a functioning mortar apparatus in operation. When the *Elizabeth* stranded on the English coast on February 18, 1808, Manby first used his mortar successfully, firing a ball with attached line to the wreck resulting in a rescue. He received well-deserved acclaim, a financial award from Parliament, and saw widespread adoption of his mortars. A particular virtue of Manby's iron mortar was that it was small enough to be reasonably portable. The mortars were so successful that both British and American life-savers used them extensively into the mid-nineteenth century.[1]

ROCKETS

Line rockets were a competing line throwing device. A rocket was placed in a long narrow trough equipped with legs to position it at an angle for flight. In 1807 the Englishman Henry Trengrouse began work with rockets as line carriers and by 1821 rockets had joined Manby's mortars as active life-saving equipment. Line rockets were more portable than even small mortars. They saved many lives in rescues and their use became accepted. Between 1870 and 1910 nearly 10,000 lives were saved in England alone using the rocket apparatus combined with a breeches buoy. Rockets eventually replaced mortars as line throwing devices in England, reportedly completely replacing mortars by 1878. Yet, rockets had liabilities, too, since they were fire hazards, expensive, subject to water damage and broken lines, and were easily effected by the wind.[2]

In the United States, mortars and line rockets were the primary means of throwing lines from shore to ship in American rescues from 1849 through 1871. In America both Manby mortars (also called eprouvette mortars) and Cunningham line rockets, invented by Robert Cunningham of Massachusetts, were standard equipment at government life-saving stations by 1849. Cunningham line rockets had a greater range than mortars, reaching distances of 700 to 1,000 yards, but were subject to the same problems other rockets faced.[3]

HUNT GUN

Both mortars and line rockets were soon to be supplanted by line throwing guns in the U.S.[4] Edward S.

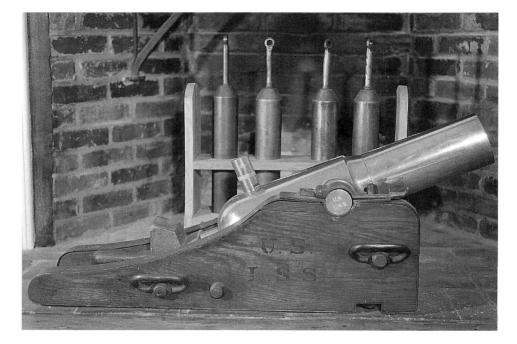

Three major line throwing tools. At left is the Hunt gun, at center a Manby mortar with ball, and at right a Lyle gun. (Richard Boonisar)

Standard method of getting a line to an offshore vessel was by this small brass cannon called a Lyle gun. Behind the Lyle gun are projectiles. (Richard Boonisar)

The rocket was an early line throwing device. A rocket with attached line ready to launch from its' tripod. (U.S. Coast Guard Academy)

Hunt of Weymouth, Massachusetts, developed the Hunt line gun about 1879 and his invention was enthusiastically adopted by the Massachusetts Humane Society to replace mortars. The Hunt gun was perfected by the Humane Society and in 1891 the Society awarded Hunt its gold medal in "recognition of his eminent services in saving life by inventing the Hunt gun and projectile." While the Hunt gun was popular with the Humane Society, it was only used at a few U.S. Life-Saving Service stations.[5]

LYLE GUN

Although the U.S. Life-Saving Service tried the Hunt gun, a different line throwing gun would be selected as standard for the USLSS. The inventor of this remarkable new line gun was Captain David A. Lyle. Ohio born and a graduate of West Point and Massachusetts Institute of Technology, Captain Lyle began his military career in the west in 1869 at San Francisco Bay's Benicia Arsenal.[6] Lyle's western tours of duty were far ranging, from freezing Alaska to California's scorching Death Valley. Perhaps Lyle had seen it all and wanted to ponder what it all meant for he then went east to become a philosophy professor at West Point.[7]

By 1877 Sumner Kimball and Revenue Marine Captain James H. Merryman, Inspector of Life-Saving Stations, needed help in developing better line throwing devices. David Lyle was assigned to help the young Life-Saving Service. Lyle spent the next two years experimenting with life-saving equipment, beginning in Springfield, Massa-

chusetts, in what is today Van Horn Park. Like Manby, Captain Lyle had problems with those who opposed his firing a dangerous projectile around the community. City officials required that he post guards since bystanders congregated about the line of fire endangering themselves. Lyle discovered what Manby had learned decades earlier: flying projectiles excited controversy.

Consequently, Lyle moved his experiments to Sandy Hook, New Jersey, then a more sparsely populated place. The officer in charge of government land was General S.V. Benét and he agreed to allow the philosopher-soldier to conduct his trials there. Perhaps General Benét was open to helping because he, too, was a bit of a dreamer. Later, his son, Steven Vincent Benét, would become a world famous poet.[8]

By 1878 Lyle had perfected his line throwing gun. It was a small 185 pound bronze cannon and carriage capable of firing a seventeen pound, fourteen and one-half inch bullet-shaped projectile with an eye bolt screwed into it. The projectile was placed in the two and one-half inch bore of the cannon's barrel with the eye bolt facing outward. The line was attached to the eye bolt which kept the line away from the cannon's mouth. Lyle guns were known to have reached a range of nearly 700 yards; however, the practical range was often much less.[9]

While the Lyle gun had a shorter range than Cunningham rockets, it possessed the advantages of lower cost, ease of handling, simpler preparation for firing and

Keeper in dark uniform pulls lanyard and fires the Lyle gun. The projectile soars above him. The sand anchor at left was made of crossed planks and buried in the beach to hold the breeches buoy lines taut. Willapa Bay Life-Saving Station, Washington. (Coast Guard Museum Northwest)

Surfmen harnessed to beach cart ready for a drill. The beach cart and all the equipment in it were collectively known as the "beach apparatus." Coos Bay Life-Saving Station, Oregon. (Coast Guard Museum Northwest)

Breeches Buoy (U.S. Coast Guard)

Breeches buoy, Lyle gun, projectiles, faking box, tally board, crotch, lines, sand anchor, shovels and lanterns were hauled to wrecks in the beach cart. (Richard Boonisar)

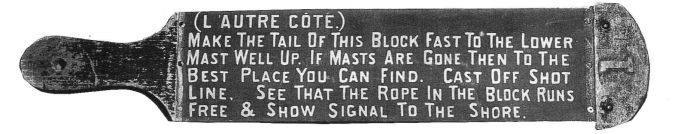

(L'AUTRE CÔTÉ.) MAKE THE TAIL OF THIS BLOCK FAST TO THE LOWER MAST WELL UP. IF MASTS ARE GONE THEN TO THE BEST PLACE YOU CAN FIND. CAST OFF SHOT LINE. SEE THAT THE ROPE IN THE BLOCK RUNS FREE & SHOW SIGNAL TO THE SHORE.

When the shot line was fired to a shipwreck, survivors had to pull aboard a heavier line, a block and a "tally board." The tally board, shown here, had instructions telling mariners to tie the block to a mast using the attached tail line and cast off the shot line. Tally boards had instructions in English on one side, French on the other. (Richard Boonisar)

better accuracy. Lyle gun projectiles could also be reused, at least during practice. The Lyle gun was used from 1878 until at least 1962. It was an invention inspired by Captain Manby's mortar, but one that would prove even more lasting and reliable.[10] Lyle described his gun as having "been a labor of love. I am deeply interested in anything bearing upon a service so noble and successful" as saving lives.[11]

The Lyle gun provided a reliable method of getting the line from shore to shipwreck, so the question became how to carry survivors safely ashore. Having them go hand over hand across a rope was dangerous and survivors were usually in no condition for such acrobatics. Tying a line about a person's waist and dragging them ashore was attempted with limited results. Charles Ellms' 1836 book illustrates an effective early Chinese life preserver which consisted of bamboo logs arranged in crossed pairs with the survivor in the very center. It was an important step forward, but still left the survivor in the water as did later European cork life jackets.[12]

BOSUN'S CHAIRS

For a time during the Life-Saving Service's early years, and on rare occasions in later years as well, the bosun's chair was used. Little more than a loop of rope, sometimes with a board added as a seat, it offered about as much safety and less comfort than a child's playground swing. It could be easily and quickly rigged, however, and it was an old and honorable sailor's device. Its greatest shortcoming was that survivors could easily fall from it and it worked poorly for conveying anyone in a weakened condition.

LIFECARS

A second device to carry mariners ashore by lines was the lifecar or surfcar. This was an American invention, invented by Joseph Francis in 1838 and perfected in 1847. Joseph Francis was born in Massachusetts in 1801 and devoted his life to designing boats and life-saving devices. He exhibited at the first fair of the Massachusetts Institute of Technology at age eighteen and a rowboat he entered won recognition. Francis went on to design and

build racing boats, an early landing barge, metal lifeboats and other craft. He worked extensively in corrugated metal and his "metallic lifeboats" became widely used.[13]

Joseph Francis is best known for his lifecar. The lifecar was a galvanized iron-sheathed boat looking much like a small submarine. It was hauled between shore and ship by lines attached to large rings mounted at each end. It had small raised air holes on the top which allowed air but little water to enter. A small hatch atop the lifecar allowed two to four occupants to enter where they generally laid down. The hatch was then closed and the lifecar pulled ashore. While the lifecar protected against being washed out by waves, it was still the world's roughest "submarine" ride. Lifecars were used up to about 1899 when the breeches buoy's ease of handling, lighter weight, greater speed and lower cost all combined to render the lifecar almost obsolete. The lifecar was, however, used during drills until about 1940.[14]

Regrettably, Joseph Francis suffered from competing claims by Capt. David Ottinger of the Revenue Marine concerning who had invented the lifecar. Ottinger, who played an important role in establishing the early life-saving stations in New Jersey, claimed to have invented the craft which he called a surfcar. Although both may have had a hand in the development of the lifecar, Joseph Francis makes a strong case for being the inventor in his book, *History of Life-Saving Appliances* and his claim was supported by the New York State Chamber of Commerce. Most importantly, Sumner Kimball stated that "I believe (the lifecar) to be the invention of Mr. Joseph Francis."[15]

BREECHES BUOY

The Life-Saving Service's most successful method of bringing survivors ashore by lines was the breeches buoy. A breeches buoy consisted of a common cork-filled life ring (a circular life preserver) with a pair of short-legged oversize canvas pants sewn inside. The person got into the breeches buoy as if putting on a pair of pants.[16]

BEACH APPARATUS

The collective name for the equipment used in a breeches buoy drill was the "beach apparatus." Main com-

The lifecar was a metal-sheathed boat which looked like a miniature submarine. It was pulled between shore and ship much like a breeches buoy. (Shanks collection)

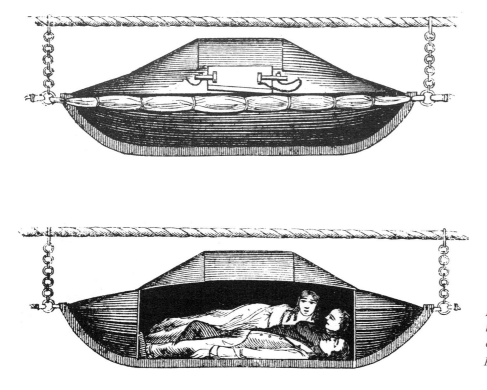

Exterior and interior views of one type of lifecar. Survivors most commonly lay down as they were pulled ashore. (Shanks collection)

The U.S. Life-Saving Service heaving-stick and throwing line. (Richard Boonisar)

Surfman with throwing line and heaving-stick. (Cape Cod National Seashore)

Heaving-stick in hand, a surfman prepares to pass a line to a sinking vessel. This 1880 illustration captures the drama of approaching a wreck. (Shanks collection)

Paul Boyton, the man who went over 25,000 miles in a rubber life-saving dress. Boyton was a pioneer in the development of survival suits and introduced the American public to water recreation. (Shanks collection)

The life-dress was the grandparent of today's survival suit. (Shanks collection)

ponents of a typical beach apparatus were a breeches buoy, Lyle gun, projectiles, sand anchor, crotch, faking box, hawser, whip lines, shovels, two tally boards, hawser cutter and block and tackle. All this equipment was hauled to the rescue scene in the beach cart. While some beach carts had two axles, most were single axle with low, raised sides and with large reels holding line. They were typically pulled to the scene by the surfmen themselves. Torch-like lanterns were carried in the beach cart. These were lighted and mounted on staffs to show a white light indicating where it was safe for survivors to land.[17]

Once the beach cart was at a wreck, the apparatus was unloaded and set up. A light-weight shot line was attached to a projectile and fired out to a stranded vessel using the Lyle gun. The projectile flew over the vessel, dropping the line down to the crew. The crew had to pull the shot line aboard which was attached to a heavier whip line. The whip line had an attached tail block (pulley) which would be tied to the ship's mast by the ship's crew. A tally board (instruction tablet) told the crew in English and French what to do. They were instructed to cast off the shot line and then tie the tail block well up on the mast or some other high place. Once the block was attached to the mast, the surfmen pulled on the whip line to haul a heavy hawser out to the ship. The hawser was then tied above the whip line tailblock. The breeches buoy rode on the hawser on a traveling block, pulled along by surfmen using the whip lines. Once the breeches buoy reached the wreck, usually only one person at a time rode the breeches buoy, although there were cases where two at a time came ashore in it.

Surfmen became so proficient at setting up breeches buoys and hauling people ashore that survivors could be brought ashore quickly. During drills the best USLSS crews could fire the Lyle gun, rig a breeches buoy and haul a person down from the wreck pole in two minutes and thirty seconds. All crews had to complete the drill in under five minutes or they faced dismissal from the service. The breeches buoy was immensely successful and became the standard rescue device for hauling survivors ashore.[18]

RUBBER LIFE-SAVING DRESSES

The rubber life-saving dress, invented by C.S. Merriman of Ohio, was also used by the Life-Saving Service in its rescue work.[19] More a suit than a dress, it was the forerunner of today's survival suit. Its goal was to protect the wearer against drowning or freezing. It consisted of full-length footed rubber pants and a double-ply rubber shirt. A steel band and rubber strap were used to firmly attach the shirt to the pants. The suit weighed about thirty-five pounds and covered the entire body except for the face. Rubber tubes hung near the face and allowed the life-saving dress to be inflated between layers at the chest, back, legs and behind the head. There apparently were

three to five inflatable areas depending on the suit. In the water, the wearer could be either horizontal or vertical.

To early Americans, the life-saving dress appeared to be some monster from the deep. Surfmen wearing them were known to unintentionally frighten persons encountering them along the beach. Some surfmen were disinclined to wear the suits because of its appearance and the fact that some felt the suits were unmanly. Calling them something other than "life dresses" might have helped.[20]

The Merriman life-saving dress was supplied to stations where surfmen would occasionally wear them to enter the breakers. The suit was used primarily in three situations. First, it was useful in allowing surfmen to enter cold water and help struggling survivors ashore. Second, the life-saving dress enabled a surfman to reach a wreck and assist benumbed crewmen in setting up life-lines for a breeches buoy rescue. Finally, on occasions it was worn when crossing deep sloughs or creeks. Life-saving dresses were used rather sparingly; in 1884, for example, they were successfully used in seven rescues.

The general public became aware of the life-dress through the efforts of a former surfman and showman named Paul Boyton who made them famous.[21] The Life-Saving Service sometimes even called the life-dress "Paul Boyton life-suits."[22] Paul Boyton was an amazing man. He said he was hired in 1873-74 "to take charge of the life saving service at Atlantic City... Paul was installed as the captain (keeper) of a station built out on the beach and equipped with all kinds of life saving apparatus... It was while in this service his attention was attracted to the life saving dress..." Boyton became fascinated with the life-saving dress and ceaselessly promoted the use of survival suits. In an era when the public feared the sea, Boyton opened up its recreational possibilities.[23]

During his career Paul Boyton swam and sailed the world, covering 25,000 miles in a rubber life-saving dress. Boyton next became a professional showman presenting "Paul Boyton's Water Circus" where he entertained by doing such feats as sailing along in his life-saving dress with all manner of sails attached to his body, sometimes even rigging himself as a square rigger. He had entire teams of life-dressed water assistants who performed ball games, mock fights and even naval "battles." Floating rubber shoes were developed and he and his performers walked on water. The Life-Saving Service used the suit conventionally but couldn't resist mentioning Boyton with pride in their 1876 *Annual Report*.[24] What Paul Boyton achieved was to demonstrate the remarkable usefulness of what we today call the survival suit. He and C.S. Merriman were founding fathers of what has become an indispensable component of rescue equipment.

Atlantic City Life-Saving Station in winter. Paul J. Pelz, architect of the Library of Congress, designed these Deal-type stations for the Life-Saving Service. There were four Deal-type stations, each originally with their distinctive towers. (U.S. Coast Guard)

Ditch Plain Life-Saving Station was guardian of the Montauk Point region of Long Island, New York. It was an 1882-type station. (Library of Congress)

Chapter 7

Life-Saving Stations of New York & New Jersey

THE LIFE-SAVING SERVICE IN NEW YORK AND NEW JERSEY

New York City was flanked by more life-saving stations than any other port. Chains of life-saving stations spread out from New York Harbor along the coasts of Long Island and New Jersey. By 1914, 71 life-saving stations stretched from Montauk Point, New York, to Cape May, New Jersey. Many of the shipwrecks that inflamed public demand for an American rescue service occurred in these waters.[1]

The life-saving stations of the New York and New Jersey sea coasts were built in the classic Atlantic Coast pattern of stations located approximately three to five miles apart. Beach patrols and lookouts covered virtually every foot of coastline. The hand launched surfboat predominated on these sandy beaches and narrow inlets. Close proximity of stations allowed for joint rescues involving two or more stations.

In contrast to the Atlantic seaboard stations, upstate New York's life-saving stations were built on the typical Great Lakes model of isolated stations located only at specific dangerous locations. These were usually harbor entrances and stations were generally too far apart to provide immediate support to one another during disasters. On the Great Lakes the lifeboat became more important than the surfboat.

New York was the only state to have life-saving stations on both the ocean and on the Great Lakes. With thirty-five stations, New York tied with Massachusetts and Michigan as having the second greatest number of life-saving stations. New York's stations were in three separate USLSS districts. By 1914, the 30 Long Island stations comprised the Fourth District, the Fishers Island station was in the Third District with Rhode Island's stations and the five upstate New York stations were in the Tenth District together with the Pennsylvania, Ohio and Kentucky life-saving stations. This complex organization illustrates the diversity of New York shores as well as their importance.[2]

New Jersey had more life-saving stations than any other state. There were 41 active New Jersey stations by 1914, all in the Fifth District which coincided with the state's boundaries. Significantly, the first federal government life-saving station was built in New Jersey, at Spermaceti Cove Station near Sandy Hook. Because the USLSS later became the Coast Guard, this station is generally regarded as the first Coast Guard station in America.[3]

There were good reasons why this coast was central to the Life-Saving Service. "This dangerous section of the Atlantic seaboard, the Long Island and New Jersey coasts, presents the most ghastly record of disaster. Lying on either side of the great metropolis of the nation…(these coasts) annually levy a terrible tribute upon its passing commerce. The broken skeletons of wrecked vessels with which the beaches are strewn…testify to the vastness of the sacrifice of life and property which these (unrelenting) shores have claimed." Offshore sand bars became watery graveyards when ships stranded off the beaches.[4]

This sandy coast, a summer playground to millions, was a nightmare to mariners during the foul weather months. Wrecks included not only New York bound ships, but many coastwise vessels bound for other ports. One of these wrecks was that of the three masted schooner *Benjamin C. Cromwell* at Fire Island, New York, on February 22, 1904. Earlier in the voyage, off Cape Hatteras, North Carolina, the *Cromwell* had encountered a succession of gales that forced the captain to jettison a considerable portion of his deck load of lumber. Fog and rain conditions became so bad that the Diamond Shoals lightship off North Carolina's Outer Banks was the last light her crew saw for the rest of the voyage. By the time the *Cromwell* was off Long Island, the ship's officers thought they were forty miles from the New York shore and did not even bother to take soundings. The ship, in fact, was just off Fire Island. She soon ran aground and quickly began to show signs she would break up. When wooden ships are broken by the sea they look as if a giant smashed them apart with a huge axe. The sailors knew what was ahead and lighted oil-soaked torches as distress signals.[5]

The burning torches were seen by a Fire Island surfman on patrol from the Bellport Life-Saving Station. Surfman Jayne promptly burned a Coston signal in reply to acknowledge that the wreck had been discovered. He then ran back to his station to report the wreck. Bellport Keeper Kremer analyzed the situation and telephoned both Blue Point and Smiths Point Life-Saving Stations for help. It was clear that this would not be an easy rescue.[6]

Long Island and New Jersey were the scene of many shipwrecks. Here surfmen launch a surfboat to go to the assistance of a stranded steamer. (Fire Island National Seashore)

Fire Island, New York, surfmen rush ashore carrying a survivor. (Fire Island National Seashore)

At dawn, the surfmen could see the ship. "Tremendous seas" swept the deck and the crew could be seen clinging to the rigging. The schooner was close enough to shore to use the Lyle gun and rig a breeches buoy, the safest option.[7]

The Lyle gun was positioned and fired. The shot was good and the captain began to haul the line in. But the motion of the ship rubbing against the line wore the thin line through and it parted. Then a thick fog moved in. The Lyle gun fired more shots, several reaching the ship, but all efforts by the ship's crew to haul aboard the breeches buoy failed. Seldom had so many good shots been fired without bringing a single person ashore.[8]

Blue Point and Smiths Point stations' surfmen arrived and joined the Bellport surfmen. The three station keepers determined to use their next option and try a rescue by boat. The high surf, direction of the current, and the large amount of wreckage being tossed about made launching a surfboat dangerous. Nevertheless, all three keepers decided to go out with a crew of the best men from the three stations. Despite the high surf, the launch was successful and the trip to the schooner began. The rescuers successfully rowed to the wreck, but the current was extremely strong and the surfboat was swept past the ship. Worse, with the seas so rough the rescue boat could not be turned around. The surfboat had to be rowed back to shore and, in a very dangerous maneuver, backed onto the beach. The surfmen quickly moved to a better site to relaunch the surfboat.

But suddenly the sailors clinging to the *Cromwell's* masts faced a new danger. The masts were falling! First the mizzenmast fell and then in quick succession the main mast and foremast fell too. The sailors had only a moment to reach the quarter deck. One of the mariners managed to climb aboard a floating cabin roof.[9]

Since the sole hope now lay with the survivors getting close to shore, the U.S. Life-Savers immediately spread along the beach carrying heaving sticks and lines. The wreckage was gradually moving toward the beach so if anyone got close enough, a heaving line would be tossed to them.[10]

But heaving lines alone would not be enough in such rough sea conditions. The life-savers had exhausted almost every rescue technique. But surfman Frank B. Raynor of Blue Point Station could see the man on the cabin roof drifting toward shore, about to enter the deadly breakers. As the man reached the surf, Raynor had to act. He ran into the sea to save the sailor.

Breakers and wreckage smashed into Surfman Raynor, knocking him off his feet. "In this desperate crisis, (surfman) Albert Latham of the Blue Point Station, rushed to his comrade's aid. Raynor succeeded in clearing himself before Latham reached him, and they both simulta-

neously laid hold of the sailor and began dragging him to shore. At times all three were under the surf, and once Raynor rescued Latham from a perilous predicament, but both bravely stood to their self-sacrificing task, and soon had their man sufficiently near the beach to hand him over to their waiting comrades, who stood shoulder deep in the surf."[11]

Other surviving sailors could be seen. A surfboat was immediately launched but the breakers beat the surfboat back and washed the keeper overboard. The defeated keeper barely managed to struggle ashore. Lead by another keeper, surfmen began firing the Lyle gun but by now the mariners were so weak they could not pick up even a light line.[12]

Then seas swept over the sailors and all the rest of them went into the sea. "It was a fearful spectacle" for the surfmen. Only two seamen were still visible. Surfmen Raynor and Latham used the only rescue resource left—their own bodies. Both again rushed into the surf after the sailors. The surfmen were repeatedly knocked down, bruised by wreckage, thrown about and pulled under by the churning sea. But Raynor and Latham were not to be stopped, they reached the two survivors and carried them safely ashore. Only two of the three men brought ashore by Raynor and Latham survived, the sole survivors of that terrible wreck on Fire Island.[13]

The United States Congress later presented Blue Point surfmen Raynor and Latham with the rare gold medal of honor for life-saving at a large gathering at Patchogue, New York, on June 15, 1904. Albert Latham recovered, but Frank Raynor "was so badly injured he had not been able to return to duty since the day of the wreck and it (was) feared that he will never regain his health." If so, surfman Raynor would have faced a future of poverty with only a gold medal to show the appreciation of a nation that cared for soldiers, but not life-savers.[14]

Both the north and south approaches to New York harbor saw some of worst wrecks in the country. Sometimes wrecks even occurred in groups. These multiple shipwrecks resulted in some of the most remarkable rescues in Life-Saving Service history. One case was during February 1880 when two storms raged along the Atlantic and Gulf Coasts. The northern storm extended from Maine south, while the southern storm extended from Louisiana north. The great storms moved toward each other meeting on February third in New Jersey and New York and resulted in "the severest tempest on the Atlantic during the year."[15]

The two storms arrived in the vicinity of New York City at midnight, beginning with snow and sleet which then turned to cold rain. For the next twelve hours shore dwellers saw the highest seas in many years, suffered winds of 84 miles per hour, had their buildings blown apart and saw coastlands flooded.[16] "It was a season of hardship

Georgica Life-Saving Station was a Long Island station built in the handsome 1882-type. (Queens Library, Long Island Collection)

Southampton Life-Saving Station on Long Island was a wonderful mix of styles. It was an 1876-type with an 1882-type tower and an inset porch designed about 1910. (U.S. Coast Guard)

Mecox Life-Saving Station was an picturesque 1875-type station on Long Island. Note lookout tower centered on roof. (Shanks collection)

Amagansett Life-Saving Station was an 1876-type station on Long Island. Many years later during World War II, Amagansett Coast Guard beach patrol captured German spies coming ashore from a submarine. (U.S. Coast Guard)

Short Beach Life-Saving Station, an 1876-type station on Long Island. There were at least twenty-six 1876-type stations, all on the East Coast. (U.S. Coast Guard)

Eatons Neck Life-Saving Station on Long Island Sound's approaches to New York City had both an 1875-type station (at left) and an 1849 station (at right). It was not uncommon for an earlier station to remain in use after a newer one had been built. (U.S. Coast Guard)

Rockaway Life-Saving Station was a fine example of an expanded red house-type station. It was one of the stations that guarded the entrance to New York Harbor. (U.S. Coast Guard)

Point of Woods Life-Saving Station with crew. A classic Long Island expanded red house-type. (U.S. Coast Guard)

and danger for the life-saving crews upon the Jersey coast… During the twelve hours the tempest lasted there were five wrecks within the field of four consecutive stations in New Jersey."

The first wreck involved the three-masted Maine schooner *Stephen Harding* that had collided in the storm with the schooner *Kate Newman*. The captain of the *Harding* briefly sighted the other vessel ahead in the darkness and then in a moment she was high above them on a great wave "almost over our heads." The ships struck, then separated, leaving one of the *Kate Newman's* crew on the deck of the *Harding*. The wounded *Stephen Harding* staggered toward shore, coming aground about a mile north of the Spermaceti Cove Life-Saving Station. On the beach, Spermaceti Cove's patrolman was making his rounds searching for wrecks. The storm was so bad that in the darkness and whirling snow, the surfman was unsure even of his own position. He saw a light, but thought it the lantern of the advancing patrolman from Sandy Hook Life-Saving Station. He struggled forward only to discover the light was in fact from the cabin skylight of the *Stephen Harding*, stranded 250 yards offshore. The surfman burned a red Coston flare to let the sailors know they were seen and then hurried back to his station to turn out the crew.[17]

Spermaceti Cove Keeper J.W. Edwards gave the standing order for such emergencies: "Open boat room doors—man the beach cart." The Number Five and Number Six surfmen had the job of securing the boatroom doors. Then each surfman slipped the drag ropes over their shoulders and took their assigned positions at the beach cart. At the command, "Forward," they commenced pulling the beach cart which carried the Lyle gun, lines, and all equipment needed for a breeches buoy rescue. "The snow was thick upon the beach, the drifts more than knee-deep and fast accumulating, badly clogging the cart wheels; and the wind, steadily increasing, impeded the advance by its force, and blew the snow and sand together straight into the faces of the men" as they struggled forward.[18]

Despite the conditions, the Spermaceti Cove crew reached the point opposite the *Harding*. In the dark amidst the blowing snow and sand, the Lyle gun was set up. Keeper Edwards carefully fired the Lyle gun and laid the life line right across the *Harding*. The ship's crew hauled the line and soon the breeches buoy was rigged. Out went the breeches buoy, disappearing into the dark night as it neared the ship's side. The surfmen then pulled the breeches buoy back ashore, expecting to find a sailor in it. But the breeches buoy returned empty. Twice again the breeches buoy went out to the ship to return empty.[19]

A fourth try was made and this time a German sailor came ashore in the breeches buoy. The German said that the captain's wife was aboard and that everyone wanted to stay with the ship until daylight and then come ashore.

But the tide was rising and the storm worsening so Keeper Edwards sent a surfman out by breeches buoy to tell those on board to leave the vessel. The schooner was beginning to pound and spray was flying twenty feet above the heads of those on board. Finally those on board the ship agreed to come ashore in the breeches buoy. A sailor was landed, then the captain's wife and the rest. It was a successful rescue, but had those on board delayed longer the rescue would not have succeeded.[20]

The great storm was by now adding to its toll of ships in the night. At about same time the *Stephen Harding* stranded, the brig *Castalia* of Bath, Maine struck the beach. She stranded about three-fourths of a mile from Seabright Life-Saving Station, the next station south of Spermaceti Cove. The *Castalia* was discovered by Seabright's beach patrolman when he looked "across the wind" after he had gone by the wreck, since it was impossible to look directly into the wind due to the stinging sand and snow. The usual red Coston signal of was burned and the patrolman returned to the station for help. Keeper A. H. West turned the Seabright crew out and the beach cart was pulled to the scene.[21]

Conditions on land and sea were terrible. Mrs. W. C. Seymore, a passenger on the *Castalia*, later wrote, "The sea was raging almost mountain high, sweeping over the vessel's decks, threatening to engulf her… The night was in inky darkness, the snow was blinding. Our boats would have been smashed to atoms, even if we could have succeeded in launching them, which was utterly impossible."[22]

The surfmen faced trying odds. A white Coston signal was burned to briefly illuminate the ship. Just to aim the Lyle gun, Seabright's keeper had to have his men shield his face from the sand and sleet. Lanterns became useless as they were coated with snow. The entire breeches buoy rescue was done by memory from drills since it was performed entirely in darkness. Yet it was done right and soon the *Castalia's* passenger and crew were being drawn safely ashore. The ship was rolling so violently that it was impossible to keep the breeches buoy hawser taut. As Mrs. Seymore and the others were drawn ashore, they were dipped into the icy sea. The surfmen plunged into the Atlantic each time the breeches buoy neared shore and dragged the ship people safely ashore. All on board were saved. Keeper West's family cared for the survivors at the station. Mrs. Seymore spoke for all survivors when she wrote, "What a grand institution is the Life-Saving Service!"[23]

That night just after midnight, the schooner *E.C. Babcock* stranded near the next station south, Monmouth Beach Life-Saving Station. This ship, too, was found by a surfman on patrol. Monmouth Beach's keeper Charles H. Valentine was quite sick when the alarm came, but he led his men to the rescue anyway. The beach cart was drawn to the scene, but the weather was so cold that the life line

A classic Long Island scene. Fire Island Life-Saving Station with Fire Island lighthouse behind it. Expanded red house-type station built in 1872. (U.S. Coast Guard)

Point Lookout Life-Saving Station on Long Island guarded shores as ships neared New York harbor. An expanded red house-type station on Long Island. (U.S. Coast Guard)

Early photo of Shinnecock Life-Saving Station, a Long Island red house-type shown before expansion. (U.S. Coast Guard)

Lone Hill Life-Saving Station on Long Island put name boards of ships over doorways to commemorate rescues. Red house-design. (U.S. Coast Guard)

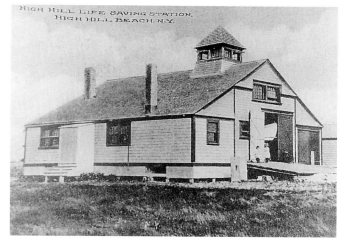

Zachs Inlet Life-Saving Station was another expanded red house station on Long Island. Located on Jones Beach it was informally sometimes called High Hill. (Alvin Penny)

Bellport Life-Saving Station was one of the early red house-type stations which was expanded as shown here during 1887-88. Long Island, New York. (U.S. Coast Guard)

Oak Island Life-Saving Station was an expanded red house-type station built in 1872 on Long Island. (U.S. Coast Guard)

Potunk Life-Saving Station on Long Island. A red house-type. (U.S. Coast Guard)

A crowd gathers at Forge River Life-Saving Station in anticipation of a breeches buoy drill. A red house-type station on Long Island. (Van Field)

Quogue Life-Saving Station survived hurricanes and time. This Lorain-type station is a Long Island private residence today. (U.S. Coast Guard)

Moriches Life-Saving Station on Long Island shore. A Lorain-style station with its boatroom at right. (U.S. Coast Guard)

Napeague Life-Saving Station on eastern Long Island was a Bibb# 2-type station, a rarity in New York but common in New Jersey. (U.S. Coast Guard)

froze and then broke, slowing the breeches buoy rescue. Yet in less than two hours, in the middle of the hurricane, all on the *E.C. Babcock* were saved.[24]

Back at Monmouth Beach Life-Saving Station, the survivors were cared for and breakfast finally served. The surfmen were getting their beach apparatus gear once again in order when suddenly a patrolling surfman bounded in with news of yet another wreck, the Spanish brig *Augustana*. Keeper Valentine, still weak from his illness, again led the Monmouth Beach crew out into the winter storm. The *Augustana* had been purposely run ashore to try to save the lives of those on board. Huge waves had pushed the ship close to the beach by the time the surfmen and beach cart arrived. Surfman Garrett H. White was the hero of the hour. "By following a receding sea, running down into the surf as far as possible, and putting forth his utmost strength, (Surfman White) succeeded in casting the heaving-stick and line on board..." The sailors pulled aboard the line with attached tally board showing lettered instructions on how to rig a breeches buoy. Unfortunately, the tally board's instructions had only English on one side and French on the other. The Spanish sailors could not decipher the instructions. The surfmen could shout to sailors, but tragically no one on the beach spoke Spanish.[25]

In desperation, the Spanish sailors began to come hand over hand ashore on the whip line. This was extremely dangerous under the best of circumstances and the lifesavers tried to signal the sailors not to attempt it. But well justified fear drove the Spaniards and they began to come

across. As the first sailor neared shore, Surfman White rushed into the sea to grab him. Driftwood filled breakers hit both men and they were knocked from their feet and torn from the whip line. But White managed to regain his footing and saved the sailor and himself. One by one more sailors came over the line and each time a surfman rushed out to get him. The surfmen were knocked down by the sea, hit by debris, and chilled beyond words, but when it was over all were safely at the Monmouth Beach Life-Saving Station. Keeper Charles H. Valentine, Surfman Garrett White and three other Monmouth Beach surfmen all received gold medals for their bravery that night.[26]

And so it went through that long New Jersey February night. There were more rescues, by Long Branch, Swan Point (Mantoloking) and Green Island (Chadwick) Life-Saving Stations and many lives were saved. Afterwards, twenty-five Congressional gold life-saving medals were awarded for the night's work, the all-time record for surfmen in a single storm.[27]

The tradition of self-sacrifice for the safety of others continued. In 1885 Shark River Life-Saving Station's keeper John C. Patterson led a rescue of three yachtsmen stranded offshore during an unusually turbulent July storm. Just as Keeper Patterson was launching the surfboat, a messenger ran up informing him that his brother, keeper of the Sandy Hook lighthouse, was dying and he must come immediately. John Patterson's face went pale. "Telegraph back that I cannot go now," was all he said as a look of determination came to his face. Taking the steering oar, Keeper Patterson ordered his crew to launch. Out Patterson

Twice a week all life-saving stations held beach apparatus drills involving firing the Lyle gun and rigging the breeches buoy. Here, Blue Point Life-Saving Station surfmen on Long Island tighten the block and tackle to make the hawser taut. (U.S. Coast Guard)

A surfman performs wig-wag signals atop Long Island's Jones Beach Life-Saving Station. A Red house-style station. (U.S. Coast Guard)

Long Island's northeast tip was watched over by Rocky Point Life-Saving Station, near Greenport. This 1896 Duluth-type station still stands as a private residence. (Shanks collection)

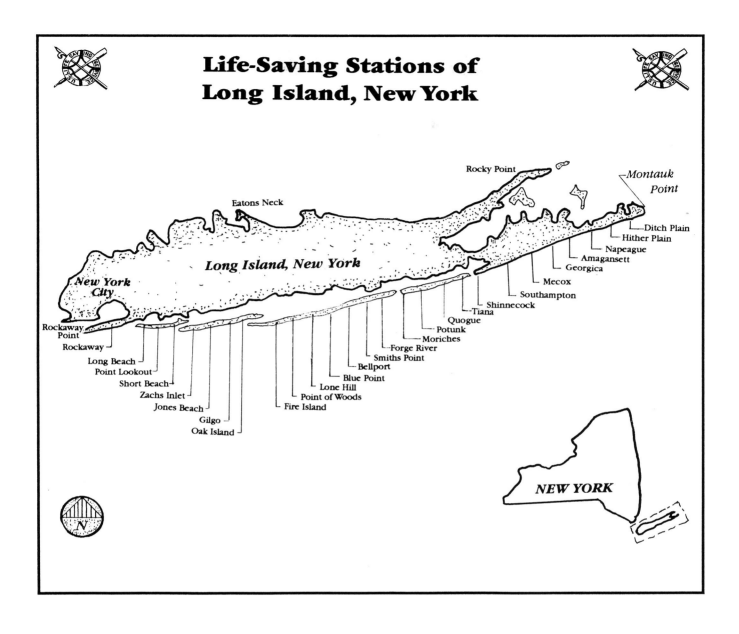

Life-Saving Stations of Long Island, New York

Long Island, New York

Rocky Point

Montauk Point

Eatons Neck

Ditch Plain
Hither Plain
Napeague
Amagansett
Georgica
Mecox
Southampton
Shinnecock
Tiana
Quogue
Potunk
Moriches
Forge River
Smiths Point
Bellport
Blue Point
Lone Hill
Point of Woods
Fire Island

New York City

Rockaway Point
Rockaway
Long Beach
Point Lookout
Short Beach
Zachs Inlet
Jones Beach
Gilgo
Oak Island

NEW YORK

and his crew went through "the fury of the gale, the high and dangerous surf" to save the three yachtsmen. Both Keeper Patterson and his surfmen received gold life-saving medals.[28]

The year 1886 proved to be one of tragedy for the Life-Saving Service. On the morning of February 11, 1886 the Austrian bark *Kraljevica* was running with all sails set before a strong northeast wind at night in dense fog. About one o'clock in the morning she fatally struck Barnegat Shoals. The crew burned a distress signal, which was seen by Barnegat Life-Saving Station.[29]

The Barnegat surfmen prepared to go to the rescue of the *Kraljevica*. Keeper Joel H. Ridgeway of the Barnegat

Life-Saving Station telephoned the Loveladies Life-Saving Station for assistance. But without waiting for the Loveladies surfmen to arrive, Keeper Ridgeway and his crew ran their surfboat down to the beach and launched. The *Kraljevica* was in an obviously bad position and could not last long. The sea was running high with a strong current along the shore and a cold wind blowing.[30]

When the surfmen rowed to the first line of breakers they were stunned, for the surf was the highest they had seen in years. It was difficult for Keeper Ridgeway to avoid being thrown from the surfboat as he stood at the steering oar. The surfmen struggled at their oars, actually being forced backwards by the sea at times. By now the hard pulling was tiring the rowers. As they approached

Surfmen to the rescue. In a scene repeated countless times on the Atlantic Coast, the surfboat is launched from the beach. (Richard Boonisar)

New Jersey's 1882-style Ocean City Life-Saving Station with surfboat on boat carriage. (The Historical Museum of Ocean City, NJ)

the wreck, sea conditions grew worse and the surfmen were near the breaking point. Keeper Ridgeway wanted to reach the wreck to tie on to it and give his men a rest but "the men were so exhausted by their arduous work that this was found impossible."[31]

Under these circumstances Keeper Ridgeway had little choice but to back toward the beach, a very dangerous technique requiring the utmost skill and caution. This was Ridgeway's only choice, other than running the boat ashore at top speed with the waves, an even riskier procedure. Trying to back ashore proved exhausting, perhaps even more than pulling out to the wreck. The surfboat was being half swamped by huge seas and one surfman bailed constantly.

With an exhausted crew and a worsening storm, Keeper Ridgeway could see only one possible chance for survival—to attempt to turn the boat around in the storm and run for the beach. Ridgeway conferred with his trusted surfman, John I. Soper, and a plan was agreed upon. The surfmen managed to turn the boat, timing their approach with the rush waves and then entered the hellish place where all seas were breaking. In the "wild turmoil of waters…a towering wave reared its frowning crest close astern (but) the boat could not rise to it. An instant later there came a thundering roar as tons upon tons of water broke with savage (force) upon the boat, twirled it around broadside and rolling it over and over like a chip, the men being thrown out in all directions." One surfman

was killed instantly, being hit in the face by either an oar or the surfboat itself. Two more, John I. Soper and Solomon Soper, died in the surf. Keeper Ridgeway and the others staggered ashore alive.[32]

This was the rarest of all Life-Saving Service fatalities, a situation where the surfmen and their boat were completely overwhelmed by the sea. Usually, when there was a loss of surfmen's lives during a rescue it was because the ship's survivors panicked and capsized the boat or in some other way failed to follow directions. The surfmen generally could manage situations where the sea was the only enemy. The Barnegat Life-Saving Station tragedy was an exception.

Ironically, there was no one left alive on the *Kraljevica,* the ship the surfmen were trying to reach. *Kraljevica* had been rapidly smashed, her bottom rent, and all hands had promptly abandoned ship in a lifeboat. Under the terrible conditions, the lifeboat quickly capsized and most were drowned, just six sailors making the beach alive. The survivors struggled ashore, found a hunter's hut stocked with provisions and settled in to rest from their ordeal. They were later found by a beach patrolman from the Ship Bottom Life-Saving Station and taken there for care. The three lost surfmen left families. Surfman John I. Soper had a wife and two children. His third child was born after his death. The families would receive the surfmen's pay for two years and then be cut off completely to face a life of poverty.[33]

Surfmen harnessed to their beach cart. Oak Island Life-Saving Station, New York (U.S. Coast Guard)

Life-Saving Stations of New York

Life-Saving Stations on New York Sea Coast

Station	Location
Ditch Plain	3½ miles SW of Montauk Lighthouse, Montauk
Hither Plain	½ mile SW of Fort Pond, Montauk
Napeague	Abreast Napeague Harbor east of Amagansett
Amagansett	Amagansett
Georgica	1 mile south of East Hampton
Mecox	2 miles south of Bridgehampton
Southampton	¾ mile south of Southampton
Shinnecock	East of Shinnecock Bay entrance
Tiana	Tiana Beach
Quogue	Quogue, ½ mile south of village
Potunk	1½ miles SW Potunk village
Moriches	Moriches Bay, ½ mile SW of Speonk
Forge River	3½ miles south of Moriches on Fire Island
Smiths Point	Abreast of Smiths Point, Fire Island
Bellport	Fire Island, 4 miles SW of Bellport
Blue Point	Fire Island south of Blue Point
Lone Hill	8 miles east of Fire Island Lighthouse
Point of Woods	4 miles east of Fire Island Lighthouse
Fire Island	½ mile west of Fire Island Lighthouse
Oak Island	East end of Oak Island
Gilgo	West end of Oak Island
Jones Beach	East end of Jones Beach
Zachs Inlet	West end of Jones Beach
Short Beach	½ mile east of Jones Inlet
Point Lookout	Point Lookout Beach
Long Beach	Near west end of Long Beach
Rockaway	Near village of Rockaway
Rockaway Point	West end of Rockaway Beach, SE of Brooklyn
Eatons Neck	East side Huntington Bay, Long Island Sound
Rocky Point	4 miles NNE of Greenport, Long Island Sound
Fishers Island	West shore of East Harbor, Fishers Island

New York Life-Saving Stations on Lake Ontario and Lake Erie

Big Sandy	North side mouth Big Sandy Creek near Woodville
Oswego	East side Oswego Harbor entrance
Charlotte	East side entrance Charlotte Harbor near Rochester
Niagara	East side entrance of Niagara River near Youngstown
Buffalo	South side entrance of Buffalo Harbor

Life-Saving Stations of New Jersey

Sandy Hook	On Bay side vicinity Sandy Hook Lighthouse
Spermaceti Cove	2½ miles south of Sandy Hook Lighthouse
Seabright	About a mile south of Navesink Lighthouse
Monmouth Beach	About a mile south of Sea Bright
Long Branch	Green Pond, Long Branch
Deal	Deal near Asbury Park
Shark River	Near mouth of Shark River, Avon-by-the-Sea
Spring Lake	2½ miles south of Shark River, Spring Lake
Squan Beach	1 mile SE Squan village near Manasquan
Bayhead	At head of Barnegat Bay, Bay Head
Mantoloking	2½ miles south of head of Barnegat Bay, Mantoloking
Chadwick	5 miles south of head of Barnegat Bay, Chadwick

Toms River	Abreast mouth of Toms River, Seaside Park
Island Beach	1¼ mile south of Seaside Park
Cedar Creek	5⁴⁄₁₀ miles north of Barnegat Inlet, south of Seaside Park
Forked River	2 miles north of Barnegat Inlet, south of Seaside Park
Barnegat	South side Barnegat Inlet, Barnegat
Loveladies Island	2½ miles south of Barnegat Inlet, Long Beach Island
Harvey Cedars	5½ miles south of Barnegat Inlet, Long Beach Island
Ship Bottom	Ship Bottom, Long Beach Island
Long Beach	Long Beach, Long Beach Island
Bonds	2³⁄₁₀ miles south of Beach Haven, Long Beach Island
Little Egg	Near lighthouse north of Little Egg Inlet
Little Beach	South side of Little Egg Inlet, north of Brigantine
Brigantine	5³⁄₁₀ miles north of Absecon Lighthouse, Brigantine
South Brigantine	1¼ miles north of Absecon Lighthouse
Atlantic City	At Absecon Lighthouse, Atlantic City
Absecon	2¾ miles south of Absecon Lighthouse
Great Egg	6¾ miles south of Absecon Lighthouse, Longport
Ocean City	South side of Great Egg Inlet, Ocean City
Pecks Beach	8½ miles north of Corson Inlet, south of Ocean City
Corson Inlet	Near Corson Inlet, north side, north of Strathmere
Sea Isle City	3¼ miles north of Townsend Inlet, Sea Isle City
Townsend Inlet	North side Townsend Inlet
Avalon	3¾ miles SW Ludlam Beach Light, Avalon
Stone Harbor	2¼ miles NE Hereford Inlet Lighthouse, Stone Harbor
Hereford Inlet	Near Hereford Inlet Lighthouse, North Wildwood
Holly Beach	6 miles NE Cape May City
Two Mile Beach	4 miles NE Cape May City
Cold Spring	½ mile east of Cape May City
Cape May	Near Cape May Lighthouse, Cape May

NEW YORK STATIONS RENAMED: Potunk was West Hampton and Tanner's Point. Tiana was once spelled Tyana. Zacks Inlet station was unofficially known locally as High Hill. NEW YORK STATIONS CLOSED: Coney Island station at Manhattan Beach, Coney Island, was manned until about 1899. Far Rockaway station (ex-Hog Island station) was located at the east end of Rockaway Beach, near Brooklyn. It was destroyed in a sudden gale while being moved across the water to a new site and was never replaced. Montauk Point station was located near Montauk Point Lighthouse on Long Island. Salmon Creek station on east side of mouth of Salmon Creek, Lake Ontario was destroyed by fire March 27, 1886 and not rebuilt.

NEW JERSEY STATIONS RENAMED: Bayhead was Point Pleasant; Chadwick was Green Island; Mantoloking was Swan Point; Ocean City was Beazley's; Sea Isle City was Ludlam's Beach; Spring Lake was Wreck Pond; Stone Harbor was Tatham's; Holly Beach was Turtle Gut. NEW JERSEY STATION CLOSED: Bay Shore station was two and half miles west of Cape May City. (In the very early years of the USLSS a few other New Jersey and New York station names appeared briefly prior to standardizing names.)

Smiths Point Life-Saving Station guarded Long Island's sandy shore. An expanded red house-type station. (National Archives)

Great Egg Life-Saving Station was a Bibb #2-type station in Longport, New Jersey. (Longport Historical Society)

Corson Inlet Life-Saving Station was a fine example of an 1872 New Jersey form of red house-type station in original form. Most of the red house stations were later expanded by adding additions on one or both sides. (U.S. Coast Guard)

Forked River Life-Saving Station, New Jersey. Some red house-type stations remained in use into the Coast Guard-era. These early stations were modified over time but were easily identifiable. (U. S. Coast Guard)

Two Mile Beach Life-Saving Station was a classic New Jersey red house-type with an addition on one side. More boats and equipment and a desire for better housing led to expansion. (U.S. Coast Guard)

Cedar Creek Life-Saving Station was an early red house-type station that was active into the Coast Guard years. After retirement this New Jersey station became a summer home for author Pearl Buck. (National Archives)

Deal Life-Saving Station at Asbury Park, New Jersey was one of the most elaborate stations. This was the first of four Deal-type stations by famed architect Paul J. Pelz. (U.S. Coast Guard)

Dining room in Deal station was a welcome goal for surfmen returning from beach patrol. Circa 1915. (U.S. Coast Guard)

Surfmen stand proudly in front of their surfboat at New Jersey's Chadwick Life-Saving Station. An expanded 1882-type station. Note the distinctive lookout tower characteristic of 1882-type stations. (U.S. Coast Guard)

Unprotected lookout atop Seabright Life-Saving Station must have been cold during a New Jersey winter. 1876-type station. (Twin Lights Historic Site—Moss Archives)

Spring Lake Life-Saving Station, an 1875-type station in northern New Jersey had a porch added which gave a distinctive look. (National Archives)

Barnegat Life-Saving Station in New Jersey lost three surfmen during the heroic 1886 rescue attempt at the Kraljevica *wreck on Barnegat Shoal. An 1882-type station. (U.S. Coast Guard)*

South Brigantine Life-Saving Station was a grandly expanded 1882-type station on the Jersey shore. (National Archives)

Little Beach Life-Saving Station in New Jersey. A Quonochontaug-type station. (US. Coast Guard)

Cold Spring Life-Saving Station in New Jersey. Crew enjoys a New Jersey coastal summer. A Bibb# 2-type station. (U.S. Coast Guard)

Sea Isle City Life-Saving Station, a Bibb# 2-style station on south Jersey coast with crew at boatroom door. (Shanks collection)

Bonds Life-Saving Station surfmen lounge on the boat ramp on a sunny day. This New Jersey Bibb #2-type station had a homey atmosphere. New Jersey had forty-one active life-saving stations by 1914, more than any other state. (U.S. Coast Guard)

Sandy Hook Life-Saving Station at the south approach to New York harbor. This Bibb #2-type station watched over busy sea lanes. (U.S. Coast Guard)

Townsend Inlet Life-Saving Station with a fine view of the boatroom and lookout tower. A Bibb #2-type station guarding the sand bars of the New Jersey coast. (U.S. Coast Guard)

Spermaceti Cove Life-Saving Station featured this fine Duluth-type station built in 1894. The station has been preserved as a museum by Gateway National Recreation Area at Sandy Hook, New Jersey. (U.S. Coast Guard)

Avalon Life-Saving Station was a Duluth-type station in southern New Jersey. Note the distinctive tall square tower and almost pagoda-like roof of the lookout tower. Avalon surfmen won four gold life-saving medals for the 1912 steamer Margaret rescue. (U.S. Coast Guard)

Cape May Life-Saving Station and lighthouse guarded southern tip of New Jersey. A Duluth-type station. (U.S. Coast Guard)

Stone Harbor (Tatham's) Life-Saving Station, a fine example of the Duluth-type in southern New Jersey. Note crew with surfboat and buggy. Surfmen won eight gold life-saving medals for the 1912 Margaret *rescue which saved ten lives. (U.S. Coast Guard)*

Monmouth Beach Life-Saving Station, a Duluth-type, guarded New York Harbor's south approaches. The historic station is being preserved. (U.S. Coast Guard)

Harvey Cedars Life-Saving Station was a handsome Duluth-type station in New Jersey. The Duluth-type was very distinctive with its tower and window arrangement (U.S. Coast Guard)

Absecon Life-Saving Station south of Atlantic City, New Jersey was a classic Duluth-type station. This was not a lonely station as numerous summer homes surround it. (U.S. Coast Guard)

Squan Beach Life-Saving Station captures the feel of the early New Jersey coast. This Duluth-type station was built in 1902. (U.S. Coast Guard)

New Jersey was the home of the Jersey Pattern-type station architecture. Holly Beach Life-Saving Station was a good example of a Jersey-type with its octagonal lookout tower topped by a peaked roof. Surfboats and beach cart are proudly on display. (Shanks collection)

Island Beach Life-Saving Station was a Jersey Pattern-type with a raised lookout tower giving it a distinctive appearance. (National Archives)

Little Egg Life-Saving Station was a Jersey-type station. There were at least eleven Jersey Pattern stations. (U.S. Coast Guard)

Mantoloking Life-Saving Station with number board looking like a giant table at left. Jersey Pattern station. (U.S. Coast Guard)

Brigantine Life-Saving Station was a Jersey Pattern station along the central New Jersey coast. There were 279 active stations at the peak of the USLSS in 1914. (U.S. Coast Guard)

Pecks Beach Life-Saving Station near Ocean City, New Jersey was a fine example of Jersey-type. (U.S. Coast Guard)

Shark River Life-Saving Station, New Jersey. A Bibb #2-type station with a rather ominous name. (U.S. Coast Guard)

Long Beach Life-Saving Station, New Jersey. Aerial view shows this Duluth-type station with an 1871 red house-type station just behind it. (National Archives)

Toms River Life-Saving Station, a Jersey Pattern station, at the entrance of Toms River, New Jersey. The Coast Guard painted huge numbers on platforms to aid in identifying stations from airplanes. In 1913 Toms River surfman Fred C. Bailey won the silver life-saving medal for rescuing the beautiful Mary Molloy from drowning. (U.S. Coast Guard)

International signal flags fly at Ship Bottom Life-Saving Station on the central New Jersey coast. A Jersey Pattern station. Ship Bottom surfmen won seven gold medals for the 1903 Abiel Abbott rescue.(Shanks collection)

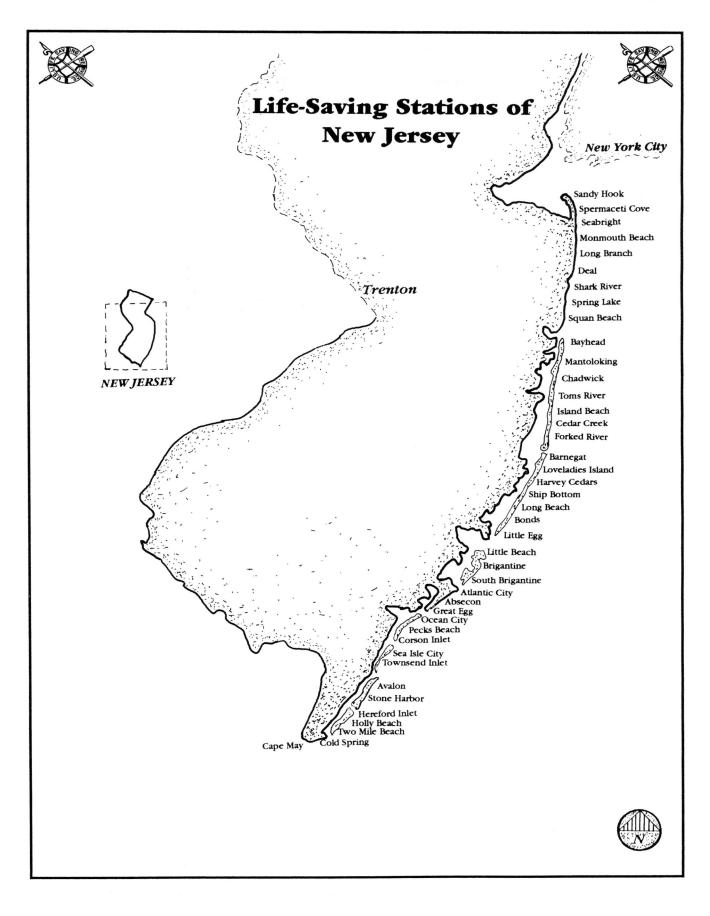

Life-Saving Stations of New Jersey

New York City

NEW JERSEY

Trenton

Sandy Hook
Spermaceti Cove
Seabright
Monmouth Beach
Long Branch
Deal
Shark River
Spring Lake
Squan Beach

Bayhead
Mantoloking
Chadwick
Toms River
Island Beach
Cedar Creek
Forked River
Barnegat
Loveladies Island
Harvey Cedars
Ship Bottom
Long Beach
Bonds
Little Egg
Little Beach
Brigantine
South Brigantine
Atlantic City
Absecon
Great Egg
Ocean City
Pecks Beach
Corson Inlet
Sea Isle City
Townsend Inlet
Avalon
Stone Harbor
Hereford Inlet
Holly Beach
Two Mile Beach
Cold Spring
Cape May

And this was only a drill! Dobbins lifeboat is lifted into the air by a breaker. Coquille River Life-Saving Station, Oregon. Train in background is building a jetty to make the river entrance safer. (National Maritime Museum)

Surfboat rescuing sailors from cruiser Milwaukee *near Eureka, California in 1917. Humboldt Bay Life-Saving Station. (Capt. George Melanson photo in Shanks collection)*

Chapter 8

Lifeboats and Surfboats

LIFEBOATS AND SURFBOATS

Lifeboats and surfboats leave port when other vessels are running for shelter. They routinely go where vessels many times larger have found conditions impossible. Their crews rescue others when most mariners struggle for survival.[1]

Lifeboats and surfboats have a long and honorable history. The Chinese river launches and rescue junks clearly deserve credit for being the first regularly employed vessels engaged in organized life-saving.[2] The Chinese, as Marco Polo noted, invented the world's first water tight compartments, one of the six most critical features in lifeboat evolution.[3] The French official de Bernieres and the English designer William Wouldhave contributed to the development of self-righting capability, another critical lifeboat feature. Water-tight compartments and self-bailing capabilities were to follow.[4]

The British designed the English lifeboat which was adopted in America and elsewhere. The American surfboat has its origins among Atlantic Coast fishermen.[5] The first American rescue boat was a Massachusetts Humane Society lifeboat, built in 1807.[6]

The names surfboat and lifeboat seem to have been rather interchangeably applied to early rescue boats. Even in modern times, a few maritime historians have mislabeled photos of these boats, sometimes even using both terms for the same vessel. Yet the difference between the two terms is clear. American rescue boats were of two basic types, surfboats and lifeboats.

SURFBOATS

Surfboats were lighter weight, smaller and of shallower draft than lifeboats. Surfboats were much more easily maneuvered in the surf, bobbing about like "floating walnut shells." They were also quicker to transport over land than lifeboats and were regularly transported on boat carriages across the beaches.

As Sumner Kimball explained, "All of these (surf)boats are so light as to be readily transported along the shore; they can be launched in very shallow water, and in the dexterous hands of our surfmen are maneuvered in the breakers with marvelous ease and (speed)."[7] During the Life-Saving Service's early and middle years, surfboats res-

cued more people than any other means, more than breeches buoy and lifeboat combined.[8] In the year 1899 (just before power lifeboats appeared), USLSS pulling surfboats made 1,089 rescue trips while pulling lifeboats made but 163 rescue trips. Roughly, these ratios had held throughout the Nineteenth Century.[9]

Surfboats were designed to be hand launched by surfmen from a beach. They were typically from 23 to 27 feet in length and weighed from 700 to 1,100 pounds. They were steered by a keeper standing in the stern using an eighteen to twenty foot long steering oar, which required "all the muscular power of a steersman" to manage.

Although surfboats became self-bailing, they were not self-righting. The ability to right a capsized surfboat was a matter of life or death and surfmen practiced righting self-bailing surfboats. The large, heavy self-bailing and self-righting English lifeboats the Americans copied from the British righted themselves. But American surfboats were not self-righting and required that the crew turn a capsized surfboat upright again.[10]

For righting capability with a good crew, the Beebe-McLellen surfboat was the star. The Beebe-McLellen surfboat was self-bailing and became equipped with a water ballast system and centerboard to speed righting after capsizing. The quickest time ever made in a capsize drill was thirteen seconds from the command "Go" starting with a crew seated in the surfboat until the crew were seated back in the surfboat in their original positions. The record was set by a crew of surfmen at the 1904 Louisiana Purchase Exposition at St. Louis under the command of Keeper Henry Cleary of the Marquette, Michigan, Life-Saving Station. American surfmen could actually right a surfboat faster than the English self-righting lifeboat could right itself.[11]

POWER SURFBOATS

By 1910 the Life-Saving Service began converting to power surfboats. The venerable Beebe-McLellen surfboats were equipped with an eight and later, twelve, horsepower motor amidships. Soon power surfboats were being used about as often as the power lifeboat and together they increased the number of persons carried to

Pulling lifeboat in heavy surf. (U.S. Coast Guard)

Vulnerability of service boats is shown by this heavily damaged surfboat. Stone Harbor station, New Jersey. (U.S. Coast Guard)

safety by about forty per cent.[12]

PULLING LIFEBOATS

The U. S. Life-Saving Service lifeboat was English in origin. A British lifeboat and boat carriage were purchased in 1873 by the U.S. Treasury Department. Most American lifeboats were built following this design and were even called the English lifeboat.[13]

Compared to surfboats, lifeboats were longer (about 29 to 34-feet in length), heavier (about 4,000 pounds in weight) and sat deeper in the water. Although they were most often rowed by eight oarsmen plus a steersman, they could also be sailed.[14]

Since lifeboats were self-bailing and self-righting, you could capsize them and they would come right back up again and empty themselves of water using relieving tubes. "Where long excursions are to be undertaken and the service is exceptionally hazardous, the men undoubtedly feel safer in a self-righting boat," Sumner Kimball pointed out.[15]

But pulling lifeboats were very heavy, in part due to an iron keel that contributed to their self-righting ability. Because of their great weight lifeboats were usually launched from a marine railway, although during the early days some were moored in the water. This limitation precluded their use at most Atlantic Coast life-saving stations where shallow water required using the lighter, hand-launched surfboat. Atlantic Coast surfmen typically had to drag their rescue boats through soft sand to launch near wrecks, a requirement that made it impossible to use heavy lifeboats. The U.S. Life-Saving Service could not depend, as did the English, on large numbers of volunteers to suddenly appear and launch heavy lifeboats at wrecks. For East Coast surfmen, the light weight, shallow draft surfboat was the boat of choice.[16]

But for the rest of the country the lifeboat was a great asset. On the Great Lakes most life-saving stations were located in man-made harbors inside river mouths where there was protected, deep water for a launchway. The Great Lakes became premier lifeboat country.[17] On the Pacific Coast, with the deepest water in the country, the lifeboat was widely used. West Coast river mouths and bays offered protected, deep water where lifeboats could be launched.[18]

THE DOBBINS LIFEBOAT

Every sailor soon learns that all boats are compromises. Each boat trades off one positive characteristic to gain another. USLSS District Superintendent David Porter Dobbins created an economical compromise between a conventional lifeboat and a surfboat. His invention was the self-bailing and self-righting Dobbins lifeboat. It was smaller and lighter than the English lifeboat, between 24 and 30-feet in length and weighing about 1,600 to 2,000 pounds. Unlike the heavy English lifeboat, a handy characteristic of the Dobbins lifeboat was that it could be hauled to a beach and launched with almost as much freedom as a surfboat.[19] This was an advantage particularly at some Pacific Coast stations where beaches had heavy breakers that would destroy a marine launchway, but where deep water just offshore allowed a lifeboat to be used. Sometimes horses assisted in pulling the heavy cart, expanding the practical range of the haul. The Dobbins lifeboat was used most extensively on the Pacific Coast and Great Lakes. By 1916, nearly every Pacific Coast station had a Dobbins lifeboat.[20] But the Dobbins lifeboat was a compromise and it never replaced the surfboat or lifeboat. If rescue boats were to be improved, some other way had to be found.

MOTORIZING THE 34-FOOT LIFEBOATS

As gasoline engines became more common in small boats it was soon obvious that a powered lifeboat could have great advantages.[21] The English had tried steam powered lifeboats, but steam had serious limitations such as loss of self-righting capability that the use of gasoline engines could avoid.[22] The Life-Saving Service's research and testing branch, the Board of Life-Saving Appliances, became interested in trying gasoline engines in lifeboats. One of the Board's members, Lt. Charles H. McLellen of the Revenue Cutter Service, was to play a key role in guiding the transition from pulling to power boats.[23] As USLSS Inspector of Life-Saving Stations, McLellen was authorized in 1899 to have a twelve horsepower, two cylinder Superior gasoline engine installed in a 34-foot pulling lifeboat.[24]

Marquette Life-Saving Station in Michigan was assigned to try the boat. Marquette Keeper Henry Cleary and his crew tested this first 34-foot power lifeboat under some very adverse weather conditions, with and without sail. Lt. McLellen reported that the vessel behaved well but he realized that 34-foot pulling lifeboats were not designed to carry a 1,350 pound engine in their stern.[25] He recommended that a new boat be designed with sufficient additional buoyancy to carry the engine more easily. During 1904-1905, a 34-foot motor lifeboat was built to USLSS specifications by the Electric Launch Company of Bayonne, New Jersey. The new 34-foot model was still not satisfactory to McLellen since it, too, was only a modified pulling boat.[26]

THE STANDARD 36-FOOT MOTOR LIFEBOAT

Finally by 1907 Charles H. McLellen designed a new 36-foot motor lifeboat that was destined to be the most successful wooden motor lifeboat ever built. "The work performed with the boats...has exceeded the highest expectations of the officers of the service and the creation of the standard 36-foot motor lifeboat was the mark of an epoch."[27]

Launching the rescue boats took plenty of muscle power. A Dobbins lifeboat is launched from its boat carriage at Ilwaco Beach (Klipsan Beach) Life-Saving Station, Washington. (Shanks collection)

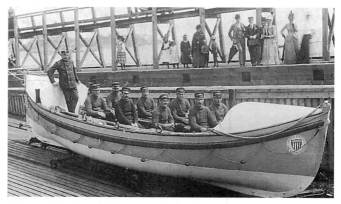

Heavy English lifeboat on launchways. Marquette Life-Saving crew, Michigan. (Richard Boonisar)

Cape Cod surfmen launching surfboat in a choppy sea. (Shanks collection)

Surfboat with lifecar in tow during drill. Pentwater Life-Saving Station on Lake Michigan. (Shanks collection)

Some crews were fortunate to have a horse assist in pulling their surfboat to launch sites. (U.S. Coast Guard)

The U.S. Life-Saving Service's 36-footers, two feet longer than the converted pulling lifeboats, were built by the Electric Launch Company of Bayonne, New Jersey and the Holmes Motor Company of West Mystic, Connecticut. The boats were powered by a thirty-five to forty horsepower engine and were capable of making speeds of up to ten knots. Besides being built with water tight compartments, these boats were self-bailing and self-righting. When capsized, they could right themselves in less than half a minute.[28]

Surprisingly, the first 36-foot motor lifeboat went to Canada. The Canadian Department of Marine and Fisheries faced extremely stormy conditions along the West Coast of Vancouver Island, British Columbia. The Canadians purchased the Electric Launch Company's first boat and sent it to their Bamfield Life-Saving Station, northwest of Victoria, B.C. Canadian authorities admired both the vessel's capabilities and its handsome double diagonal planking of Honduras mahogany.[29]

In 1907 Captain W.H. Gillen was appointed Bamfield's coxswain, earning him the honor of being the first 36-foot motor lifeboat coxswain in North America. Gillen's crew included an engineer and two seamen. In yet another ironic turn of fate, within a year a storm tore the Bamfield motor lifeboat from its moorings and wrecked it on Robber Island in Barkley Sound. A replacement boat was soon ordered. Motor lifeboats were here to stay.[30]

The U.S. Life-Saving Service's first standard 36-foot motor lifeboat was ready early in 1908. It, too, was sent to the Pacific Coast to Waaddah Island Life-Saving Station at Neah Bay, Washington. Named the *Conqueror,* the lifeboat performed at the 1909 Alaska-Yukon Pacific Exposition in Seattle.

It was appropriate that the first two true motor life-

boats went to the Pacific Coast. Although initially the Great Lakes and Atlantic Coasts would have slightly more motor lifeboats, a higher percentage of Pacific Coast stations would have motor lifeboats than any other region. It is also significant that both Canada and the U.S. sent their first standard 36-foot motor lifeboats to the same location—the entrance of the Strait of Juan de Fuca northwest of Seattle.[31]

With the older 34-foot power lifeboats augmented by the new 36-footers, motor lifeboats were soon at stations on all coasts. The *Annual Report of the Life-Saving Service* for 1908 raved that motor lifeboats "have more than doubled the scope of life-saving service at the stations where they are used, multiplying the opportunities for rendering assistance to distressed vessels and persons because of the advantage their speed affords, and increasing the effectiveness of…operations by enabling life-savers to reach scenes of disaster in good physical trim for the performance of their most difficult and perilous work."[32] By 1914 there were 147 power lifeboats and surfboats in commission. Ten of these were new state of the art 36-foot power lifeboats.[33]

The feeling for the new power lifeboats was best expressed by surfman Cornelius Sullivan of San Francisco's Fort Point Life-Saving Station. After all the countless hours of rowing pulling boats, Fort Point's power lifeboat finally arrived on the deck of a steamer about 1908. She was unloaded at San Francisco's Union Iron Works and the Fort Point crew rowed along the Embarcadero to pick up their new boat. When they took possession of the power lifeboat, they tied the old pulling boat astern and motored back to the station. Surfman Sullivan was a member of that pioneer crew. When asked what it felt like to have a motor lifeboat after all that rowing, in his fine Irish accent

Surfboat bringing survivors ashore.
(Cape Cod National Seashore)

First standard Class E 36-foot motor lifeboat. Although the motorized 34-foot former pulling lifeboats predated them, the 36-footers were the first purposely built motor lifeboats. Note how despite an engine, the crew sits facing stern as if ready to row. A long open mid-section and long stern compartment distinguished the Class E motor lifeboats. This is the first of the 36-footers, the Conqueror *from Waaddah Island (Neah Bay) Life-Saving Station in Washington. (U.S. Coast Guard)*

Class H 36-foot motor lifeboats succeeded the early Class E 36-footers. Class H motor lifeboats had a distinctive short engine compartment amidship and short bow and stern compartments. This is the Point Reyes, California Class H motor lifeboat aground after fouling its propeller in tow line. (Howard Underhill)

Last group of the wooden motor lifeboats were the various Class T 36-footers. Note the bow compartment and amidships engine compartment are much longer than on the preceding Class H vessels. Number 36542, shown here, has been restored and placed on exhibit in the lifeboat station at Point Reyes National Seashore in California. (Ralph Shanks)

he replied with deep emotion, "Ah, it was a day of great rejoicing!"[34]

IN THE WAKE OF THE 36-FOOTERS
CLASSES OF 36-FOOT MOTOR LIFEBOATS

The Life-Saving Service called their boats "power lifeboats" and the Coast Guard called them "motor lifeboats." They were different names for the same vessels. However, there were different classes of 36-footers built over the years and it is possible to distinguish them visually. The first 36-footers became classified as "Class E" 36-foot motor lifeboats. The "E" simply stood for "Early." Class "E" 36-foot motor lifeboats were easy to identify because they had a very long stern compartment (which housed the engine) and a long, open midsection in the style of pulling boats. Some early photos show all the station crew riding along in the "Class E" thirty-six footers seated in the midsection facing aft as if ready to row. They were beautiful, popular boats that revolutionized life-saving. Some of the "Class E" boats stayed in service at least as late as 1929 or 1930.[35]

The next group of 36-footers were designated "Class H" types. During the early 1920s Commander Frederick Honeywell was in charge of motor lifeboat construction and his naval engineer was Al Hansen. Because both men's surnames began with the letter "H," this group was called "Class H." The "Class H" 36-foot motor lifeboats featured a center engine compartment which for the first time broke up the long open area where oarsmen formerly sat. "Class

H" motor lifeboats had an amidships engine compartment that was shorter in length than any other class and had the shortest bow and stern compartments of any class. Visually it was almost as if an engine compartment had been dropped into place in the center of a pulling lifeboat. Eventually a revised "Class H" type was built which was called the "Class HR," or "Class H Revised" type. The difference between the "H" and "HR" was one of forward cabin construction.

In 1929 Alfred Hansen developed yet another type, the "Class T" 36-foot motor lifeboats. These were built from 1929-31. Slight modifications of the "Class T" types called "Class TR" (for "Class T-Revised" and built 1931-37) and "Class TRS" (for "Class T-Revised & Simplified" and built 1937-1956) extended the production of wooden 36-foot motor lifeboats by the Coast Guard into 1956. These three classes of 36-foot motor lifeboats, "Class T," "Class TR" and "Class TRS," featured the longest bow compartment and the longest amidships engine compartment of any classes.[36]

The wooden 36-foot motor lifeboats were built by the Coast Guard at their Curtis Bay, Baltimore, Maryland, facility as late as 1956 and served until the last one, *Number 36535*, was retired from the Depoe Bay, Oregon, Coast Guard station in 1987.[37] Thirty-six foot wooden motor lifeboats had continued to do rescue work for over seventy years after the end of the Life-Saving Service.

Last active 36-foot motor lifeboat in heavy surf. Preserved, this vessel is now on display at the Mariners Museum in Virginia. (U.S. Coast Guard)

Early photo of Smith Island Life-Saving Station showing the crew prior to the adoption of uniforms. Smith Island station guarded the entrance to Chesapeake Bay at Cape Charles Lighthouse, Virginia. An 1874-type station. (National Archives)

Little Island Life-Saving Station, an 1876-type Virginia station which lost its keeper and two surfmen in heroic 1887 rescue attempt. (U.S. Coast Guard)

Chapter 9

Delaware, Maryland and Virginia

DELAWARE, MARYLAND & VIRGINIA STATIONS

The life-saving stations of Delaware, Maryland and Virginia guarded the approaches to Chesapeake Bay and Delaware Bay. Sumner Kimball wrote: "The commerce passing to and from the great marts of Philadelphia, Baltimore, and Norfolk…contributes its proportion to make up the record of disasters" on these coasts.[1] Hurricanes ravaged the beaches, flooded low areas and took a toll in sailors and surfmen.

Little Island and Dam Neck Mills Life-Saving Stations on the Virginia coast faced some of the most dangerous wreck situations in the region. Early on a cold, stormy morning in January 8, 1887 surfmen from both Little Island and Dan Neck Mills went to the rescue of the German ship *Elisabeth*. The vessel had struck a treacherous offshore bar and was doomed.

Because the wreck was in the jurisdiction of Little Island Keeper Abel Belanga, both station crews were placed under his leadership.[2] Keeper Belanga first attempted a breeches buoy rescue, but repeated shots with the Lyle gun failed. Yet another shot was about to be fired when the surfmen saw a dark object along side the *Elisabeth*. The sailors were abandoning ship, a terrible mistake under such severe sea conditions. The much safer breeches buoy rescue had been possible until the German sailors took to their lifeboat. Even so, more shots were fired with the Lyle gun and one line landed safely on the *Elisabeth*. But with the sailors all in their small boat no one was on board the ship to grab the line.[3]

Since the sailors were now in the small boat, the only way to assist them would be by surfboat. It was very cold, snow covered the beaches, and the sea was quite rough. The German crew could not last long in an open boat. Keeper Belanga and two of his surfmen returned to Little Island station to get the surfboat.[4]

Keeper Belanga gave orders to prepare the surfboat and ran to his house for something to eat. There was little time and breakfast was not yet ready, so Mrs. Belanga hurriedly set out a piece of pie and a cold cup of coffee. Abel Belanga stood while he ate. His wife knew what the sea conditions were and she anxiously asked her husband what he intended to do with the boat since the sea

was so rough. Mrs. Belanga realized the danger and perceived her husband's foreboding. They must have looked at each other the way only a husband and wife can do. He kissed her and walked to the door, turning to say, "The worst has not yet come! I would give fifty dollars if the men were out of that boat."[5] Abel Belanga then stepped out the door and into the storm.

Hauling the surfboat back to the wreck scene, Keeper Belanga hand-picked his crew. It would be a very dangerous rescue and he wanted the best surfmen. Among those he selected was his brother James E. Belanga of Dan Neck Mills station. Two others he chose were his brothers-in-law.[6]

His crew chosen, Abel Belanga and his men launched the surfboat "in handsome style." As they pulled away toward the ship, the keeper urged his surfmen to row hard, shouting cheerily, "Drive her, boys! Drive her!" The surfmen reached the doomed ship quickly, transferring the Germans from the ship's boat into the USLSS surfboat. The survivors were immediately given life preservers and Keeper Belanga was at the point of turning toward shore when "an immense wave swept around the rear of the ship, combed over the two boats…swamped them and turned them completely over and over. Thus, in a moment every man was thrown into the sea."[7]

Disaster was almost total. All twenty-two German sailors drowned. Two Dam Neck Mills surfmen were also lost, one of which was Keeper Belanga's brother James. Two Little Island station surfmen also died, including Joseph Spratley, Keeper Belanga's brother-in-law. Keeper Abel Belanga was drowned. All the lost surfmen were family men.[8]

Just two surfmen, both of Little Island Life-Saving Station, survived. One of them, Frank Tedford, was another brother-in-law of Keeper Belanga. Surfman Tedford had reached shore, made signs that he was all right and walked toward the station. He almost got to the station when he collapsed in the snow. At that moment, miraculously, Surfman Tedford's wife appeared and with another woman dragged her husband to the station. She saved her husband's life.[9]

Cobb Island Life-Saving Station, Virginia, boasted a boathouse with launchway, an unusual feature on the Atlantic Seaboard. An expanded 1876-type station. (U.S. Coast Guard)

Dam Neck Mills Life-Saving Station was involved in the tragic 1887 Elizabeth rescue attempt. This Quonochontaug-type station stood south of Virginia Beach. (U.S. Coast Guard)

Virginia Beach Life-Saving Station has been preserved as Virginia Beach Maritime Museum. Note surfmen on porch. A Quonochontaug-type station. (Shanks collection)

Surfman Ethridge was the only other survivor. While in the water, Keeper Belanga had saved Ethridge's life by helping him get his long rubber boots off and by offering great encouragement. Always thinking of his surfmen to the last, the keeper was unable to remove his own boots which made swimming difficult. Ultimately, further struggle was impossible and Keeper Belanga perished. His body was carried home to his wife.[10]

Life was harsh on the Delmarva Peninsula. With such challenging conditions the lifecar was still an important asset on this treacherous coast. In February 1892 the Spanish steamer *San Albano* rammed the outer shoals of Hog Island, Virginia, having missed the entrance to Chesapeake Bay due to fog. Earlier, a surfman on patrol from Hog Island Life-Saving Station had seen the vessel and tried to warn it off by burning a red Coston signal. The surfman quickly returned to the station and informed Keeper John E. Johnson of what he had seen. Keeper Johnson climbed the station lookout and spotted the steamer with his telescope. She was stranded on the outer shoals. Johnson called for his crew and soon the beach cart was rolling through flooded beaches toward the wreck.[11]

The wreck was reached but "confused surf, impelled by a forty mile gale, fell in tumult on the beach." First attempts at rescue by breeches buoy failed since the ship was so far offshore. An approach by surfboat was also tried but rescue was prevented by heavy breakers surrounding the steamer. Even with all necessary equipment on scene, rescue appeared impossible.[12]

Then Keeper Johnson decided to attempt a desperate and dangerous plan. The Lyle gun was lashed to the beach cart and the cart run out into the surf into waist deep water. The surfmen actually entered the Atlantic breakers pushing their beach cart to get within range of the *San Albano*. Waves smashed against the beach cart threatening to sweep the surfmen off their feet. It was a wild desperate action. Yet amidst the surf at the right moment, the Lyle gun was aimed and fired. There was a moment of breathless suspense as the projectile and shot line flew toward the steamer.[13]

It was a perfect shot and a line was soon rigged to the ship. The lifecar was attached to the whip lines in the same manner as a breeches buoy and run out to the ship. The lifecar was chosen as it could best pass through the heavy breakers. Eight trips were required to bring the nineteen survivors safely ashore. Hog Island Keeper Johnson was awarded America's gold life-saving medal for ingenuity and bravery and his surfmen all received silver medals. The Spanish government, in appreciation, also bestowed life-saving medals upon the life-savers. Hog Island did not have a pretty name, but it had an admirable record of life-saving.[14]

Maryland's North Beach Life-Saving Station with white picket fence and lots of sand. An 1882-type station that stood in what is now Assateague Island National Seashore. (U.S. Coast Guard)

Faded glory preserved in a yellowing photograph. Isle of Wight Life-Saving Station in Maryland, a Quonochontaug-style station amid the sand dunes. (U.S. Coast Guard)

Fenwick Island Life-Saving Station served the Delaware and Maryland Coast. An 1882-type station in Delaware. (U.S. Coast Guard)

Delaware had six stations guarding the southern approach to Delaware Bay. Among them was Rehoboth Beach Life-Saving Station, an 1876-type station. (U.S. Coast Guard)

Cape Henlopen Life-Saving Station, a vastly expanded 1875-type, was less than a mile north of Cape Henlopen lighthouse in Delaware. The 1875-design was used nationally. (Richard Boonisar)

Life-Saving Stations of Delaware, Maryland and Virginia

Life-Saving Stations of Delaware

Station	Location
Lewes	East of Lewes
Cape Henlopen	Cape Henlopen
Rehoboth Beach	Opposite north end of Rehoboth Bay
Indian River Inlet	North of Inlet
Bethany Beach	Bethany Beach
Fenwick Island	1½ miles north of Fenwick Island Lighthouse

Life-Saving Stations of Maryland

Isle of Wight	3 miles south of Fenwick Island Lighthouse
Ocean City	Ocean City
North Beach	Assateague Island, 10 miles south of Ocean City
Green Run Inlet	Assateague Island, 13½ miles north of lighthouse

Life-Saving Stations of Virginia

Popes Island	Assateague Island, 10 miles north of lighthouse
Assateague Beach	Assateague Island, about a mile south of lighthouse
Wallops Beach	1½ miles south of Chincoteague Inlet
Metomkin Inlet	East of Accomac on Metomkin Beach
Wachapreague	South end of Cedar Island off Wachapreague
Parramore Beach	Parramore Island east of Quinby
Hog Island	South end of Hog Island east of Nassawadox
Cobb Island	South end of Cobb Island east of Eastville
Smith Island	At Cape Charles Lighthouse east of Kiptopeke
Cape Henry	¾ mile SE Cape Henry Lighthouses
Virginia Beach	5½ miles south of Cape Henry Lighthouses
Dam Neck Mills	10 miles south of Cape Henry Lighthouses
Little Island	On beach abreast of North Bay
False Cape	On beach abreast of Back Bay

NAME CHANGE: Virginia Beach was formerly called Seatack.

Bethany Beach Life-Saving Station awaits a distress call. A Delaware station constructed in the Duluth-type by architect George R. Tolman. (U.S. Coast Guard)

International signal flags were flying at Wallops Beach Life-Saving Station, Virginia. An 1882-type station destroyed by the 1933 hurricane. (Richard Boonisar)

The crew of the Hog Island Life-Saving Station in Virginia won gold life-saving medals for the 1892 San Albano *rescue. (U.S. Coast Guard)*

False Cape Life-Saving Station was the southern-most station in Virginia. An Quonochontaug-type station. (U.S. Coast Guard)

Ocean City Life-Saving Station in Maryland is now the Ocean City Lifesaving Museum. An 1882-type station. (U.S. Coast Guard)

Assateague Beach Life-Saving Station, an 1874-type in Virginia. This station no longer stands but a historic lifeboat station of the same name built by the Coast Guard Station is preserved in Assateague National Seashore. (U.S. Coast Guard)

Cape Henry Life-Saving Station served the critical south approach to Chesapeake Bay in Virginia. A Quonochontaug-type station. (Shanks collection)

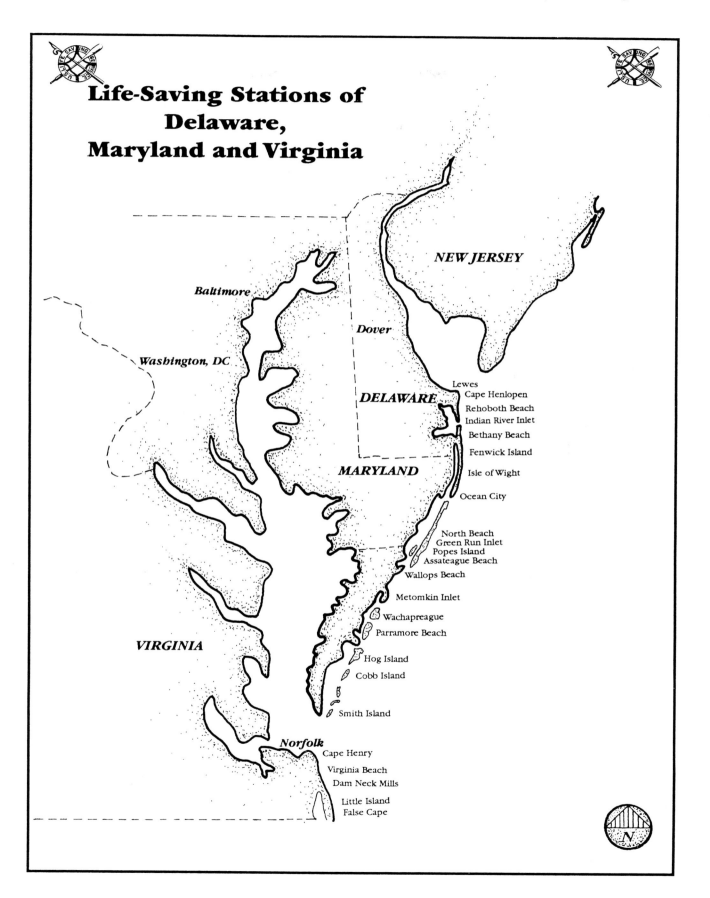

Life-Saving Stations of Delaware, Maryland and Virginia

Martha J. Coston perfected the famed Coston signals which prevented hundreds of shipwrecks and saved thousands of lives. She was a brilliant, dynamic woman a century before it became acceptable for women to excel. (Library of Congress)

Chapter 10
Women and Minority People

WOMEN AND MINORITY PEOPLE IN LIFE-SAVING

Two of the great hidden stories of American life-saving concern the bravery and leadership of women and minority people. During the existence of the Life-Saving Service, American society systematically down played the accomplishments of women and minorities. This was reflected in hiring practices, promotions and reports of the USLSS. Such conditions were not specific to the Life-Saving Service, but occurred almost everywhere. Minority people and women took a back seat—often literally.

It is easy to follow the traditional recounting of the Life-Saving Service history and focus only on white men. European-American men dominated life-saving—as they dominated society. But despite incredible discrimination, minority people and women earned important places in life-saving history.

THE WOMEN

No one contributed more to live-saving than Martha Coston. Intelligent and innovative, Mrs. Coston was a tall woman with blonde hair and blue eyes who was considered a great beauty in her time. By age sixteen she met, fell in love with and married Benjamin Franklin Coston who, at twenty-one, was already a well-known and respected inventor. In the 1840s, B. Franklin Coston was considered a "prodigy" and had become particularly well known for his work with "submarine boats." By his early twenties he rose to become head of the U.S. Navy scientific laboratory in Washington, D.C. His wife Martha was busy raising their children.[1]

Benjamin Franklin Coston's research included experiments with his "Coston Night Signals," color coded flares for nighttime communication between ships. This was a great innovation in the pre-radio era, having both commercial and military value. But Coston's other naval research was more pressing and he was unable to complete his work on the signals. In the course of his other research at the U.S. Navy laboratory, Coston inhaled chemical gases which injured his health. He also became dissatisfied with the treatment he received while working for the Navy. As a result he left the lab and, since one of his inventions was the world's first portable gas apparatus, was offered the presidency of a gas company in Boston.

About a year later while traveling, Mr. Coston became critically ill. His wife cared for him for three months but it was to no avail, and at age 26 one of America's most promising inventors died.[2]

Amidst her grief, Martha Coston, now a twenty-one year old mother of three children, realized that without her husband she was penniless. She recalled that her husband had told of a valuable box of materials containing his Coston Night Signals. Martha Coston's only hope of income lay with her husband's incomplete research papers for the proposed signals.[3]

A business associate, realizing the potential worth of the signals, tried to swindle Martha Coston out of the research materials. She did, however, succeed in regaining possession of all her husband's signal plans. The future of the Coston Night Signals was thereafter entirely in Martha Coston's hands.

Upon careful investigation, Martha Coston found her deceased husband's life work was not only incomplete, but apparently economically unfeasible and overly complicated. The "recipes" for the chemicals needed were inadequate or missing. She found herself in possession "of merely a rough chart of (her husband's) ideas, without good recipes for the perfect combination of chemicals necessary for its perfection."[4] Undaunted, Martha Coston hired successive teams of chemists and, under her direction, the Coston Night Signals were painstakingly perfected. She then found a reliable manufacturer to produce the signals. In an era when few women had careers, young Martha Coston became a business owner, director of a scientific research project and a high-level saleswoman.[5]

But her work was not easy. The world's navies were slow to grasp the incredible value of what Martha Coston had achieved. She had to convince the admirals and political leaders of the potential of her new signals. At the outbreak of the American Civil War in 1861, Martha Coston pressed her flares on the Navy. She knew their value, even if many were slow to see it. Her flares were finally adopted by a reluctant U.S. Navy but Mrs. Coston received much less than their real worth. Yet she was glad to help her government and knew the signals would help win the Civil War. Her signals soon proved their value by allowing nighttime naval communication, and the *New York*

Coston Signals light up the night as surfmen gather at a rescue scene. Martha Coston's signals were always carried on patrol and in rescue boats. Her signals warned ships away from shore, communicated messages between vessels and land, and called surfmen to wrecks. (Richard Boonisar)

Coston signal with wooden holder at left, flare at top right and brass flare holder at lower right. Besides the Life-Saving Service, the U.S. Navy used Coston night signals. The modern highway flare is a descendant of Martha Coston's signals. (Richard Boonisar)

Times called Coston signals "a remarkable and valuable invention."[6]

After the Civil War, Martha Coston traveled to Europe and spent the next difficult years selling her signals to the kings, queens and admirals who commanded European navies. It was very difficult for a single woman to be taken seriously as a manufacturer of highly technical maritime equipment, but Ms. Coston persevered. She lived under sometimes economically difficult conditions, was ignored and bullied and made to wait long months for replies to her inquiries. But her strength of character, determination and the great potential of Coston signals won over many of the most famous people of the day. Her work in Europe led her to deal with famed nobility of the era, including the court of Napoleon III in France and other royalty. When visiting Queen Victoria in London, Martha Coston found herself being transported in a glass carriage. She discovered Italy to be special and almost married a handsome Italian count. The kings and queens of Europe became familiar with the beautiful and remarkable American woman. France, The Netherlands, Italy, and Denmark all adopted the Coston signals. Ultimately, the Coston signals would be used world-wide and the Coston Signal Company (later the Coston Supply Company) became an important New York firm.[7]

Much of this was romantic, but Martha Coston made clear it was years of hard work that built her company and brought her life-saving signals to the maritime world. She had several far-sighted Navy admirals supporting her, including her good friends Admiral Joseph Smith and Admiral and Mrs. David Farragut, the latter the commander of Union naval forces in the Civil War. But other officers opposed her and she wrote later that "to me, it was a most bitter thing to find that in that lofty institution of our country, the Navy, men so small minded that they begrudge a woman her success, though achieved after long years of struggle and patient industry."[8]

Perhaps Martha Coston's greatest contribution involved the U.S. Life-Saving Service. Every life-saving station in American became equipped with Coston flares, often mounted on the boatroom wall ready for use. Surfmen carried Coston signals on all patrols and in the rescue boats. Thousands of mariners were saved over the decades when their ships were warned away from shore or sand bar by a surfman burning a Coston signal. When a wreck was seen, it was Martha Coston's flares that were burned as signals of hope.

The reports of the Life-Saving Service are filled with the name Coston: "At 3 a.m. the flash of a Coston light, set off by the patrol, warned a schooner of her approach to danger, and she kept away...to avoid stranding." And "Patrolman displayed red Coston light to two steamers...on a course that threatened to carry them upon a dangerous reef."[9]

In 1902 Martha Coston died at age seventy-four, honored on two continents.[10] She had become a friend of American presidents, kings and queens and had improved the lives of countless surfmen and thousands of mariners who owed their lives to her Coston Night Signals. She refined her husband's dream, made it practical, continually improved it and brought it to a world that was slow to see its value. Her company lived on under family management, surviving into the Twentieth Century. Her signals were used by the Army and Navy, on merchant and military vessels and even in aviation. Most highway flares today use the same ingredients Martha Coston perfected.[10]

Other women helped in life-saving. The Women's National Relief Association (later the Blue Anchor Society) headquartered in New York City was a humanitarian organization dedicated to providing for survivors brought to the life-saving stations. The Association was organized in 1880 by women who realized that survivors frequently needed clean, dry clothing once they were ashore. Survivors sometimes had to remain at a life-saving station for days or weeks before they could resume their journey. Providing the destitute with clothing and other articles was a major need. Poorly paid surfmen were usually unable to provide needed clothing and the USLSS had little funding. The women gathered clothing and other items that were shipped to life-saving stations as needed. The reports of the Life-Saving Service mention hundreds of cases where cold, wet, needy people were aided. Lucretia (Mrs. James A.) Garfield, wife of the U.S. president, was especially active in the Women's National Relief Association.[11]

While there were some life-saving stations with few women about, at most stations the women played important roles. This was no easy task since the USLSS only provided family housing for the keeper. All married surfmen had to provide their own housing. As a result many stations came to have clusters of small cottages about where wives and children of married surfmen lived. At some stations a considerable community of life-saving families developed and the station really became a village.[12]

At many stations when the men went out to a rescue, the women, often with their children, prayed for their husband's safety and for the rescue of those on the wrecked vessel.[13] Besides praying, the women might build beach fires as signs of hope and to provide warmth as the rescued and their husbands returned ashore. Warm clothing was gathered and coffee and food was prepared.[14] Survivors and surfmen were often in poor condition when they returned to the station and the women's care could be a matter of life or death. Wives of keepers or surfmen were known to rush into the water to save people. In the aftermath of a wreck, a concerned wife might go searching for her surfman husband, find him exhausted on a frozen beach and bring him safely to the station. The women

Women riding breeches buoy for enjoyment. Given the opportunity, women proved themselves as capable and daring as men. Note beautifully dressed lady bravely riding the breeches buoy standing up! (Shanks collection)

Woman enjoying breeches buoy ride. (Sleeping Bear Dunes National Lakeshore)

There were many women and girls at most stations. Vermilion Life-Saving Station on Lake Superior, was one of the most isolated stations in the country. (Lake Superior State University)

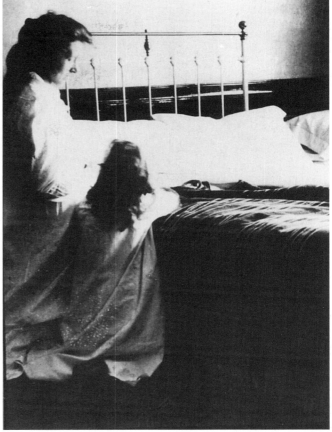

Mrs. William Sparrow was the wife of the Point Allerton, Massachusetts, keeper. She gave lantern slide presentations and talks aimed at making the public aware of the work of surfmen and the need for retirement benefits and decent health care. She is shown here preparing breakfast for surfmen and survivors as they return from the wreck of the Belle J. Neale *in January 1904. (Richard Boonisar)*

Mrs. Sparrow and her daughter praying for surfmen and survivors of a shipwreck. Once survivors reached a station the women's care often made the difference between life or death. Point Allerton Life-Station, Massachusetts. C. 1910 (Richard Boonisar)

saved more lives than the public ever knew.

Edith Morgan was a woman of courage. She was the daughter of Keeper Sanford W. Morgan of Grande Pointe au Sable Life-Saving Station in Michigan. During a storm in the winter of 1878 two men were seen off the station in a capsized boat. It was the off-season, so no crew was at the life-saving station. The only persons present were Keeper Morgan, Edith and her two brothers, one a child. The surfboat could not be launched with such a tiny crew, so the family launched a little fishing boat. Out they rowed, the youngest son steering since he had the least strength. Edith, her father and oldest brother all rowed through the winter seas, but breakers pounded the boat and nearly swamped it. The family was forced to return to shore and the oldest boy sent to round up the off duty surfmen. Edith and her father then fell to work clearing driftwood and logs from the beach so that the surfboat could be launched. When the surfmen arrived, Edith helped the

men launch the surfboat which succeeded in the rescue.

Edith Morgan's "service was no less useful and noble" in December 1879, a year later. The steamer *City of Toledo* was wrecked offshore south of the Grande Pointe au Sable Life-Saving Station during a snow storm. The ship was so iced up "she resembled an iceberg rather than a vessel. The weather was so cold that the surfmen were unable to get out to the wreck in the boat, the oars and thole-pins clogging up with ice so rapidly as to arrest the rowing, and the rescue had to be effected by the slow process, terribly retarded under the circumstances." The beach apparatus was brought out and the Lyle gun fired a line to the vessel. But the winter ice conditions with all "the ice upon the vessel prevented (the breeches buoy lines) from being fixed at a sufficient height above the deck to keep them from immersion in the water, where the ice formed on them so quickly as to make them hard to manage, and where (the lines) were at the same time subjected to the

Native Americans were surfmen in several regions of the country. Wampanoag Indian surfmen of the Massachusetts Humane Society won medals for the 1884 City of Columbus *rescue off Gay Head, Martha's Vineyard. Joseph Peters, a Wampanoag, mans the steering oar, at right. (Dukes County Historical Society)*

heavy drag of a strong current." There was little help at hand, so Edith Morgan took her stand with the few men upon the ice banks, in snow a foot and a half deep. Having to pull heavy, ice encrusted lines was extremely hard work. She "tugged away with them upon the whip line for five or six hours, until every one of the eighteen persons on board were safely landed. It is testified that if not for her assistance some of the persons on board must have certainly perished." In recognition of her conduct on these two occasions, Edith Morgan was awarded the Congressional silver life-saving medal.[15]

There were other heroines. At Florida's Santa Rosa Life-Saving Station, the keeper's two daughters helped pull the beach cart with the Lyle gun to the wreck of the ship *Catherine* on August 7, 1894. It was a "hard struggle through the sand with the beach apparatus." Although some male volunteers also helped, it was in large measure due to the spirit and energy of the two young women that the beach cart could be hauled to the scene and the Lyle gun set up and successfully fired. The entire crew was then rescued by breeches buoy.[16]

In many ways the women were as courageous as the men. It was no easy task to live at an isolated station working for an organization that failed to provide for its families. The leading cause of death and disability among surfmen was occupational induced disease, often respiratory diseases. The job was the kind that broke men's health and the women saw it. Each time the surfmen went out, there was the possibility of loss of a surfman's life or health. Either meant both grievous personal loss and financial ruin for the family. Yet the women were there even at the most isolated and rugged of stations adding to the odds for survival.

MINORITY PEOPLE IN LIFE-SAVING

Just as women struggled to rise above the discrimination of the era so too did minority men. Life-saving ability has never been limited by artificial boundaries of race or gender. Native Americans, African-Americans and Asian-Americans all made significant contributions.

Many American Indian tribes were people of the sea or Great Lakes. Consequently, Native Americans served as surfmen both in the Massachusetts Humane Society and the U.S. Life-Saving Service. Among the best known were the Massachusetts Human Society surfmen of the Wampanoag Indian tribe at Gay Head on Martha's Vineyard. The Gay Head branch of the Wampanoag were a small tribe and by 1880 lived in a community of about 160 people. The tribe had a Humane Society boathouse and surfboat, and engaged in rescues.[17]

On January 18, 1884 one of the most tragic wrecks in New England history occurred when the *City of Columbus* with 130 people on board struck the shoals off Martha's Vineyard. In short order, the Wampanoag surfmen were dragging the Massachusetts Humane Society boat down to the surf line. Joseph Peters, a Wampanoag Indian, was a veteran whaler and respected boatman who took charge and manned the steering oar. Every surfman in the boat was a Gay Head Wampanoag. When these small Eastern Indian tribes went to the rescue more than the lives of loved ones were at risk. These communities were so small that to lose their strongest and often finest men would be a blow to their survival as a culture.

Perhaps thoughts of what had happened to the Shinnecock Indians were in the minds of some of the Wampanoag when the rescue call came. The Shinnecock Indians of Long Island were long-time whalers, salvors and life-savers, who had been employed in salvaging the iron ship *Circassian* in December 1876. Many of the workers in the dangerous salvage operation were Shinnecocks. A huge storm arose and the white manager of the operation insisted, against the advice of the Life-Saving Service, that everyone stay on board to complete the work. In the end the *Circassian* was destroyed along with the senseless loss of 28 people on board. Ten of those lost were Shinnecock salvors, a devastating blow to a tiny tribe.[18]

But the Gay Head Indians, like the Shinnecock, had been watermen for centuries and they went out knowing they might not come back. The breakers were very rough at Gay Head and ice quickly formed on the boat. Huge breakers picked up the surfboat and threw it back upon the beach. The surfmen struggled back ashore. This would be dangerous rescue.[19]

The boat was launched again and in an exhausting effort rowed to the wreck. In the excitement, the surfmen went out without wearing life preservers and at least one surfman was barefoot. It was freezing cold, with a strong current and there were large waves and whirlpools about the *City of Columbus*. Wreckage made the waves even more dangerous, yet seven survivors were brought ashore safely by the Indian surfmen. While the first boat was at sea, another Wampanoag crew launched a second Massachusetts Humane Society boat, but it was destroyed by heavy seas. This second boat's crew, however, made it safely ashore, wet and cold.[20]

The first boat returned with the seven survivors, but the surfmen were exhausted. Quickly, another crew of Wampanoag Indian surfmen stepped forward and the surfboat was off. Again, a successful trip was made and then another. Still, it was not enough. Other rescue vessels offshore were having less success and tragically, time had run out for 103 persons on the *City of Columbus*.[21]

Yet a total of 13 persons were saved by the Indian surfmen in one of the most difficult rescues in Massachusetts history. The survivors were taken to Wampanoag homes where Indian women cared for the survivors. The Indian surfmen had risked all, their own lives and perhaps even their culture. The Gay Head surfmen received Massachusetts Humane Society silver life-saving medals.[22]

Other heroic Native American surfmen were found on the Pacific Coast and on the Great Lakes. On Washington's Olympic Peninsula there are Indian nations with long seafaring traditions. At Waaddah Island (Neah Bay) Life-Saving Station during the 1870s the entire crew except the keeper were Makaw and Quileute Indians.[23] Chehalis and Quinault Indians were surfmen at Shoalwater (Willapa) Bay Life-Saving Station.[24] The Quinault Indians produced two renowned life-savers, Jonas Johns and Sampson Johns. They rescued the entire crew of fourteen men from the schooner *Lily Grace* wrecked near Grays Harbor, Washington, in January 1887. The two brothers plunged into the surf, each with a line attached to his body, and swam out to the wreck. The *Lily Grace* was fast breaking up and the Johns brothers were exhausted by their swim in the cold water. Yet they managed to rig a dugout canoe and pull it back and forth to the wreck like a lifecar. All on board were saved by dugout canoe. About a year later the Johns rescued three more sailors from the British ship *Abercorn* at Grays Harbor. Dangerous Grays Harbor had not yet received a life-saving station and the Johns brothers were the greatest life-savers of the region. Both received the silver life-saving medals from the Life-Saving Service.[25]

On Michigan's Upper Peninsula, Native Americans were present as surfmen and as wives of both Indian and White surfmen. For example, the best surfman at the lonely Vermilion Life-Saving Station on the Upper Peninsula was an American Indian, probably Ojibwa.[26]

Asian-Americans contributed to early life-saving as well. Chinese-Americans were the first commercial fishermen on San Francisco Bay and some other West Coast ports. They made up a large portion of many crews on American trans-Pacific ships and earned a reputation for heroism during shipwrecks. On the East Coast an Asian-American, F. Miguchi, won a USLSS medal. Mr. Miguchi was serving aboard the U.S. Revenue Cutter *Gresham* at Arundel Cove, Maryland. In August 1904 another Revenue Cutter crewman went under in deep water off the *Gresham*. All efforts to rescue the seaman failed, and Miguchi heroically leaped overboard and went after the drowning sailor. To lift the unconscious man's head above water, Mr. Miguchi got under the sailor and had to submerge himself while keeping the man's head above water until more help arrived. "The witnesses testified that this act of Miguchi was one of heroism deserving of high praise, and that his own life was seriously jeopardized." Revenue Cutterman Miguchi received the Congressional silver life-saving medal.[27]

On North Carolina's Outer Banks in the stormy Cape Hatteras region known as the "Graveyard of the Atlantic," some of America's greatest surfmen were to be found. Among this elite group were African-American surfmen. When the tragic *Huron* wreck occurred in 1877 Captain J.J. Guthrie, the District Superintendent of the Life-Saving Service, choose a black man, James Saxton, "one of the ablest surfman on the coast" as steersman for the perilous small boat trip to the wreck scene. In the finest tradition of the Outer Banks, Guthrie, Saxton and a crew of both

Courageous African-American surfmen braved the sea, wind and discrimination to earn an honored place in life-saving history. Surfman at Pea Island Life-Saving Station, North Carolina. (Cape Hatteras National Seashore)

African-American surfmen at Pea Island Life-Saving Station in North Carolina. Keeper Richard Etheridge, at left, was the first African-American to command a life-saving station. Descendants of Pea Island surfmen serve in the Coast Guard to this day, some as officers. (North Carolina Department of Cultural Resources)

white and black Americans went out against tremendous odds. All these surfmen, both black and white, gave their lives in this famous rescue attempt.[28]

The Outer Banks had African-American surfmen at a number of Life-Saving Service stations. Pea Island Life-Saving Station had a white keeper and a mixed white and black crew. At the wreck of the *M & S Henderson* in November 1879 the keeper and his crew failed to keep a proper watch and generally mishandled the rescue. The white keeper also lied in reporting events to USLSS officials. Four lives had been lost in the wreck.[29]

Revenue Cutter Service Lt. Charles F. Shoemaker, an outstanding officer, was charged with the investigation. Shoemaker knew how to make situations right. He fired the white keeper and those of his crew deemed guilty. Thus in 1880, Lt. Shoemaker recommended that Richard Etheridge be made keeper of Pea Island Life-Saving Station. Mr. Etheridge was one of the best surfmen on the North Carolina coast: skilled, strong, literate, intelligent and a leader. In short, the ideal surfman. Richard Etheridge was also a Black American. As Shoemaker wrote, Etheridge "has the reputation of being as good a surfman as there is on the coast, black or white."[30]

Shoemaker felt Etheridge was the best man for the job and USLSS General Superintendent Sumner Kimball approved the nomination. There had been black surfmen before, but Captain Etheridge was the first African-American to be a keeper of a Life-Saving Station. Shoemaker stated he was aware that he was breaking new ground with the appointment, but that black surfmen were "among the best on the coast of North Carolina."[31] He then ordered Etheridge to hire an all black crew. This accomplished two objectives: it provided additional jobs to highly qualified black surfmen and it avoided placing Etheridge in command of potentially racist whites. The black surfmen were drawn from those already serving in the USLSS, plus newly hired men. A short time after Keeper Etheridge's appointment, Pea Island station was burned, probably by arsonists. Keeper Etheridge did not let that stop him or his surfmen. His station began a long career of honorable service.

One of the worst wrecks Keeper Richard Etheridge and his surfmen faced was the October 11, 1896 stranding of the American schooner *E.S. Newman*. During a tremendous hurricane the schooner was forced ashore. The ship's captain had his wife and three year old daughter on board and his signal for help must have been a particularly heartfelt one. The distress signal was seen by a beach patrolman and a Coston flare burned by the surfmen acknowledged the call for help. Keeper Etheridge and his crew immediately started for the wreck pulling the beach cart. Huge seas were sweeping over the beach and threatened to prevent reaching the scene of disaster. Despite the waves and hurricane force winds, the Pea Island surfmen reached a point near the wreck. The beach was inundated by flood water and it was therefore impossible to bury the sand anchor necessary to secure the shore end of the breeches buoy.

It was one of those rare desperate situations where neither a boat nor a breeches buoy could be used. Two of the black surfmen voluntarily stepped forward and offered to go into the water and attempt to reach the ship. They tied shot lines around themselves and waded into the howling Atlantic. Nearing the ship, the surfmen threw a line on board with a heaving stick. The line was made fast to the three year old child who was soon in the caring arms of a Pea Island surfman. The surfmen on shore hauled on the shot lines, pulling the surfman with the child as he battled ashore. Next the captain's wife was carried ashore in a similar manner and then all the rest of those on board. The survivors "were rescued under great difficulties and with imminent peril," the Life-Saving Service reported. All were taken to the station and furnished with food, dry clothing and shelter for the next three days.[32]

Pea Island Life-Saving Station had a long, distinguished career. North Carolina historian David Stick later called Richard Etheridge "one of the most experienced, able, and daring lifesavers in the entire service."[33] Ethridge and his crews proved that race had nothing to do with being a great surfman. To this day, descendants of Pea Island surfmen serve as commissioned officers and enlisted personnel in the U.S. Coast Guard.[34] Today, when the breeches buoy drill is enacted for demonstration at Cape Hatteras National Seashore, both white and black surfmen perform the drill. The finest spirit of the Outer Banks lives.

Nags Head Life-Saving Station guarded North Carolina's treacherous Outer Banks. Note exposed lookout platform of this 1874-type station. (North Carolina Department of Cultural Resources)

Penneys Hill Life-Saving Station had a lookout tower which provided protection for surfmen from foul weather along the coast. This 1876-style station has been expanded to meet the growing challenges of rescues at "The Graveyard of the Atlantic." (Cape Hatteras National Seashore)

Chapter 11

North Carolina and South Carolina

THE LIFE-SAVING SERVICE AT THE CAROLINA STATIONS

The Outer Banks of North Carolina is a dangerous region known as the "Graveyard of the Atlantic." To this day Outer Banks Coast Guardsmen call themselves the "Guardians of the Graveyard."[1] Because of numerous shipwrecks in these waters, North Carolina had twenty-nine life-saving stations.

The *Atlantic Coast Pilot* describes "the coast of North Carolina is a long barrier beach" in the form of islands known as the Outer Banks. "The banks are constantly shifting sand dunes varying in height. Three capes, with their offshore shoals, project from the islands, namely: Hatteras, Lookout and Fear."[2] To encounter a genuine hurricane in these waters was often synonymous with disaster.[3]

The first crew of surfmen ever lost by the USLSS was from North Carolina's Jones Hill (soon renamed Currituck Beach) Life-Saving Station. These brave men went out into the dark night of March 1, 1876 in their surfboat to rescue the crew of the stranded Italian bark *Nuova Ottavia*. Taking a lantern with them in their surfboat, the life-savers rowed out through the breakers. In the darkness, those on shore could see nothing but the lantern in the surfboat rising and falling as great waves tossed the surfboat about. Suddenly, a scream was heard, the lantern went dark and all was quiet except the sea. The surfmen were lost.[4]

In such a place, it became tragically clear that fully manned life-saving stations with professional, paid surfmen was necessary. On November 24, 1877 the Navy vessel *U.S.S. Huron* wrecked off Nags Head, North Carolina, with the loss of 98 persons. Ironically, the disaster occurred just three miles south of a life-saving station that could have saved many lives, but it was closed for the inactive season. The life-saving station was scheduled to reopen in just six days.[5]

Then on January 31, 1878, barely three months after the *Huron* tragedy, the steamer *Metropolis* was dashed to pieces four and a half miles south of the Currituck Beach station, with the loss of 85 lives. Unfortunately, funding had been denied to build stations close enough together and "the fundamental cause of the loss of life upon this occasion was the undue distances which at that time separated the stations upon the North Carolina coast."[6]

These three North Carolina wrecks had a national impact. *Harper's New Monthly Magazine* reported that "as this page of horrors came before (the Congress and President)...it was remembered that the chief of the (Life-Saving) Service had been laboring in vain for two years to convince the Congressional mind of the unreasonable distances between stations on the North Carolina coast, and the consequent extent of patrol. The tide of public sentiment was with the Service, and misplaced economy was universally condemned. Before the end of the following June, a bill, under the championship of Hon. S.S. Cox, of New York, and Hon. Charles B. Roberts of Maryland, was carried through both Houses which elevated the institution to its proper rank as a separate establishment, instead of a branch of the Revenue Marine. The President immediately nominated Mr. (Sumner) Kimball as General Superintendent, who was promptly and unanimously confirmed, without the usual reference to a committee." Events in North Carolina had directly contributed to the formation of the Life-Saving Service as an independent agency.[7]

The Life-Saving Service would become an honored way of life on the Outer Banks. Large extended local families—the Midgetts, Etheridges and others—produced numerous sons who became surfmen and keepers. The Life-Saving Service became a part of the local heritage, a very symbol of the region. It was during the great hurricanes that the surfmen usually earned their reputations.

On August 16, 1899 a terrible hurricane "on evil wings" struck North Carolina's Outer Banks. It was, according to the United States Weather Bureau, "the most severe in the history of Hatteras." At 4 p.m. the hurricane, still sweeping northward, was furious around Cape Hatteras and its winds were recorded at 70 miles per hour. The life-savers knew they were in for trouble.[8]

The three masted schooner *Aaron Reppard,* loaded with anthracite coal, already appeared to be in trouble. Surfman William G. Midgett was on patrol from Gull Shoal Life-Saving Station and had seen the ship first. No one knew the ways of the Cape Hatteras region better than the Midgetts and William studied the vessel carefully. The

Keeper Malachi Corbell saved two African-American fishermen whose boat capsized near Caffey's Inlet, North Carolina and in June 1877 became the first member of the U.S. Life-Saving Service to win the Congressional life-saving medal. Awarded the silver medal, he is shown at a 1905 Surfman's Mutual Benefit Association convention. He became keeper at Wash Woods station. (U.S. Coast Guard)

Congressional gold life-saving medal was awarded only when loss of life was risked by the rescuer. Both gold and silver medals were rarely awarded to Life-Saving Service members because there was an attitude that risking their lives was just part of the job. (Pictured Rocks National Lakeshore)

Wash Woods Life-Saving Station was one of the stations which faced serious problems from encroaching sand dunes. This 1876-type station was the northern-most station in North Carolina. (Cape Hatteras National Seashore)

schooner would make a little headway and then drop back. "I knew she would come ashore, and I then made my way back to the station and reported her." Surfman Midgett met the USLSS patrolman from Little Kinnakeet Life-Saving Station and asked him to keep a close watch on the ship while Midgett went for help.[9]

Upon William Midgett's arrival at Gull Shoal station, Keeper Pugh telephoned Chicamacomico and Little Kinnakeet Life-Saving Stations and soon all three life-saving crews set out for the beach opposite the stranded schooner. They found the sea "as high as it could possibly be." Breakers were sweeping entirely across the island, from the Atlantic Ocean into Pamlico Sound. No surfmen outranked the Outer Banks crews in bravery and determination, but these men were not fools either. "No number of men, no matter how skillful, could have launched a boat" in such seas and lived.[10]

The schooner was about 700 yards offshore, beyond Lyle gun range. However, the vessel was slowly drifting toward shore and might come within range of the Lyle gun. As she was battered closer to shore, the schooner came within 500 yards of shore. This was the first opportunity for rescue and the Lyle gun was carefully aimed and fired. The projectile soared toward the ship, but fell short. A second charge was prepared and the Lyle gun again fired. This time the line landed perfectly across the schooner.[11]

The ship was rolling too violently for anyone on board to haul in the line to rig a breeches buoy. Then the masts began falling and the situation worsened. In desperation, the *Reppard's* captain attempted to swim ashore, but conditions were impossible and he was drowned.[12]

On the beach, the surfmen began their own desperate actions. Two or three surfmen from each station began putting on cork life-belts and tying 50 yards of shot line around themselves. Two surfmen held the landward end of each line while the third surfman prepared to enter the sea. The breakers were filled with wreckage—planks, timbers, broken spars—each flying piece a deadly battering ram that could kill a surfman. The Atlantic was so furious that no boat could survive it, yet the surfmen would challenge the sea with nothing more than a light line.[13]

There was simply no other way left to attempt the rescue. The ship quickly broke up, throwing the surviving sailors into the sea. Then Chicamacomico, Gull Shoal and Little Kinnakeet surfmen entered the deadly Atlantic breakers. Keeper E.O. Hooper of Little Kinnakeet Life-Saving Station refused the entreaties of others to leave the work to much younger men and rushed in. Flying debris struck the keeper, fracturing Hooper's right leg, but he and the younger surfmen kept going. It was a nightmare of huge breakers filled with deadly wreckage. But there were three terrified sailors to save. When the surfmen finally emerged from the sea, all three of the *Reppard's* survivors were with them.[14]

The hurricane continued along the Outer Banks. The *Diamond Shoal Lightship,* anchored off Cape Hatteras, was blown ashore and its crew saved by the Creeds Hill Life-Saving Station surfmen. Portsmouth Life-Saving Station went to the assistance of the schooner *Lydia A. Willis* and eventually rescued the survivors in their surfboat. Little Kinnakeet Station's surfmen set out for the wreck of the schooner *Robert W. Dasey,* only to have the beach cart "become mired in quicksand." The rescuers managed to save the ship's crew anyway. Chicamacomico life-savers saw the schooner *Minnie Bergen* sinking as huge seas washed over the deck. The Chicamacomico surfmen were undaunted and rescued all on board with their breeches buoy. Gull Shoal Surfman Rasmus Midgett, acting entirely alone, rescued the crew of the barkentine *Priscilla.* When it was over another historic chapter in Outer Banks rescues had been accomplished. Outer Banks heroism was everywhere.[15]

One winter five years later, conditions were very serious further south at Cape Lookout Life-Saving Station. It was February 9, 1905 and an influenza epidemic had hit the station and nearly all the surfmen were sick. Sometime after noon Keeper William H. Gaskill, ill and weak, climbed the lookout tower to relieve the watch. The coast was fogged in, but a momentary rift in the fog occurred and the keeper caught a glimpse of a sailing ship's topmost spars. That was all Keeper Gaskill saw, but it was enough. He knew that any vessel in such a position had to be upon the shoals. The keeper also knew that sea conditions were very rough.[16]

Gaskill called his sick crew to the pulling lifeboat. It would be a rough eighteen mile row in wintry weather. This would be a hard toll on the most fit of crews and Keeper Gaskill must have wondered at the condition of his men. Despite their potentially deadly illness, every man made ready to go out. The lifeboat pulled away, eight surfmen at the oars and Keeper Gaskill steering.[17]

It was not until 4 p.m., after a long row, that the wreck was reached. The surfmen found the three masted schooner *Sarah D.J. Rawson* of Georgetown, South Carolina, on her side with two masts, her deck houses and most rigging ripped away by the sea. Six sailors could be seen alive on board the vessel. The entire ship lay "in a seething mass of breakers" filled with lumber and wreckage which threatened the safety of the lifeboat. Keeper Gaskill tried to approach the schooner, but the seas nearly tossed the lifeboat end over end and the timbers in the water threatened to bash holes in the rescue boat. Only the veteran keeper's skill saved the lifeboat from destruction.[18]

Cape Lookout Life-Saving Station was home to Keeper William H. Gaskill and his surfmen. They won nine gold life-saving medals for the 1905 Sarah D.J. Rawson *rescue. Cape Lookout was an 1882-type station. (North Carolina Department of Cultural Resources)*

Ocracoke Life-Saving Station oversaw wrecks on Ocracoke Island south of Cape Hatteras. The station was built in 1882-83 and was a modified 1882-type. (Alvin Penny)

Surfboat racing out across the breakers of the Outer Banks. Oregon Inlet station, North Carolina. (Cape Hatteras National Seashore)

After repeated attempts, Keeper Gaskill realized that to approach the ship was too dangerous. Darkness was falling and the USLSS crew would spend the night in their lifeboat awaiting a chance to save the sailors. During the night the wind increased and the sick surfmen suffered terribly from "exposure, fatigue and hunger."[19]

Dawn arrived, but rescue was still impossible. Finally, about 11 a.m. conditions moderated somewhat and the lifeboat was worked in close. Despite breakers and debris, a heaving line was thrown on board the *Sarah D.J. Rawson*. Following the keeper's instructions, a seaman tied the line about his waist, jumped in the sea and was pulled on board the lifeboat. One by one, his companions followed. The sailors were chilled and needed warmth so the sick, exhausted Cape Lookout surfmen took off their own oil coats and gave them to the sailors. Then the eighteen mile row back to Cape Lookout Life-Saving Station began. It was even harder now, with the added weight of the rescued sailors and weariness of the surfmen.

Finally all safely reached the station. In the middle of winter, the sick "life-saving crew had spent twenty-four hours in an open boat, without food, and with no other nourishment other than cold water, their limbs cramped with cold and the lack of room to move about, and their bodies aching from maintaining so long a sitting posture."[20]

The Cape Lookout Life-Saving Station keeper and all eight surfmen were awarded the rare gold life-saving medal. These were selfless heros and they had pride in government service.

Chicamacomico Life-Saving Station compiled a fine record of rescues including the famous Mirlo *rescue during the Coast Guard era when life-savers braved fiery oil-covered seas to reach the steamer. This station is the namesake of the Chicamacomico-type and today is preserved by Cape Hatteras National Seashore. Excellent breeches buoy demonstrations are presented here. (Cape Hatteras National Seashore)*

Kitty Hawk Life-Saving Station was a Chicamacomico-type station. Note gables, short lookout tower and distinctive roof. The Chicamacomico-type station was built only in North Carolina during the 1911-13 period. (National Archives)

Portsmouth Life-Saving Station guarded the Portsmouth Island area. This Quonochontaug-type station is preserved by Cape Lookout National Seashore. (North Carolina Department of Cultural Resources)

Cape Hatteras National Seashore now owns the Little Kinnakeet Life-Saving Station, a rare example of the Southern-type life-saving architecture. Note massive lookout tower and distinctive porch. (U.S. Coast Guard)

Oregon Inlet Life-Saving Station had a long history of many rescues. Quonochontaug-type station. (Cape Hatteras National Seashore)

Life-Saving Stations of North Carolina and South Carolina

Life-Saving Stations of North Carolina

Station	Location
Wash Woods	On beach abreast Knotts Island, Deals
Penneys Hill	5¾ miles north of Currituck Lighthouse, Corolla
Currituck Beach	About a mile north of Currituck Lighthouse, Corolla
Poyners Hill	6½ miles south of Currituck Lighthouse
Caffeys Inlet	10¾ miles south of Currituck Lighthouse
Paul Gamiels Hill	Near Duck, 5 miles north of Kitty Hawk
Kitty Hawk	On beach north end Kitty Hawk Bay, Kitty Hawk
Kill Devil Hills	Kill Devil Hills
Nags Head	Nags Head
Bodie Island	About a mile north of Bodie Island Lighthouse
Oregon Inlet	South of Oregon Inlet, near Manteo
Pea Island	2 miles north of New Inlet, near Manteo
Chicamacomico	5 miles south of New Inlet, near Rodanthe
New Inlet	3 miles south of New Inlet, near Rodanthe
Gull Shoal	11¾ miles south of New Inlet, near Salvo
Little Kinnakeet	1½ miles north of Cape Hatteras Lighthouse, near Avon
Big Kinnakeet	5½ miles north of Cape Hatteras Lighthouse
Cape Hatteras	1 mile south of Cape Hatteras Lighthouse, Buxton
Creeds Hill	4 miles SW of Cape Hatteras Lighthouse, near Frisco
Durants	3 miles east of Hatteras Inlet, near Hatteras
Hatteras Inlet	1½ miles SW of Hatteras Inlet, near Ocracoke
Ocracoke	3 miles NE of Ocracoke Inlet, Ocracoke
Portsmouth	NE end of Portsmouth Inlet, Portsmouth
Core Bank	Core Bank, near Atlantic
Cape Lookout	1½ miles south of Cape Lookout Lighthouse
Fort Macon	Beaufort entrance, north of fort
Bogue Inlet	Inner shore Bogue Banks, near Swansboro
Cape Fear	On Smith Island, Cape Fear, near Southport
Oak Island	West side of mouth of Cape Fear River

Life-Saving Stations of South Carolina

Sullivans Island	At Moultrieville, Sullivans Island
Morris Island	Near Charleston Lighthouse

NAME CHANGES: *Currituck Beach was formerly Whale's Head and Jones Hill; Penneys Hill was once called Currituck Inlet. Durants was called Hatteras for a brief time.*[21]

Sullivans Island Life-Saving Station was one of only two US Life-Saving Stations in South Carolina. Sullivans Island was very unusual in that it was a Marquette-style station with a lookout tower on the roof. Marquette-type stations were common on the Great Lakes and Pacific Coast, but were rare on the Atlantic Coast. This station is located near Charleston and is still owned by the Coast Guard. (U.S. Coast Guard)

The very names seemed to warn mariners on the North Carolina coast. This is Cape Fear Life-Saving Station, an 1882-type station. (Richard Boonisar)

Famed Cape Hatteras Life-Saving Station stood in the heart of North Carolina's Outer Banks coast. Many shipwrecks occurred in the waters off this 1882-type station. Cape Hatteras Station won one gold and seven silver medals for the 1909 Brewster rescue on Diamond Shoals. (Cape Hatteras National Seashore)

Big Kinnakeet Life-Saving Station was a very active North Carolina station on a dangerous coast. Surfmen and boy stand beside their 1876-type station. (Cape Hatteras National Seashore)

Caffeys Inlet Life-Saving Station with crew. This Quonochontaug-type station stood at Duck, North Carolina. Built in 1897-98 this was one of the second generation of stations that replaced many 1870s vintage structures. (Cape Hatteras National Seashore)

Paul Gamiels Hill Life-Saving Station, a much expanded 1876-type station in North Carolina. This center portion of the building is original with the lean-tos and lookout added later. (Cape Hatteras National Seashore)

Durants Life-Saving Station was an attractive 1876-type station in North Carolina. Note distinctive lookout tower and facade. (Cape Hatteras National Seashore)

The power of the sea on North Carolina's Outer Banks is demonstrated by the destruction of Hatteras Inlet Lifeboat Station. The Chatham-type structure was totally destroyed. (U.S. Coast Guard)

Bogue Inlet Life-Saving Station stood amid marshlands. Southern Pattern-type station built in 1904. (U.S. Coast Guard)

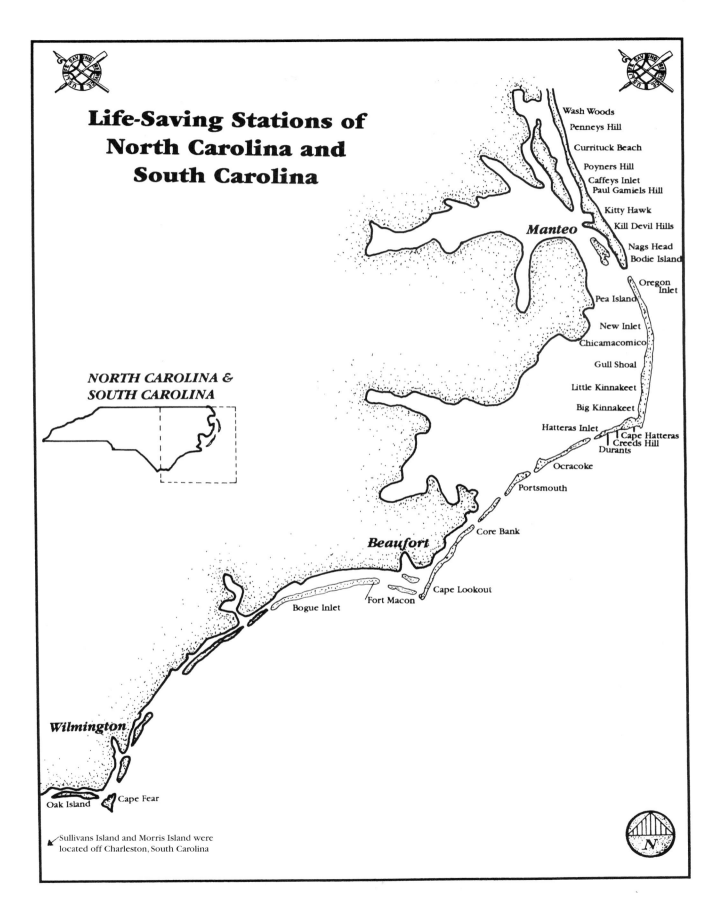

Life-Saving Stations of North Carolina and South Carolina

Wash Woods
Penneys Hill
Currituck Beach
Poyners Hill
Caffeys Inlet
Paul Gamiels Hill
Kitty Hawk
Kill Devil Hills
Nags Head
Bodie Island
Oregon Inlet
Pea Island
New Inlet
Chicamacomico
Gull Shoal
Little Kinnakeet
Big Kinnakeet
Hatteras Inlet
Cape Hatteras
Creeds Hill
Durants
Ocracoke
Portsmouth
Core Bank
Cape Lookout
Fort Macon
Bogue Inlet

Manteo

Beaufort

Wilmington

Oak Island
Cape Fear

NORTH CAROLINA & SOUTH CAROLINA

Sullivans Island and Morris Island were located off Charleston, South Carolina

A floating life-saving station far from the sea. Louisville Life-Saving Station was on the Ohio River at Louisville, Kentucky. It had an appropriate riverboat-like appearance and could be moved as the river level changed. (U.S. Coast Guard)

Louisville surfmen rush out of their floating station in their life-skiff. Two life-skiffs were kept in the stern of the floating station. Louisville was a busy station manned year round. (U.S. Coast Guard)

Chapter 12

Floating Life-Saving Stations

FLOATING LIFE-SAVING STATIONS

Many of the Life-Saving Service's shore stations were designed so they could be moved fairly readily and inexpensively if threatened by encroaching seas. However, the ultimate moveable stations were the Life-Saving Service's two floating stations: Louisville Life-Saving Station at the Falls of the Ohio River in Kentucky and City Point Life-Saving Station off Boston, Massachusetts.

The oldest and best known floating station was Louisville Life-Saving Station, established in 1881. A dam had been built across the Ohio River at Louisville and vessels bound upstream bypassed the dam and gained elevation by the conventional method of locks. But for vessels bound downstream, passage was by way of two dangerous chutes that allowed rapid descent of vessels. "This dam is a constant source of danger to small boats that attempt to cross the river, as they are liable to be drawn down through the chutes. Large vessels are also exposed to the same perils if they become disabled or unmanageable."[1]

Because of recurring floods no suitable site for a land based life-saving station could be found. A floating station was required because it could be easily relocated as the river banks changed. The floating life-saving station could also be moved up and downstream to be closer to seasonally changing danger spots. Normally, the station was moored above the dam because this was where the most accidents occurred. During floods, however, the station could be towed wherever needed.

Since 1875 three courageous boatmen—William Devan, John Tully, and John Gillooly—had been voluntarily saving lives at the Falls of the Ohio, often at great personal risk. They had already won the gold life-saving medal and by 1881 had saved forty-five lives and achieved national fame.[2] The first crew of the Louisville Life-Saving Station consisted of these three men, plus one other, a crew of just four (later six) surfmen under the command of Keeper William Devan.[3]

Louisville Life-Saving Station was a handsome, wooden, riverboat-like vessel specially built as a life-saving station. It had a scow-shaped hull with a two story house-like superstructure topped by a lookout tower. Two boats, called life-skiffs, were kept in a boatroom inside the station and could be launched bow first at a good speed. They were appropriately named the *Ready* and the *Reckless* and were low, fast, pulling boats apparently unlike any others in the Service. Besides the life-skiffs, two reels of five inch manila line were kept on-hand to attach to disabled vessels.[4] The chutes were dangerous even at low water and surfmen were employed year round.

Louisville Life-Saving Station was still new when, on March 5, 1882, the stern-wheel riverboat *James D. Parke* wrecked nearby. She had a crew of 50 plus 55 passengers, including women, men and children.[5]

The river was running high but no problem had been anticipated. The riverboat positioned herself above the Indiana chute ready for her descent. All seemed well when suddenly, her bow went under. The *James D. Parke* then "wobbled," her smokestacks toppled over, and a cloud of steam burst from her. The stern-wheeler went down in eighteen feet of water. Word spread that the riverboat had blown up.

On deck, there was a scene of "utmost horror and confusion" as people scrambled for safety. The riverboat was "a mass of crushed and splintered timbers, bales, boxes of merchandise...crowded with wild and desperate figures." The whole catastrophe took place in just ten minutes. In fact, the vessel had not blown up. Rather, she was unequally loaded and had sunk.[6]

The lookout atop the Louisville floating station saw the danger immediately and the surfmen were underway in the life-skiffs in minutes. Three men manned the *Ready* and three more the *Reckless*.[7]

Rowing to the *James D. Parke* the surfmen found that the vessel had heeled over and sunk, but that a slanted portion remained above the water where the survivors had taken refuge. A doorway was ripped off the riverboat and a gangplank was used to take people off. Keeper Devan shouted, "Get into these lifeboats quick!" and *Ready* and *Reckless* filled to capacity. It took twelve trips to get everyone ashore, but the surfmen took all 80 people left on the riverboat safely ashore. Other vessels arrived to help save those washed downstream and in the end everyone was miraculously saved.[8]

In rare situations unusual floating life-saving stations were established. City Point Life-Saving was a ship-like station established in 1895 and moored on Dorchester Bay at Boston. (Shanks collection)

City Point floating station kept its rescue boats in a stern boat bay. City Point probably was the first station in the country to have gasoline powered rescue boats. (Richard Boonisar)

Louisville surfmen were also impressive in time of flood. During the great river floods of 1883-84 at Louisville, the Ohio River burst its banks, endangering the lives of thousands of people. Keeper Devan and his crew saw the river embankment break and heard the "heart-shaking roar" as the pent up water had surged into Louisville. After launching their boat, they "dangerously steered through a wild riffraff of rushing debris (and) the rowers saw fences, shanties, sheds and outhouses fly up from their fastenings on every side and whirl away to ruin." Houses floated past and debris was covered with rats. "A hundred screams rent the air in all directions." The task seemed impossible, but the surfmen were everywhere in their life-skiffs. The Louisville Life-Saving Station surfmen ultimately "rescued and took to places of safety over 800 imperiled persons, men, women and children—among them many sick and infirm—and supplied food and other necessities to more than 10,000." They performed one of the most remarkable rescues in U.S. history.[9]

In 1928-29 the wooden Louisville floating station was replaced by a fine 98-foot long steel floating station which was also two stories high with a lookout tower. This floating station also performed many rescues and remained active until 1964 when it was retired and preserved at Louisville.[10] It is the last historic floating life-saving station in America.

The USLSS's other floating station, City Point Life-Saving Station, was established at Dorchester Bay, Boston, Massachusetts. Numerous fatal boating accidents had occurred in Dorchester Bay and vicinity, usually involving small craft. Locating a station closer to the boating public would be a great advantage. As a result, the Life-Saving Service in 1895 decided to construct a floating life-saving station to be anchored in Dorchester Bay.[11]

The following year the USLSS announced that "the floating station...in Dorchester Bay, near City Point, Boston Harbor, designed to render assistance in the numerous casualties occurring to yachts and sailboats in that vicinity, has been completed, anchored in position, and put into commission."[12] This floating station looked much more ship-like than did the riverboat type station at Louisville. City Point had a pointed bow and a ship-like superstructure with a flying bridge where lookouts stood watch. There was no tall lookout tower, but City Point launched its boats from its stern into the water as did Louisville. Significantly, City Point station was equipped with a gasoline powered launch, the *Relief*, probably the first life-saving station in the country to have a power boat.[13] Later a second power boat was added.

City Point had nine surfmen. City Point followed a pattern of seasonal employment with closure during winter months, as was done on the Great Lakes. Winter layoffs meant City Point surfmen transferred to shore sta-

tions where they were hired as the "winter man," the extra surfman New England shore stations needed for added winter patrols and other seasonal duties. Some City Point surfmen sought permanent transfers to shore station because they offered more months of employment.[14]

City Point's rescue calls primarily involved aiding small boats that were adrift, capsized, dragging anchor, or dismasted. At least two different vessels served as City Point floating station. The floating station was renamed the Boston Lifeboat Station and served until 1950 when it sunk.[15] Both Louisville and City Point represented important and unusual station types. They were specialized adaptations to unique locations and they performed their frequent rescues well.[16]

Stern view of Louisville Life-Saving Station showing floating station's boat room with river skiff on launchway. Louisville was the only inland life-saving station in the country. (U.S. Coast Guard)

Florida was the only state where the Life-Saving Service built houses of refuge. A keeper and his family had no crew and were the only occupants of these stations. Mariners had to reach shore without help from rescue boats, then were cared for at a house of refuge. Indian River Inlet House of Refuge, Fort Pierce, Florida. (St. Lucie County Historical Museum)

Orange Grove House of Refuge near Delray Beach, Florida seems relaxed as the keeper and his wife sit on the porch and laundry hangs from railings. The keeper and his family patrolled beaches looking for wrecks, particularly after storms. (Delray Beach Historical Society)

Chapter 13

Houses of Refuge and Life-Saving Stations of Florida

FLORIDA HOUSES OF REFUGE

Florida has a unique coast which resulted in a fascinating type of rescue facility. While the coast of Florida is well-known for its hurricanes and lightning storms, the state is more famous for its beautiful beaches and warm waters. What made Florida so unusual was that "when vessels strand, they usually come well up on the shore, so that sailors find little difficulty in reaching the land." However, during Florida's early years and well into the Life-Saving Service era "these shores were almost uninhabited, and mariners cast upon them were exposed to the terrors of starvation and thirst."[1]

To deal with a coast where rescue by surfboat or beach apparatus was unnecessary, but where lack of food and water were dangers, the Life-Saving Service reached back to the Massachusetts Humane Society for a solution. The Life-Saving Service decided to build houses of refuge to provide shelter and food for shipwrecked mariners. The original house of refuge system had faltered in New England because shipwreck victims needed surfmen and boats to assist them in reaching shore. In addition, unmanned houses of refuge had been subject to vandalism, theft and neglect.

In Florida the old house of refuge concept was revived and improved. Houses of refuge were to be staffed by a full time keeper and his family. There would be no crew of surfmen, but there would always be someone there to maintain the house and protect its contents. Besides being living quarters for keeper and family, the houses of refuge contained cots, food, water, clothing and medicine for rescued mariners. The goal was to be able to provide accommodations for up to 25 people for ten days.[2]

The difficulty, of course, was that the shipwrecked sailors generally would have to get to the house of refuge on their own. There was real fear that mariners completely unfamiliar with the nearly uninhabited Florida coast would stray blindly into the bush and die of thirst or starvation. Guideposts were thus placed along the Florida east coast beaches indicating the direction and distance to either the nearest house of refuge or the nearest lighthouse, whichever was closer. The houses of refuge averaged 26 miles apart and in some cases there were lighthouses in between the houses of refuge.[3] Using lighthouses as a back-up rescue facility was an ancient and honorable practice.

House of refuge keepers and their families patrolled the beaches. Mosquitoes, sandflies, blazing sun, soft sand and lonely isolation made patrols long and hard. These conditions were endured by the keeper, his wife and older children—any of whom might be on beach patrol. The houses of refuge more than any other Life-Saving Service facilities were family operations.[4]

The keeper of a house of refuge was without crewmen, breeches buoy, lifecar, lifeboats or surfboats. But the keeper did have his own strength and courage, his family, a heaving stick and line, Coston signals, lanterns and occasionally helpful passers-by. Neighbors still were very few and the beaches nearly deserted.

In later years, conditions improved when a small boat, boathouse and lookout tower were added to at least some houses of refuge. The number of neighbors also began to increase, but the house of refuge families were true pioneers who brought search and rescue services, law and order and a much needed government presence to Florida.[5]

There were major shipwrecks on the Florida coast. One was the brig *J.H. Lane* of Searsport, Maine, which wrecked in heavy, rainy weather five and a half miles south of the Gilberts Bar House of Refuge on April 19, 1886. The ship was discovered early in the morning by Keeper Samuel Bunker during a break in the storm. Enlisting the aid of two boatmen bound down Indian River, Keeper Bunker and his two volunteers went down the beach to the wreck. Since the *J.H. Lane* was stranded on a reef three quarters of a mile offshore, the sailors would have to come ashore in the ship's boat. It was obvious that the brig was breaking up. At same time, the surf at beach was becoming smoother. Waiting longer to abandon ship would only increase the danger. The only thing the house of refuge keeper could do was to signal the ship's crew to come ashore in their own boat.[6]

Mosquito Lagoon House of Refuge did not have an inviting name, but offered the only shelter available to shipwrecked sailors. (National Archives)

Gilberts Bar House of Refuge on Hutchinsons Island near Stewart, Florida was active in important rescues. It is the only House of Refuge known to survive today and it is preserved as Gilbert's Bar House of Refuge Museum. (Florida State Archives)

Chester Shoal House of Refuge near Cape Canaveral had inviting landscaped grounds. Houses of Refuge, designed by architect Francis W. Chandler, were built in Florida during 1875-85. (U.S. Coast Guard)

The Life-Saving Service always hated to allow deep water sailors unfamiliar with local surf conditions to come ashore in their own boats. The USLSS had witnessed too many such tragedies, but house of refuge keepers had no other option. No sooner had the ship's boat been launched than it capsized, throwing the sailors into the sea. One sailor was washed away and drowned, but the rest grabbed their boat's lifelines and hung on. The boat and crew drifted slowly along the shore, gradually nearing the beach. But landing was nearly impossible because a boat in such poor condition could never make it through the heavy surf. So Keeper Samuel Bunker tied his heaving line around his waist and gave the end of the line to his two volunteers. Bunker watched the breakers and when a momentary lull occurred he rushed in and grabbed a sailor and dragged him safely ashore. Again and again Keeper Bunker followed a receding wave out and grabbed a sailor, shouting for the two men on the beach to pull on the heaving line and haul them ashore. The seven survivors were saved by Keeper Bunker in this heroic manner. All were taken to the Gilberts Bar House of Refuge and given water, food and dry clothing.[7]

The sailors were cared for at the House of Refuge for a week. Then they were given directions and provisions to reach Indian River Inlet House of Refuge, the next station north, some twenty miles up the coast. There Keeper Stoekel cared for them and provisioned the shipwrecked sailors so that they could continue their long walk up the Florida coast to the nearest railroad station, at Titusville, over eighty miles away. Living on the Florida coast in those days was reminiscent of being on a desert island, except for the presence of the Life-Saving Service.[8]

Generally help from the houses of refuge did not involve spectacular shipwrecks, but more modest actions. Typical help was illustrated by this grateful quote from a mail carrier whose boat sunk off the Biscayne Bay House of Refuge in April 1891: "I was sailing on Biscayne Bay, going south with the United States mail, when a terrific gale set in from the northeast causing the waves to run so high as to swamp my boat. She sunk in ten feet of water with the mail on board. By the greatest exertions and risks (the mail carrier and two companions) succeeded in crossing the bay. We arrived at the House of Refuge all played out. The keeper (Captain Fulford) and his wife at once took us in hand, giving us dry clothes and something to eat. I reported the swamping of the mail boat to the keeper. It being by that time pitch dark nothing could be done just then. Long before daylight, however, Captain Fulford was up, and his wife soon had breakfast ready." Keeper Fulford, his wife and the three stranded men went to scene of the wreck and managed to salvage both the boat and the soggy mail. "It was the prompt assistance of the keeper, Captain Fulford, that saved boat and the (U.S. mail, which included cash). Mrs. Fulford gave us material aid in handling the gear in raising the boat. The Life-Sav-

ing Service is doing much good here, and certainly has an efficient officer in charge of their Biscayne Bay Station, he being always on the alert to save life and property."[9]

Perhaps the busiest time at a house of refuge was on October 16-17, 1904 at Gilberts Bar House of Refuge. On the sixteenth, the Italian bark *Georges Valentine* was actually "knocked down broadside to the sea" by a terrific squall accompanied by torrential rain. Of twelve persons on board, just seven remained alive. Two of these managed to reach the House of Refuge where they were cared for. The keeper immediately set out in search of others, finding all five of the other survivors. He extricated them from the drifting wreckage and brought them to the station. The sailors were in poor condition and the keeper anticipated having to care for them for several days.[10]

The day after the *Valentine* wreck, the Spanish ship *Cosme Colzada* stranded three miles from Gilberts Bar House of Refuge. The keeper was busy tending to the health of the first group of survivors and could not patrol the beaches. Fortunately, an African-American neighbor found the shipwrecked crew and cared for them, taking the sailors to the house of refuge the following day. The facility was nearly at capacity by now with 23 shipwrecked sailors present, but the Life-Saving Service cared for all. Florida's houses of refuge may have been few and modestly staffed, but they rose to all challenges and saved many lives.[11]

Besides its unique Houses of Refuge, Florida also had two fully manned life-saving stations. Santa Rosa Life-Saving Station was near Pensacola. An 1882-type station, it was destroyed by a hurricane in 1906. The other full-fledged life-saving station was Jupiter Inlet at Jupiter. (Shanks collection)

Bulow House of Refuge near Daytona Beach was the northern-most Florida House of Refuge. Note long gabled windows on roof. Life-Saving Service House of Refuge-style architecture was unique to Florida. (U.S. Coast Guard)

Picnic day on the porch of Biscayne Bay House of Refuge at Miami Beach. (Florida State Archives)

Florida Houses of Refuge and Life-Saving Station

Station	*Location*
Bulow	20 miles south of Matanzas Inlet
Mosquito Lagoon	Near Oak Hill on beach outside lagoon
Chester Shoal	11 miles north of Cape Canaveral
Bethel Creek	16 miles north of Indian River Inlet
Indian River Inlet	South side of Inlet, Fort Pierce area
Gilberts Bar	Hutchinsons Island, near Stuart
Fort Lauderdale	9 miles south of Hillsboro Inlet Lighthouse
Biscayne Bay	Miami Beach

Life-Saving Station	*Location*
Santa Rosa	Santa Rosa Island near Warrington

NAME CHANGE: Bulow House of Refuge was for a time called Smith's Creek.

DISCONTINUED HOUSES OF REFUGE: As with all other chapter station lists, the above listing is from 1914 when Florida had eight Houses of Refuge plus one regular life-saving station. For some years there were three additional Houses of Refuge along the Florida coast. Orange Grove House of Refuge was in the Delray Beach area and was discontinued October 1, 1896. Cape Malabar House of Refuge was located 20 miles south of Cape Canaveral and was discontinued March 30, 1891. In 1885, Indian River House of Refuge was renamed Bethel Creek House of Refuge. This was probably done to avoid confusion with the newly established Indian River Inlet House of Refuge. Thus, Florida had a total of ten Houses of Refuge, all on its east coast.[12]

DISCONTINUED LIFE-SAVING STATION: Jupiter Inlet station on the south side of the inlet at Jupiter was a completely equipped life-station with surfboat and a full crew of surfmen. It was a regular life-saving station, not a House of Refuge. It was discontinued January 21, 1899.[13]

Biscayne Bay House of Refuge was a pioneer structure at Miami Beach. (U.S. Coast Guard)

Hurricanes were a danger as Houses of Refuge were built close to the beach. Biscayne Bay House of Refuge was badly damaged by the 1926 hurricane. (U.S. Coast Guard)

Santa Rosa Life-Saving Station was one of two Florida life-saving stations. This was the second Santa Rosa station as the first station was destroyed in a hurricane. A Quonochontaug-type station built in 1908. (Florida State Archives)

Jupiter Inlet Life-Saving Station was a fully manned and equipped life-saving station, not a House of Refuge. An 1882-type station built in 1885. (Florida State Archives)

Keeper's wife and boathouse at Chester Shoal House of Refuge. Keeper and his wife sometimes used a small boat to assist mariners in salvage operations. (U.S. Coast Guard)

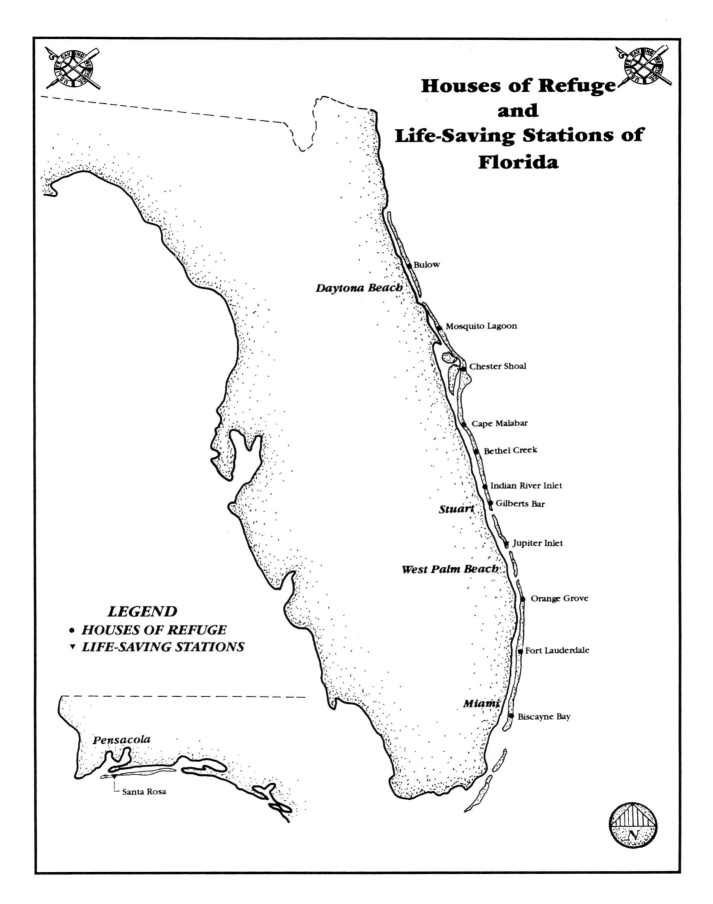

Houses of Refuge and Life-Saving Stations of Florida

Bulow

Daytona Beach

Mosquito Lagoon

Chester Shoal

Cape Malabar

Bethel Creek

Indian River Inlet

Gilberts Bar

Stuart

Jupiter Inlet

West Palm Beach

Orange Grove

Fort Lauderdale

Miami

Biscayne Bay

LEGEND
- **HOUSES OF REFUGE**
- ▼ **LIFE-SAVING STATIONS**

Pensacola

Santa Rosa

N

International signal flags fly at San Luis Life-Saving Station at the west end of Galveston Island. Surfmen pose proudly beside their surfboat. An 1880-type station. (U.S. Coast Guard Academy)

Sabine Pass Life-Saving Station in Texas was a classic example of Gulf-style life-saving station architecture. Note construction atop piles, the large verandah and lookout tower atop roof. A surfboat is moored ready for use. (Surfman Authur Barr)

Chapter 14

Texas

THE LIFE-SAVING SERVICE IN TEXAS

The Gulf Coast was a challenge to the Life-Saving Service with its hurricanes and floods. Life-saving stations built on low ground in exposed locations meant surfmen, survivors and stations were especially vulnerable to the forces of nature.

The USLSS came to Texas later than other regions, in part because life-saving station construction in Texas had been delayed by yellow fever epidemics in the late 1870s.[1] By 1880, however, the Life-Saving Service had expanded its operations to the Gulf of Mexico. Seven stations were built in Texas, most located at the entrances to the state's more important harbors.

Due to Gulf Coast hurricanes and floods, crews and stations would pay a high cost to guard this coast. A critical problem was the underfunded Life-Saving Service's inability to employ crews year round. The worst hurricanes often struck during the "inactive season" when the surfmen were off duty and only the keepers were in attendance. The Life-Saving Service was slow to understand Texas weather patterns.[2]

Stations were primarily equipped with pulling surfboats along this low coast. Pulling surfboats and, later, power surfboats dominated here, supplemented by small skiffs. As late as 1915 only Galveston would be equipped with a motor lifeboat.

Although many early stations were built flush to the ground in conventional life-saving station construction, all or nearly all later Texas stations (plus the one in Louisiana) came to be constructed in a unique Texas Gulf architectural style. Stations were built on piles or pillars well above ground. This allowed water from floods and hurricanes to pass safely under the station and cooled the facility in hot, humid weather. Spacious verandahs surrounded the buildings giving them a traditional southern look. A lookout tower normally topped the center of the roof. Stations were built on pillars either on low, sandy beaches or on piles in the water. Because of a shallow coast, boathouses were sometimes placed far offshore at the end of long piers. While the Texas stations responded to shipwrecks, the great floods and hurricanes were the most challenging rescue work.[3]

Early in July 1899 extraordinarily heavy rains drew the nation's attention to Texas' flood-swollen Brazos River. In places the river was reported at fifty feet above mean water level and hundreds of square miles of lowlands were flooded. Life-Saving Service District Superintendent William A. Hutchings at Galveston, went into action. Hutchings dispatched the keepers of the Galveston and Aransas Life-Saving Stations by train to rush boats and men to the rising Brazos River.

Arriving at the Brazos, the life-savers found that strong currents appeared unexpectedly in strange locations and that they needed the help of local pilots. Local African-American pilots were especially knowledgeable and were sought out.[4]

Everyone in the rescue operation risked their health. With heavy rain pouring down upon the rescuers, water soon became contaminated by sewage and industrial chemicals. Rescue operations progressed slowly as the USLSS rowed about seeking survivors. Life-savers had to move through thick woods where tree branches could capsize a boat and sunken fences became snags. But many people were rescued, sometimes in groups of over a hundred. They were usually fearful, hungry and stranded atop a building or mound. Plantations and humble cabins were searched, sometimes without result and sometimes with huge success.[5]

Life-Saving personnel suffered from both disease and industrial poisoning as a result of their rescue work. The Life-Saving Service reported that "in addition to the severe and exhausting exposure suffered by all (the rescuers) Keeper (Edward) Haines (of Galveston station) and District Superintendent Hutchings were afflicted with poison, while the ever faithful surfman Jacob Jacobson contracted fever of which he died a short time after his return to the (Galveston) life-saving station." This single, tiny U.S. Life-Saving Service contingent had managed to rescue 257 people of all races with their surfboat.[6] The Life-Saving Service always had brave men ready to lay their lives down for others in need.

Many other Gulf storms were to follow. The life-saving stations, necessarily built at exposed locations suf-

Saluria Life-Saving Station near Port O'Connor was a fine example of the earliest Texas stations. These stations were built conventionally on the ground and had to be replaced by the raised Gulf-style stations. Note the unusually narrow lookout tower found on the 1880-type Texas stations. (Surfman Arthur B. Barr)

Texas surfmen at Saluria Life-Saving Station. Keeper Andrew Rasmussen stands at center. (Shanks collection)

Aransas Life-Saving Station on Mustang Island near Port Aransas shows the vulnerability of 1880-type Texas stations built on very low shores without the piles of Gulf-style stations. (U.S. Coast Guard)

fered great damage. The September 1900 hurricane "wrought untold damage to the city of Galveston" and swept away the Galveston Life-Saving Station.[7]

Galveston station was rebuilt, but in July 1909 yet another devastating hurricane struck the Gulf coast. It was the inactive season and all the stations were undermanned and had to rely in part on volunteers which made work much more difficult. Three adjacent stations, Galveston, San Luis and Velasco, suffered the worst.[8]

When the storm hit, the life-saving crews of these three stations immediately went to the rescue, even though their own stations were in grave danger. The Galveston station crew pulled to the rescue in their surfboat. The wind was blowing so hard an oar was whipped out of its oarlock and went flying through the air, narrowly missing the Galveston keeper. The surfboat crashed into a pier and when District Superintendent Hutchings waded out in the surf to help his surfmen he was painfully injured by the floating wreckage that battered everything.[9]

At the San Luis Life-Saving Station, on the west end of Galveston Island, salt cedar trees measuring ten inches in diameter "were snapped off like reeds" by the great wind. San Luis Life-Saving Station was built on sandy ground and its foundation washed away. The station was then literally pushed about by the sea. The station horse disappeared when the stable washed away.

The San Luis surfmen, along with some fishermen they had rescued, fled to the surfboat as the station buildings were being carried away. Then the surfboat, with everyone in it, broke its moorings and was swept clear over the island and across the bay, not stopping until it hit the mainland. Providentially, all survived their harrowing surfboat ride and as soon as the conditions moderated a bit, the surfmen rowed back to the station and looked for other survivors. They rescued several more people and rowed them into Galveston to safety.[10]

During this time, at Velasco Life-Saving Station, the next station south, Keeper John P. Steinhart was on watch in the lookout when he saw a sloop in the Brazos River dragging out to sea. As at the other two stations, most of the crew was off for the "inactive season" and the keeper found it impossible during a hurricane to find enough willing volunteers. Consequently, the sloop drifted away in obvious peril. "The sloop…was swept out to sea and its occupants lost. The two men aboard the vessel proved to be Columbus A. Maddox and Edward Juelsen, surfmen belonging to the Galveston life-saving crew. They had purchased the sloop with the view of earning a little money during the inactive season. When overtaken by the hurricane, they were on their way back to Galveston to reenlist in the service for the ensuing year beginning August 1." Ironically, as they were on their way to save the lives of others, these two surfmen lost their own lives.[11]

Meanwhile, at the Velasco Life-Saving Station the storm danger was growing worse. Keeper Steinhart had not returned from a rescue and the station was facing destruction. If anyone was to survive, Velasco station would have to be evacuated immediately. The keeper's wife and two men volunteers got everyone in the 27-foot Monomoy surfboat to try to survive the storm. In all 34 people, nearly all women and children from the station and nearby were huddled in the surfboat for five hours, "exposed to the fury of wind, rain and sea." During this time in the open surfboat, it was the keeper's wife who "personally administered to the needs of the others." Eventually the keeper returned from his rescue attempts and everyone finally made it safely to the town of Velasco.[12]

In the following years when hurricanes struck the Gulf Coast surfmen managed to save hundreds of lives. But conditions could become so bad that even the survival of the surfmen was in doubt. "Upon the occurrence of these hurricanes the crews of stations within the storms have been accustomed, under extreme conditions, to man their larger (surf)boats at the beginning of the flood, in the hope of surviving the storm, riding at such available mooring as seemed to offer the best holding ground. The predicament of the crews (and their families) during these occasions can be well imagined. Driven from their stations by the rise of water, there is nothing else for them to do, on the low, flat beaches of the country, but to take to their boats, make them fast the best they can, and trust to good fortune to bring them through the storm."[13]

After another hurricane destroyed the Velasco and San Luis stations on August 16, 1916 killing six surfmen and five of the wives and children, the lessons of the Texas coast were finally hammered home. The Velasco and San Luis stations were rebuilt on steel pilings and elevated above the high water during hurricane seasons, techniques long used by the Lighthouse Service to protect their structures. Some stations were relocated to more protected sites and built in the safer Gulf Coast architectural style. It became a common architectural style for stations in the region and some contemporary Coast Guard stations use the style to this day.[14]

Life-Saving Stations of Texas

Station	Location
Sabine Pass	West side of pass near Sabine
Galveston	On Pelican Spit, near Galveston
San Luis	West end of Galveston Island
Velasco	2¼ miles NE of mouth of Brazos River
Saluria	NE end of Matagorda Island near Port O'Conner
Aransas	NE end of Mustang Island near Port Aransas
Brazos	North end of Brazos Island near Port Isabel

A LOUISIANA STATION: In 1918 the Coast Guard built its Barataria Lifeboat Station at Grand Isle, Louisiana. Its Gulf-style architecture and duties place Barataria Bay station in the same class as the circa-1915 Texas life-saving stations.[15]

Velasco Life-Saving Station, an 1880-type station with surfmen and boat. Shallow coastal waters and frequent inland floods meant Texas was surfboat country. (U.S. Coast Guard Academy)

Barataria Life-Saving Station, Louisiana. Lone Louisiana life-saving station was built by the Coast Guard using USLSS Gulf plans in 1918. (U.S. Coast Guard)

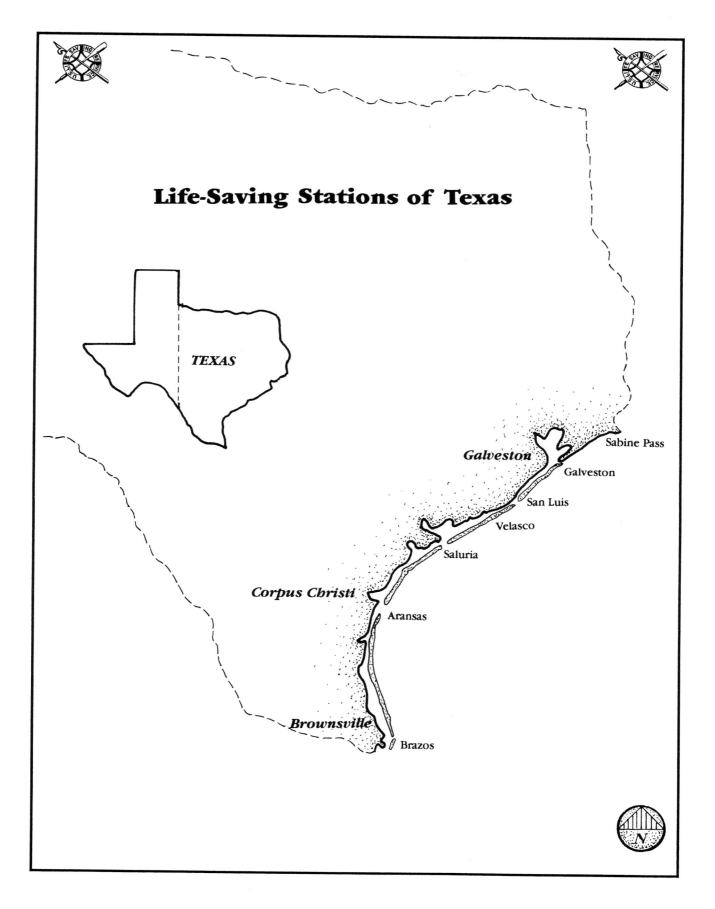

Life-Saving Stations of Texas

TEXAS

Galveston

Sabine Pass

Galveston

San Luis

Velasco

Saluria

Corpus Christi

Aransas

Brownsville

Brazos

Americans loved to watch life-saving drills. Surfboat hits Lake Michigan at Michigan City Life-Saving Station in Indiana. A Bibb #3-type station with distinctive "witch's hat" lookout. (U. S. Coast Guard)

Frankfort Life-Saving Station with surfboat in Lake Michigan and lifeboat on launchway. This Bibb #3-type station is being preserved at Elberta, Michigan. Bibb #3 stations were unique to Lake Michigan. (Shanks collection)

Chapter 15

Great Lakes

THE LIFE-SAVING SERVICE ON THE GREAT LAKES

The Great Lakes, the largest body of freshwater in the world, are oceanic in character. Although lake waves are not as large as the biggest ocean waves, they present unique challenges. Freshwater waves are steeper and closer together than most ocean waves. Storms strike very quickly on the Great Lakes and "at certain seasons (the lakes) are visited by violent gales which throw their freshwater into furious convulsions with a suddenness unknown upon the ocean."[1]

Because there are also relatively few natural harbors on the Great Lakes, ships must frequently pass through constricted man-made harbor entrances with limited room for maneuvering. Such passages are especially dangerous during storms. "Vessels unable to hold their own against the severity of these (Great Lakes) storms, being land-locked and with scant sea room, are likely to be left with only the choice between stranding wherever they may be driven (or) seeking refuge in the harbor that seems most accessible. The latter course is naturally the one taken. To effect an entrance within the narrow space between the piers at such times with sailing vessels, and even with steamers, is frequently a task of extreme difficulty, and the luckless craft are liable to strand upon the bar on one or the other side of the piers" which extend into the lake on both sides of the entrance channel.[2]

Great Lakes weather was notoriously cold and windy. Ice was so severe that navigation ceased for several months each winter. Seeking economic gain, shipping companies tried to operate their vessels as late into the winter season as possible, even into November. November, the eleventh month, was when the most vicious storms often set in and the ice began to arrive. So many of the Great Lakes worst shipwrecks occurred in November that lake sailors spoke of "The Curse of the Eleventh Month."[3]

Great Lakes life-saving stations were first built in 1854 with small structures operated by volunteers. These facilities soon fell prey to the usual theft, vandalism and neglect.[4] To secure the economic development of the region, it became increasingly obvious that real life-saving stations were needed. After a period of operating yet another group of inadequately manned "lifeboat stations," the Life-Saving Service finally recognized the importance of Great Lakes shipping and completed a chain of fully manned, fully equipped life-saving stations.

Some regions of the Great Lakes were among the most isolated in the nation. Few stations anywhere were as lonely as those along eastern Lake Superior's "Graveyard Coast." Vermilion, Crisps, Two Heart River and Deer Park life-saving stations were all located on Michigan's Upper Peninsula between Grand Marais and Whitefish Point. Mosquitoes, black flies, extreme isolation, frigid weather, cutting winds, low pay and danger came with these stations. One surfman on patrol fell in an ice cave and was only saved after his dog returned to the station without him. Ghosts were said to pursue beach patrolmen and in such an empty land who knew if it were true.[5]

It was the lonely stations along the Lake Superior shore that seemed to produce the strangest tales. Benjamin Truedell was a young surfman at Deer Park Life-Saving Station on Lake Superior east of Grand Marais, Michigan. On the stormy night of August 30, 1892 Surfman Truedell was sleeping before his scheduled midnight patrol. The wind blew and Deer Park station groaned and creaked in the wind. Rain and sand battered the windows. Benjamin Truedell tossed about on his cot.

"At midnight when I was awakened to go on patrol, I leaped from my cot trembling and perspiring, and glanced about wildly, for I had been dreaming of a wreck, a dream so realistic I still fancied myself on the beach. The delusion persisted in spite of (being among) my comrades, dressed in oilskins and carrying lanterns, and the familiar surroundings" of the station. The other surfmen asked Truedell what was the matter. "I've had a most peculiar dream. A ship is going down somewhere. And a lot of people will go with her." The others were skeptical, but Benjamin Truedell was insistent. "Mark my words. Tomorrow we'll hear of a wreck."

Surfman Truedell continued, "I had dreamed I was walking down the beach through the storm. I had not gone far before I became aware of another presence. It was a well dressed man, obviously someone of position." The man stepped out of the spray in front of Truedell. With a pleading look, he muttered something the lifesaver could not understand and then pointed three times

Great Lakes surfboat crossing Lake Superior breakers. Freshwater surfmen faced great storms and frigid weather. Keeper Benjamin Truedell at steering oar, Grand Marais Life-Saving Station, Michigan. (Michigan State Archives)

Great Lakes surfboat entering stormy Lake Superior. Vermilion Life-Saving Station, Michigan. (Lake Superior State University)

out toward the lake. The apparition's white face drew close to Surfman Truedell, and then, still appearing to beg for help, slowly vanished back into the mist.

The other Deer Park surfmen laughed at Benjamin Truedell's story. However, a short time later the station lookout shouted that a shipwrecked sailor was approaching the station. He turned out to be from the steamer *Western Reserve* that had gone down off Deer Park with all passengers and crew, except for this lone survivor. Among those on board were Peter Minch, the distinguished owner of the ship, his wife and children. The surviving sailor told how Minch had struggled valiantly to save his family, but all had drowned.

The Deer Park surfmen began a search of the beaches looking for bodies. Wolves were plentiful in the area and the life-savers needed to get there first. Eventually, Surfman Truedell found a body of a well-dressed man. Truedell was stunned. It was the person from his dream. It was Peter Minch, the *Western Reserve's* owner. The surfman's dream had been true.[6]

Benjamin Truedell stayed in the Life-Saving Service,

rising to become keeper of Grand Marais Life-Saving Station, the next station west of Deer Park. Keeper Truedell went on to lead many rescues and build a great name as a brave and skilled life-saver. But he never forgot his strange dream that foretold the wreck of the *Western Reserve*. Sitting at home in his older years, when the wind off Lake Superior rattled the shingles and mist rose from the lake, Keeper Truedell would recount his experience.

The remote surfboat stations of Michigan's Upper Peninsula were not typical freshwater stations. Most Great Lakes life-saving stations were built at man-made harbor entrances at port communities.[7] Every important Great Lakes harbor had a life-saving station. The Chicago area had four stations.

While Great Lakes man-made harbors were treacherous, they offered two major advantages for life-savers. First, life-saving stations could be built just inside harbor entrances which gave some protection during launching. Second, harbor entrance stations provided deep water necessary for launching heavy self-righting, self-bailing lifeboats and thus Great Lakes surfmen could use life-

Grande Pointe au Sable Life-Saving Station on Lake Michigan, a Duluth-style structure. It is a hot summer day and all the windows are open in the lookout tower and both boat bay doors are also open, revealing the rescue boats ready for action. Circa 1916. (U.S. Coast Guard)

Tawas Life-Saving Station on Lake Huron is almost magically decorated with a Victorian exterior stairway to the lookout. Compare this 1875-type station without clipped roof to North Manitou Island and Beaver Island stations in adjacent photos. (U.S. Coast Guard)

Beaver Island Life-Saving Station stood beside the lighthouse on a remote island in Lake Michigan. Keeper stands in front of his 1875 clipped gable-type station with its two surfboats. (Michigan State Archives)

Signal flags flying at North Manitou Island Life-Saving Station. This 1875 clipped gable-type station served Lake Michigan. (National Archives)

Thunder Bay Island Life-Saving Station (above) and Sturgeon Point Life-Saving Station (below) were neighboring 1875-types built in 1875-76 on Lake Huron in the area of Alpena, Michigan. Note differences in gables, presence or absence of roof-top lookout, stairway and other features. Even within a single architectural type there were interesting variations. Both, however, clearly display the diamond-shaped end wall braces common on 1875-type stations. (U.S. Coast Guard)

Four remote Lake Superior stations were built in 1876 on the "Graveyard Coast" of Lake Superior west of Sault Sainte Marie. They served one of the most remote and wild coasts on the North American continent. Vermilion Life-Saving Station, shown here, is the only one still standing and is owned by Lake Superior State University. (Pictured Rocks National Lakeshore)

Deer Park Life-Saving Station keeper, surfmen and station dog all pose for the camera. This 1876 Lake Superior-type station was the one where Benjamin Truedell was serving when he encountered a ghostly plea for help. (Pictured Rocks National Lakeshore)

Two Heart River Life-Saving Station crew in front of their 1876 Lake Superior-type station. The four stations shown here were the only ones of their type and they were only found on Lake Superior. Architect was J.L. Parkinson. (Pictured Rocks National Lakeshore)

Crisps Life-Saving Station was so remote that for a time it did not even have a name. It was simply known as the "Station Seven Miles West of Vermilion Point." These stations were the 1876 Lake Superior-type. (Pictured Rocks National Lakeshore)

boats when going to rescues. Both the English lifeboat and the Dobbins lifeboat were common on the Great Lakes.[8]

Great Lakes life-savers earned many life-saving medals. Keeper Jerome Kiah of Michigan's Pointe aux Barques Life-Saving Station won the gold medal under the most tragic of circumstances. His entire crew of surfmen had drowned during a gallant rescue attempt. On April 23, 1879 they had rowed out into Lake Huron intending to rescue the crew of the *J.H. Magruder*. Jerome Kiah was in charge when the lifeboat capsized and all on board but the keeper drowned. When saved, Kiah's first words were, "Poor boys, they are all gone." Despite an agonizing physi-

cal and psychological ordeal, Kiah regained his health. He later rose through the ranks to become a District Superintendent of life-saving stations on Lakes Huron and Superior.[9]

No port on the lakes knew the joy and sorrow of life-saving better than Cleveland, Ohio. Cleveland could claim Frederick T. Hatch, the only person to win the gold life-saving medal both as a surfman and as a lighthouse keeper. Hatch earned his first gold medal in November 1883 as a surfman at Cleveland Life-Saving Station. Surfmen Hatch, Lawrence Distel and seven other Cleveland life-savers won the gold life-saving medal for daring rescues saving 29 lives from the schooners *Sophia Minch*, *John B. Merill* and

John T. Johnson, during a two day period in a tremendous Lake Erie gale.[10]

A decade later Frederick Hatch had transferred to the Lighthouse Service and was keeper of the lighthouse at the entrance to Cleveland harbor. Here he earned his second gold life-saving medal by saving a woman's life near the lighthouse in 1890. Hatch's fellow gold medalist, Lawrence Distel, had also done well. Distel had risen to become keeper of Cleveland Life-Saving Station.

On the afternoon of May 17, 1893 during a storm described as "one of the worst ever known in northeastern Ohio," Keeper Distel led his surfmen on a rescue attempt off Hatch's lighthouse. Two men had capsized in a small boat and the surfmen had been called to the rescue. The Cleveland lifeboat had gone where no one else dared to go, entering ten to fifteen foot high breakers where the flood swollen Cuyahoga River met Lake Erie. The surfmen could not find the two men and it was all they could do to handle their boat.

Then "a monstrous wave" rushed toward the USLSS lifeboat. Keeper Distel deftly began to turn his lifeboat to meet the huge wave, but at exactly the wrong moment a surfman's oar snapped in half. The wave struck the USLSS lifeboat "over the starboard bow, knocked the boat upside down, and hurled its occupants into the surf with such violence that (to quote Keeper Distel) it seemed as though they 'were plunged to the bottom of the lake.'"[11]

Lighthouse keeper Hatch saw the capsize and used his fog signal and a white flag to call for assistance. But before any other vessels could get to the scene, four Cleveland surfmen drowned. Only Surfman George Loher and Keeper Distel, Hatch's old friend, survived.

"It would be gratifying if the story of the misfortunes of these two faithful men could terminate here, but the painful facts remain to be recorded that George Loher lost his life a few weeks later at the post of duty. Surfman Loher, while on night patrol which took him along the railroad tracks of the Lake Shore & Michigan Southern Railroad was struck by a train and killed. Keeper Distel, now the only survivor of the Cleveland lifeboat, had suffered such serious injuries in the capsizing that he was disabled and unable to continue as a member of the Life-Saving Service. Frederick Hatch had witnessed both Cleveland's saddest and proudest hours.[12]

There were many other brave Great Lakes life-saving crews. One of the most interesting was on Lake Michigan at Evanston, Illinois, near Chicago. Evanston Life-Saving Station was located on the campus of Northwestern University. The entire crew, except veteran keeper Lawrence O. Lawson, were college students. Due to Lawson's teaching, they became some of the best and bravest surfmen in the Life-Saving Service, as demonstrated at the wreck of the steamer *Calumet* on November 28, 1889.

On that frigid morning late in "the Eleventh Month," Keeper Lawson received an urgent message, "There is a large vessel ashore off Fort Sheridan. Come!" Fort Sheridan was an army installation over ten miles up the lake shore at Highland Park, Illinois. The thermometer was at twenty-two degrees below zero and the "furious gale" blowing made the wind chill factor far colder. The wind howled off the lake and "the mad rush of waves" left a coating of ice wherever they struck. Keeper Lawson immediately prepared to go to the rescue.[13]

Traveling by train, horse and on foot the keeper and his "student crew" made the trip north to the wreck. The shipwreck was off a steep 75-foot high lake bluff. Breakers regularly swept across the beach below. A fire was built atop the bluff for warmth and to encourage those on the *Calumet*. Soldiers from the fort soon arrived to offer help.[14]

Keeper Lawson saw that the steamer was well offshore and submerged almost to her main deck. Her eighteen man crew was trapped aboard her by waves sweeping the ship. It was clear that with the destruction of their vessel eminent, the sailors could not last much longer.

Keeper Lawson wanted "to attempt to reach her by (breeches buoy) rather than risk the lives of the men and the destruction of the boat in an attempt to launch through the surf which lashed at the foot of the bluff and practically left but scant foothold on the narrow strip of beach." The Lyle gun was aimed and fired twice from atop the bluff to attempt a breeches buoy rescue, but the ship was too far offshore and both times the projectile fell short. "Boat service was therefore the only alternative; so discarding the gun, the men made immediate preparations for a launch, regardless of the danger involved." The old motto "You have to go out, but you don't have to come in" was once again being tested.[15]

Just getting down to the beach was arduous. A pathway down through the thick brush had to be cut to get the boat through. Steps and footholds had to be dug in the thick blue clay so the men could descend. Soldiers and civilians helped with cutting the pathway, but the most dangerous work would be that of the surfmen.

Once the boat was lowered to the beach it had to be dragged windward along the narrow shelf to a better launch site. Heavy surf rolled across the beach and half the time the surfmen were waist deep in icy water. The breakers were so big they completely filled the boat three times as it was dragged along the beach. The surfmen had to constantly dodge breakers that threatened to crush them against the boat's side. At the same time, they had to continue to move the boat along so that it would not be smashed to pieces by the waves. Merely keeping their footing was a challenge, but finally a launching site was reached.

Students from Northwestern University were the surfmen at Evanston Life-Saving Station in Illinois. Keeper Lawrence O. Lawson (with beard) was the only non-student. Student crew won the gold life-saving medal for their 1889 rescue of the Calumet *wreck. (U.S. Coast Guard)*

Evanston Life-Saving Station on the campus of Northwestern University. This Lake Michigan station was a unique design by architect J.L. Parkinson, built in 1876-77. (U.S. Coast Guard)

Despite the crashing surf, the rescue boat was launched. At Keeper Lawson's command, the boat was pushed into the breakers. Off the surfmen rowed, pitching and rolling in the freshwater waves. "In crossing the inner bar they met an immense breaker which nearly threw the boat end over end, the shock of its impact being so great as to almost throw Keeper Lawson overboard from his post at the steering oar, and before he could recover himself a second wave dashed over the boat and filled it to the thwarts. This made the boat almost unmanageable" and the stroke oarsman had to use the bailing bucket furiously to keep her going.[16]

But the Evanston surfmen did get through the heaviest line of surf. "Flying spray from every wave-crest left a glaze of ice on every object it struck, the men's clothing being covered" with ice and even the oars encrusted in ice. These surfmen were not weather-hardened fishermen, but college students and yet they rowed in professional USLSS manner. They were Great Lakes bred and Arctic conditions were nothing new to them.[17]

When the surfmen finally reached the *Calumet* the grateful ship's captain told them, "I never thought you'd make it, boys." But make it they did—three times in all. There were eighteen on the *Calumet* and they could only safely take off six each trip and so it was back and forth through the icy breakers.[18]

When it was over, all on board were saved. The Evanston Life-Saving Station keeper and young surfmen were awarded the rare gold life-saving medal "for the display of extraordinary courage and heroism."

Most Great Lakes rescues occurred at harbor entrances and along the lake shore. But some freshwater rescues were far offshore. The Charlotte Life-Saving Station near Rochester, New York, answered such a call.

About 5:30 p.m. on December 14, 1902 the local New York Central Railroad train master received a telegram asking him to notify Charlotte Station's Keeper George N. Gray that a vessel in distress lay off Lakeside shore twenty-three miles east. The shipwreck message was rushed to the life-saving station and the keeper "instantly prepared to go to her relief. The harbor tug was frozen in the ice up the river and, therefore, could not tow the surfboat to the scene, while to undertake to (row) 23 miles against a head sea on a winter night…would have been useless and foolhardy." Besides, a storm was brewing and it would do no one any good for the surfmen to arrive exhausted.[19]

The keeper requested that a special train be prepared for Windsor Beach to transport the surfmen, surfboat and equipment to a site closer to the wreck. The snow and ice were so bad it took an entire gang of railroaders just to shovel the snow away from the two needed flatcars. It also took two hours for the surfmen to haul their surfboat on the beach wagon to the railroad siding. It was another hour before the railroaders could get the train ready to go. Conditions on land were harsh. On the lake, they were worse.

It was 9:30 p.m., four hours after the message was first received, when the rescue train reached Lakeside. Horses were waiting to pull the boat on sleds, but "the journey of four miles (to the lake shore) was accomplished with extreme difficulty, great drifts of snow, in places at least six feet deep obstructing progress…" The crew frequently had to help the four horses struggle through the snow with the surfboat on the sleds. The lake shore was finally reached at 11:30 p.m. and Keeper Gray immediately burned a Coston flare as a signal to show that the life-savers had arrived. There was no way of knowing if the Coston signal had been seen.

Before embarking, the keeper carefully discussed the

Photo at left:

Charlotte Life-Saving Station was home of the crew that earned gold life-saving medals for the 1902 John R. Noyes *rescue. This 1875-type station with clipped gable roof was located on Lake Ontario near Rochester, New York. (Shanks collection)*

Pennsylvania's lone life-saving station was at Erie. Keystone state surfmen relax in front of their 1875-style station. (Shanks collection)

"Death's Door" was the name of the area guarded by Baileys Harbor Life-Saving Station in Door County, Wisconsin. This Duluth-style station is now a restaurant in Baileys Harbor. (U.S. Coast Guard)

A USLSS launch arrives at Plum Island Life-Saving Station on a remote island off Door Peninsula, Wisconsin. This Duluth-style station served "Death's Door" coast. (U.S. Coast Guard)

probable position of the vessel with the person who had seen the ship's distress signal. The Charlotte Life-Saving crew then launched their surfboat into the choppy waves of Lake Ontario. It was bitter cold and the air filled with thick vapor enshrouding the lake in dense fog. Using only a compass as a guide, the surfmen rowed through the fog, burning several Coston signals en route. "Finally, however, the bewilderment proved so disheartening that (the keeper) felt compelled to wait for daylight, and therefore ordered the boat ashore." At his request the people of the vicinity kindled a large bonfire. The keeper then permitted his crew to lie down for an hour and a half upon straw brought by local farmers.

After this brief rest and breakfast at a farmhouse, the keeper sent his entire crew along the cliffs to try and sight the distressed vessel once daylight broke. No one could see the vessel, but Keeper Gray launched the surfboat anyway. A man was left on shore and told to climb to the top of a windmill, the highest place in the area. If he sighted the ship, he was to signal which way the surfboat was to go. Sure enough, as soon as the lookout had mounted the windmill it was just light enough to see a distant speck that proved to be the endangered ship. He signaled the surfboat which returned to shore for directions. Launching yet again, the keeper turned in the correct direction, his crew pulling hard on the oars.

The route to the ship was a sailor's nightmare. The wind increased in speed, the surfboat being compelled to take strong seas that hit her on the side and threw frigid water on the crew, covering everyone with ice. The surfmen rowed twenty miles off shore, reaching the wreck just before noon. The wind was now blowing very hard and the sea running high.

"The vessel and her crew were in a most pitiable condition." The ship was the schooner *John R. Noyes* and she had lost her sails, yawl boat, and both anchors, had her cabin smashed in, was leaking fast, and was heavily en-

cumbered with ice. "She was simply a helpless wreck, drifting about at the mercy of the storm. All on board were suffering from exposure and from lack of food. The surfmen found five people on board, a woman and four men. The mariners "had lost hope, bidden one another good-by, and were lying on the deck benumbed, disparing, and some of them hysterical. In a little while all would have perished."

Despite the cold, the keeper gave the woman his overcoat and his mittens. All on board were transferred to the surfboat and brought safely toward shore. Landing through the built-up ice was very difficult, but the five survivors were safely ashore and cared for. A kindly woman then fixed the surfmen dinner.

The life-savers had rowed sixty frigid miles! All the surfmen suffered from frostbite, some quite seriously. But they had saved everyone on board. Keeper Gray and his heroic crew of New York surfmen were later awarded the Congressional gold life-saving medal.

On the world's oceans sailors talk of the "seven seas," but lake sailors know that there is an "eighth sea," the Great Lakes.

Middle Island Life-Saving Station on Lake Huron. An 1879-type station. (U.S. Coast Guard)

Life-Saving Stations of the Great Lakes

Life-Saving Stations of Illinois

Lake Michigan

Station	Location
South Chicago	South Chicago
Jackson Park	1524 East Sixty-fourth Street, Chicago
Old Chicago	In Chicago Harbor
Evanston	On Northwestern University campus

Life-Saving Station of Indiana

Lake Michigan

Michigan City	North side entrance of Calumet Harbor

Life-Saving Stations of Michigan

Lake Huron

Lake View Beach	5 miles north of Fort Gratiot Lighthouse, Port Huron
Harbor Beach	Inside Harbor Beach harbor
Pointe aux Barques	Near lighthouse, Huron County
Port Austin	About 2 miles NE of Port Austin
Tawas	Near lighthouse, East Tawas
Sturgeon Point	Near lighthouse north of Harrisville
Thunder Bay Island	West side of island, east of Alpena
Middle Island	North end of Middle Island, north of Alpena
Hammond	Hammond Bay, Presque Isle County
Bois Blanc	Eastside of Bois Blanc Island off Cheboygan

Lake Michigan

Beaver Island	Near lighthouse, Beaver Island, NW of Charlevoix
Charlevoix	South side harbor entrance, Charlevoix
North Manitou Island	On North Manitou Island, NW of Leland
South Manitou Island	On South Manitou Island, west of Leland
Sleeping Bear Point	Near Glen Haven
Point Betsie	South of lighthouse at Point Betsie, north of Frankfort
Frankfort	South side of harbor entrance, Frankfort
Manistee	North side entrance of harbor, Manistee
Grande Pointe au Sable	1 mile south of Big Sable Lighthouse, north of Ludington
Ludington	North side harbor entrance, Ludington
Pentwater	North side harbor entrance, Pentwater
White River	North side entrance of White Lake, west of Whitehall
Muskegon	South side harbor entrance, Muskegon
Grand Haven	North side harbor entrance, Grand Haven
Holland	In south side of harbor, Macatawa
South Haven	North side harbor entrance, South Haven
Saint Joseph	East side harbor entrance, St. Joseph

Lake Superior

Vermilion	10 miles west of Whitefish Point
Crisps	18 miles west of Whitefish Point
Two Heart River	Near mouth of Two Heart River, Two Heart
Deer Park	Near mouth of Sucker River, Deer Park
Grand Marais	West side of harbor entrance, Grand Marais
Marquette	Near lighthouse, Marquette
Eagle Harbor	Near lighthouse, Eagle Harbor
Portage	Portage Ship Canal, ¾ mile from north end

A classic Great Lakes scene at Kewaunee Life-Saving Station with a Lake Michigan steamer. If the vessel should experience trouble, this Wisconsin station would spring into action and go to the rescue. An expanded Bibb #3-type station built in 1893. (Nautical Research Center)

Sturgeon Bay Canal Life-Saving Station shared the grounds with the lighthouse of the same name. Lookout tower is at right. This Bibb #3-type station is still an active U.S. Coast Guard station. (U.S. Coast Guard)

Life-Saving Stations of Minnesota
Lake Superior
Duluth	On Minnesota Point, Upper Duluth

Life-Saving Stations of New York (Upstate)
Lake Ontario
Big Sandy	North side mouth Big Sandy Creek, near Woodville
Oswego	East side harbor entrance, Oswego
Charlotte	East side entrance Charlotte Harbor, Rochester
Niagara	East side Niagara River mouth near Youngstown

Lake Erie
Buffalo	South side harbor entrance, Buffalo

Life-Saving Stations of Ohio
Lake Erie
Ashtabula	West side of Ashtabula Harbor
Fairport	West side entrance to Fairport Harbor
Cleveland	West side entrance to Cleveland Harbor
Lorain	East side entrance to Black River, Lorain
Marblehead	Port Marblehead, near Sandusky

Life-Saving Station of Pennsylvania
Lake Erie
Erie	North side entrance to Erie Harbor

Life-Saving Stations of Wisconsin
Lake Michigan
Kenosha	Washington Island, Kenosha Harbor
Racine	In Racine Harbor by lighthouse
Milwaukee	Near south harbor entrance, Milwaukee
Sheboygan	North side entrance to Sheboygan Harbor
Two Rivers	North side entrance to Two Rivers Harbor
Kewaunee	North side entrance to Kewaunee Harbor
Sturgeon Bay Canal	Northeast side of entrance to canal by lighthouse
Baileys Harbor	Easterly side of Baileys Harbor
Plum Island	Near NE point of Plum Island, Door County

STATION DISCONTINUED: *Salmon Creek Life-Saving Station on Lake Ontario in New York was destroyed by fire on March 27, 1886. It was not rebuilt.*

NAME CHANGES: *MICHIGAN stations had a number of name changes including: Crisps station was formerly Crisp Point and was also for a time simply known as the station "7 miles west of Vermillion Point"; Deer Park station had two previous names, Muskallonge Lake and Sucker River; Hammond station was Hammonds Bay and Forty Mile Point; Harbor Beach station was Sand Beach; Point Betsie station was Point Betsy and also Point au Bec Scies; Port Austin station was Grindstone City; Portage station was Ship Canal; Tawas was Ottawa Point; Vermilion was Vermilion Point. In ILLINOIS Evanston station was formerly Grosse Point; Jackson Park station was called Chicago. PENNSYLVANIA'S Erie station was once called Presque Isle.[20]*

ADDITIONAL STATIONS: *Great Lakes lifeboat station construction continued on well after 1915. Important classic Coast Guard lifeboat stations built later included: In Minnesota: North Superior station at Grand Marais; In Michigan: Munising station at Munising; Whitefish Point station at Whitefish Point; Mackinac Island station on Mackinac Island; In Illinois: Wilmette station at Wilmette and Calumet Harbor station in the Chicago area.[21]*

White River Life-Saving Station on the eastern shore of Lake Michigan was a Bibb #3-type station. It stood just inside the man-made harbor entrance. (Michigan State Archives)

Marblehead Life-Saving Station drew a crowd as the surfboat was launched. This was an 1875-type station with clipped gable roof located near Sandusky, Ohio. (U.S. Coast Guard)

Holland Life-Saving Station was a Bibb #3-type station in Michigan. Bibb #3 stations were built only on Lake Michigan during 1886-93. (Shanks collection)

Sheboygan Life-Saving Station in Wisconsin was a classic Bibb #3-type station with the hat-like lookout tower roof often favored by architect Albert Bibb. (Shanks collection)

Fairport Life-Saving Station on Lake Erie in Ohio was an 1875 clipped gable-type station expanded on both sides. Original station is center portion. (U.S. Coast Guard)

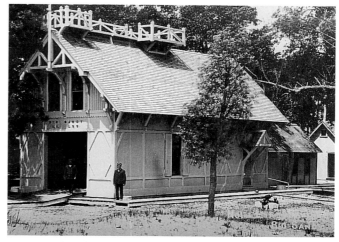

Grand Marais Life-Saving Station on Lake Superior showing marine railway used to launch lifeboat. Duluth-type station. (Michigan State Archives)

Big Sandy Life-Saving Station on Lake Ontario was the eastern-most Great Lakes station. This upstate New York station was an 1875-type station. (U.S. Coast Guard Academy)

Niagara Life-Saving Station on Lake Ontario in New York. There were only two Niagara-type stations, this and one at Cape Disappointment, Washington, both built in the 1890s. (U.S. Coast Guard)

Oswego Life-Saving Station on New York's Lake Ontario shore. Crew with beach cart stand in front of their 1875 Clipped Gable-type station. The 1875 clipped gable-type stations were a distinctive Great Lakes design. (Shanks collection)

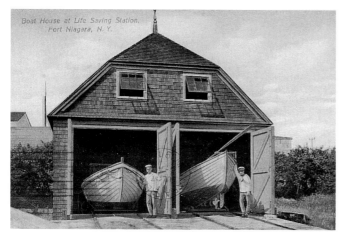

Boathouse with surfboats at Niagara Life-Saving Station. Note how the Niagara-type boathouse used the same architectural style as the station. (Shanks collection)

Surfmen and children at Michigan's Charlevoix Life-Saving Station. Duluth-type stations such as this were built during the 1894-1908 period on the Great Lakes and East Coast. (Michigan State Archives)

Duluth Life-Saving Station in winter. This Minnesota station was the prototype of the Duluth-style stations built on the Great Lakes and East Coast. (U.S. Coast Guard)

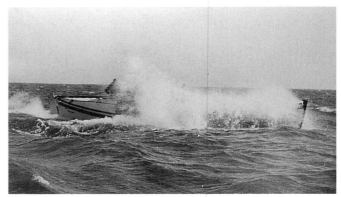

Racine 36-foot motor lifeboat searches Lake Michigan after a major storm. Cold spray nearly hides the boat. (U.S. Coast Guard)

Portage Life-Saving Station on Lake Superior endured hard winters. Keeper Thomas H. McCormick and his crew won eight gold life-saving medals for the 1913 Waldo rescue. Eagle Harbor station also participated in the heroism of this rescue. A Marquette-style station in upper Michigan. (U.S. Coast Guard)

Ice-covered 36-foot motor lifeboat returns to Cleveland after searching for survivors of a Lake Erie shipwreck. Surfmen faced Arctic conditions on the Great Lakes. (U.S. Coast Guard)

Marquette Life-Saving Station on Lake Superior was the prototype of the Marquette architectural style, although many Marquette-style stations lacked the porch shown here. This was the station of Keeper Henry Cleary, record-holder for the fastest capsize drill. (U.S. Coast Guard)

Sleeping Bear Point Life-Saving Station with lookout tower at left, Marquette-style station center and boathouse at right. Today the station and boathouse are restored and can be visited at Sleeping Bear Dunes National Lakeshore in Michigan. (Sleeping Bear Dunes National Lakeshore)

The Great Lakes were rich in architectural diversity. Ashtabula Life-Saving Station in Ohio was both charming and unique. A one-of-a-kind design by architect George R. Tolman. (U.S. Coast Guard)

Eagle Harbor Life-Saving Station a Lorain-type station at the extremity of the remote Keweenaw Peninsula on Lake Superior. Under the leadership of Keeper Charles A. Tucker this station received nine Congressional gold life-saving medals for the Waldo *rescue in 1913. (U.S. Coast Guard)*

Port Austin Life-Saving Station on Lake Huron. Port Austin surfmen earned seven silver medals for the 1911 Wyoming *rescue. Lookout tower at left could weather any storm. An 1879-type station. (National Archives)*

Chicago area was rich in life-saving station architecture. Old Chicago Life-Saving Station, shown here, had a massive lookout tower and ornamental facade with four boat bays. This was the archetype of the Old Chicago-type station. (Shanks collection)

Jackson Park Life-Saving Station in Chicago was built to be an impressive addition to the city. Mansion-like station was a unique Victor Mendleheff design built in 1908. (Shanks collection)

South Chicago Life-Saving Station amid Great Lakes industrial might. Life-saving stations were built even among heavy industry, not only on tree-lined coves or picturesque beaches. An expanded Bibb #3-type station. (U.S. Coast Guard)

Buffalo Life-Saving Station on Lake Erie. Buffalo was of the same design type as the Old Chicago Station. Note the massive lookout tower and distinctive facade. Only two stations were built in the Old Chicago-style. (U.S. Coast Guard)

Capsize drills were done in good weather at the keeper's discretion. While some surfmen hated capsize drills because they had to spend the rest of the day cleaning and drying equipment, the public loved to watch and big crowds frequently attended. Jackson Park Life-Saving Station, Chicago. (Shanks collection)

Surfboat capsized and about to be righted. Note heads of surfmen appearing at upper side of boat. In a moment it will be upright and the crew back in the sitting position. South Manitou Island Life-Saving Station, Michigan. (Sleeping Bear Dunes National Lakeshore)

A calm day on Lake Huron. Class E motor lifeboat is a handsome sight at Hammond Life-Saving Station, Michigan. Station at center was 1875-design by architect Francis W. Chandler. (National Archives)

International signal flags give Racine Life-Saving Station a festive appearance. This Wisconsin station was the prototype of the rare Racine-type, a style found only on Lake Michigan. (U.S. Coast Guard)

Harbor Beach Life-Saving Station's large boathouse with (left to right) surfboat on boat carriage, beach cart, crew, lifeboats in water, surfboat on launchway with small boat nearby. This was an important Lake Huron station. (National Archives)

Point Betsie Life-Saving Station on Lake Michigan was a Chatham-style station north of Frankfort, Michigan. This lovely station still stands today. (U.S. Coast Guard)

Surfmen relax on bench beside Harbor Beach Life-Saving Station on Lake Huron in Michigan on a summer day. An 1879-type station. (National Archives)

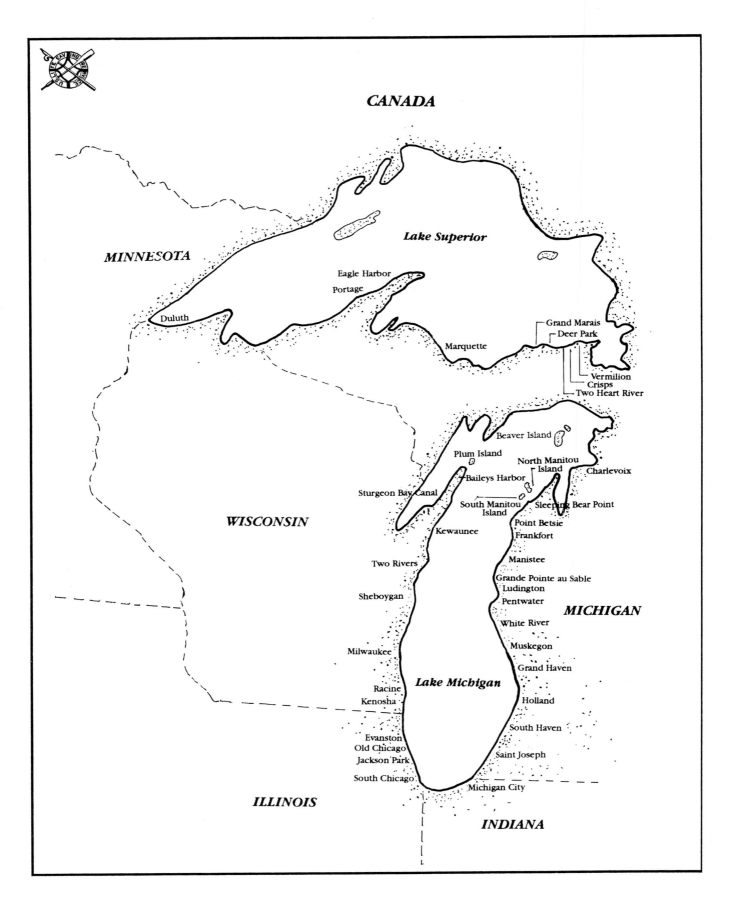

CANADA

Lake Superior

MINNESOTA

Eagle Harbor
Portage

Duluth

Grand Marais
Deer Park

Marquette

Vermilion
Crisps
Two Heart River

Beaver Island

Plum Island

North Manitou
Island

Charlevoix

Baileys Harbor

Sturgeon Bay Canal

South Manitou
Island

Sleeping Bear Point

WISCONSIN

Point Betsie
Frankfort

Kewaunee

Manistee

Grande Pointe au Sable
Ludington

Two Rivers

Pentwater

MICHIGAN

Sheboygan

White River

Muskegon

Milwaukee

Grand Haven

Lake Michigan

Racine
Kenosha

Holland

South Haven

Evanston
Old Chicago
Jackson Park

Saint Joseph

South Chicago

Michigan City

ILLINOIS

INDIANA

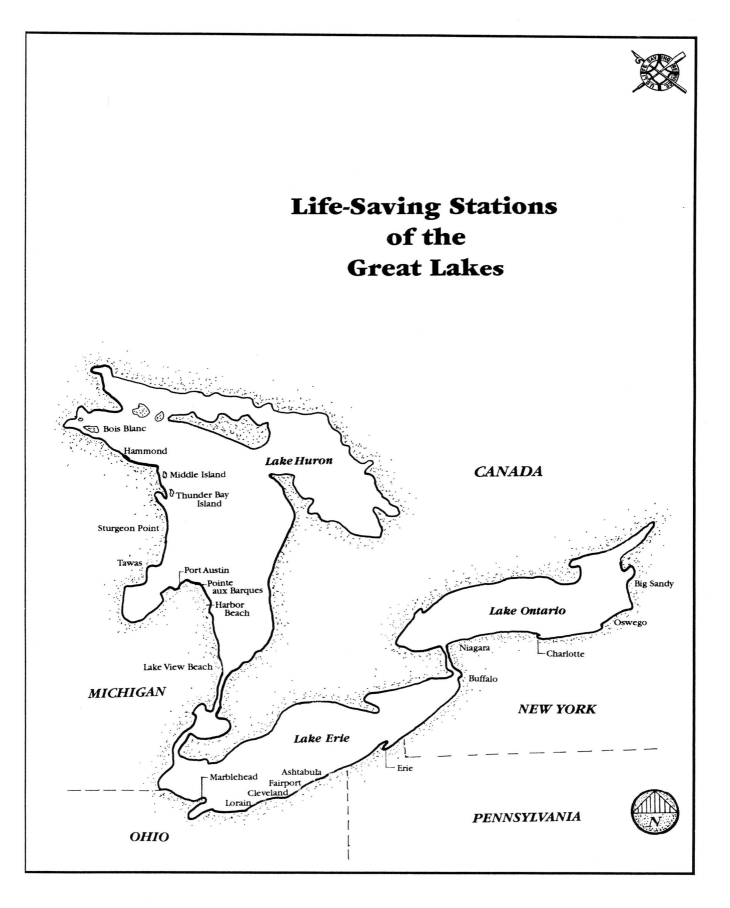

Life-Saving Stations
of the
Great Lakes

Bois Blanc

Hammond

Lake Huron

Middle Island

Thunder Bay
Island

CANADA

Sturgeon Point

Tawas

Port Austin

Pointe
aux Barques

Harbor
Beach

Big Sandy

Lake Ontario

Oswego

Niagara

Charlotte

Lake View Beach

Buffalo

MICHIGAN

NEW YORK

Lake Erie

Erie

Marblehead

Ashtabula
Fairport
Cleveland

Lorain

OHIO

PENNSYLVANIA

N

The first life-saving station on the Pacific Coast was Shoalwater (Willapa) Bay Life-Saving Station built in 1877 on the Washington coast. Life-savers in surfboat with keeper's dwelling at left and 1875-type station at right. Most Pacific Coast stations were built with designs or modifications unique to the West Coast. (Coast Guard Museum Northwest)

Some life-saving station architecture was unique to the West Coast. Point Adams Life-Saving Station in Oregon was done in architect Albert B. Bibb's Fort Point-type. Note the Fort Point-style "witch's hat" boathouse (nicknamed for hat-like vent atop roof) at right and beach cart. Point Adams crew won gold life-saving medals for the 1913 Rosecrans rescue. (Coast Guard Museum Northwest)

Chapter 16
Pacific Coast

RESCUE WORK ON THE PACIFIC COAST

The Pacific Ocean is the largest geographic feature in the world. It is larger than the Atlantic Ocean, Indian Ocean and Great Lakes combined. It produces the world's largest waves. Wind generated storm waves have reached up to 200 feet in height in northern California. Earthquake generated tsunami waves in Alaska have roared even higher up a mountainside.[1] Fearsome bars surround most northern California, Oregon and Washington harbors and have been the scene of many of the region's worst wrecks.

The West Coast had few harbors of refuge, providing mariners with less options for safety and forcing them to make long runs for shelter. While storms were less common than on the Atlantic Coast and the Great Lakes, the waves were bigger and the storms, when they did occur, often lasted longer.[2] Fog was a danger during many months of the year and Lighthouse Service records showed that northern California was one of the two foggiest locations in the country.[3] Even the land could be dangerous and virtually all the California life-saving stations suffered earthquake damage during their careers.

The Pacific Coast Life-Saving District comprised California, Oregon, Washington and Alaska. It was by far the largest district in the Service. The area was too extensive to build stations all along the shore, so stations were built at the largest and the most troublesome harbors. The San Francisco Bay Area boasted six stations and the Columbia River and its approaches had three stations. Everywhere else a single station stood watch over a particularly horrendous coast, usually a treacherous harbor entrance. The names ring like a list of Pacific Coast shipwreck hells—Cape Disappointment, Coos Bay, Coquille River, Point Reyes, Point Bonita, Humboldt Bay, Yaquina Bay, Tillamook Bay, Umpqua River, Grays Harbor and others. In such places, it was not just the old pulling boats of the USLSS that could be overwhelmed, but also the powerful motor lifeboats of the Life-Saving Service's later years.

For most of the Life-Saving Service's existence, the West Coast was politically weak and General Superintendent Sumner Kimball was slow to recognize the enormity of danger. Just 20 stations were built on the Pacific Coast by the USLSS and that includes the disrupted career of California's Bolinas Bay Life-Saving Station. Up in Alaska, Keeper Tom Ross and his crew at Nome Life-Saving Station were the only surfmen in the nation's largest state. The Pacific Coast was so under-supplied with life-saving stations that the Coast Guard would later spend decades building more West Coast stations.[4]

Life-saving stations were in such short supply that in 1909 the Life-Saving Service made an unprecedented move to improve rescue services. The lighthouse keepers on the Farallon Islands, twenty-three miles off San Francisco, were equipped with a Lyle gun and breeches buoy and trained to operate them. A small building was erected on Southeast Farallon Island near the light station to house the beach apparatus. The practice of training lighthouse keepers did not become widespread, probably because the number of keepers stationed at a lighthouse was too small for full scale rescue work.[5]

The Life-Saving Service had difficulty understanding the Pacific Coast. Sumner Kimball once wrote, "The Pacific coast is not a dangerous one...the climate is remarkably bland and shipwrecks are of rare occurrence... The weather, therefore, is easily forecast, and navigation can not in general be regarded as hazardous."[6] Kimball granted, "There are, however, a few extremely dangerous points, mostly situated at the entrances to the important ports." He was right about his last statement; there were some "extremely dangerous points" but there was far more danger than he initially recognized.

By the end of the Life-Saving Service era in 1915, Kimball had completely revised his opinion of Pacific Coast waters. Terrible wrecks increasingly claimed lives on the West Coast, often despite the USLSS's best efforts. The distances were so great that after the turn of the century motor lifeboats became standard fare on the Pacific Coast. Breakers were so fearful at some stations that even routine drills claimed lives. Point Reyes Life-Saving Station, north of San Francisco, lost three surfmen in four years during boat drills (and a fourth surfman to illness).[7] Coquille River Life-Saving Station, Oregon's southern-most station, had three of its crew drowned during a single practice.[8] Washington's Waaddah Island (Neah Bay) Life-Saving Station had two of its surfmen drown while trying to get ashore at the station from their motor lifeboat in rough weather.[9] The Pacific Coast had stations where waves 40-feet high were reported by keepers.[10]

Facing the Pacific surf. Point Reyes, California was one of the roughest beaches in America. During its first four years of operation Point Reyes Life-Saving Station lost four surfmen, three to the rogue waves of this beach. (Point Reyes National Seashore)

Photos of actual rescue scenes are rare, but here the Bolinas Bay Life-Saving crew approaches steam schooner Yosemite *in their 36-foot motor lifeboat. The ship was loaded with dynamite and the crew had abandoned her. Despite peril, surfmen boarded* Yosemite *and attempted to save the ship. February 7, 1927. (National Maritime Museum)*

Many of the most important Life-Saving Service activities on the West Coast occurred during the final decade of the USLSS's existence. Power lifeboats and Dobbins pulling lifeboats were beginning to dominate rescue work at Pacific Coast stations, although pulling surfboats were still used.[11] Coastal cliffs, some hundreds of feet high, rimmed the Pacific shore and auxiliary boathouses were common here. The idea was to have a second equipped boathouse at a convenient launching site to eliminate time-consuming trips dragging boats overland. Although auxiliary boathouses were used at some other locations in the country, they were particularly valuable on a coast with few long beaches, high headlands and often impassable cliffs. This Pacific Rim was a new world for the Life-Saving Service.

Earthquakes were also a new experience for the USLSS. The 1906 San Francisco earthquake was one of the Life-Saving Service's greatest challenges. The Life-Saving Service "sustained considerable loss in the earthquake and fire disaster which devastated San Francisco… (The USLSS) storehouse in that city was wrecked and burned, and life-saving apparatus and miscellaneous station supplies…were destroyed." Every life-saving station in the state, except Humboldt Bay, was reported as damaged. Station chimneys toppled, plaster rained down from walls and ceilings and foundations groaned and cracked.[12] But when the shaking stopped every surfman was alive and uninjured. Then the real challenges began.

In San Francisco, "close on the heels of the earthquake spread the destroying fire, which ate its way rapidly through the debris of the fallen buildings and swept over portions of the town that the earthquake had failed to raze." Surfmen from Golden Gate Park, Southside, Fort Point and Point Bonita Life-Saving Stations fought the flames alongside firemen, soldiers and citizens. Miraculously, people were found alive in the rubble and the surfmen helped dig them out. Keeper Varney of Golden Gate Park station directed endless wagon loads hauling relief supplies. Destitute San Franciscans sought out the life-savers for help. As many as 150 persons a night were sheltered at the station. The surfmen fed the public from their own supplies until they had no more. Additional food was obtained and the surfmen issued 30,000 meals. During the entire time, the life-savers manned fire hoses, hauled refugees in wagons and did ambulance duty. Across the Golden Gate, Point Bonita Life-Saving Station's crew "rescued some women and children, the families of the assistant light keepers of the Point Bonita Light Station, from a wrecked brick building. They also furnished to refugees a total of 208 night's shelter and 802 meals, all at the crew's expense. They made no charge for either food or lodging, but accepted $20 from one grateful family…" At Arena Cove Life-Saving Station, hundred miles north of San Francisco, the life-saving station was damaged and nearby Point Arena Lighthouse was devastated. The light-

A dramatic rescue in progress. In extreme cases keepers would take the Lyle gun from shore and fire it from a vessel. Here Keeper Johnson of Coos Bay Life-Saving Station in Oregon is about to fire his Lyle gun from the steam schooner Cleone to the Columbia, which had stranded on the Coos Bay bar. The shot was good and no lives were lost. February 17, 1924. (Carl Christensen photo in Shanks collection)

Golden Gate Park Life-Saving Station built in San Francisco in 1878 was California's first station. This station played a heroic role in saving lives and feeding the hungry after the 1906 San Francisco earthquake. Golden Gate Park Station at left was a one-of-a-kind design by architect J. Lake Parkinson. Keeper's dwelling at right was a design by architect John G. Pelton, used only here and at Willapa Bay, Washington. Crew and families stand beside surfboat. (National Maritime Museum)

Fort Point Life-Saving Station in San Francisco was the prototype of the rare West Coast Fort Point-style station. Fort Point was the last life-saving station to be used by the Coast Guard on the Pacific Coast. It was disestablished on March 23, 1990 in a ceremony where Coast Guard Commandant Admiral J.W. Kime and historian Ralph Shanks were the speakers. The station is now a part of Golden Gate National Recreation Area and may be seen about a half-mile east of the Golden Gate Bridge. It is the only surviving example of a Fort Point-style station. (U.S. Coast Guard)

Across the country surfmen's drills were immensely popular with the American people. Boat drills drew large crowds. Golden Gate Park Life-Saving crew launching Dobbins lifeboat about 1908. (Shanks collection)

Southside Life-Saving Station in San Francisco was southwestern-most life-saving station in the country. This Marquette-type station was built using Albert Bibb design in 1893-94. San Francisco had three life-saving stations: Southside, Golden Gate Park and Fort Point. (U.S. Coast Guard Academy)

Proud crew stands beside their Dobbins Lifeboat and boat carriage. Dobbins boats were most often selected for capsize drills on the West Coast. Southside Life-Saving Station at San Francisco. (Alvin E. Penny)

Point Reyes Life-Saving Station guarded a very dangerous northern California beach. Four of this crew lost their lives in the first four years of the station's existence. This was a Fort Point-type station with a "witch's hat" boathouse. (Point Reyes National Seashore and U.S. Coast Guard)

An auxiliary boathouse at Point Reyes Life-Saving Station. Many Pacific Coast stations had both a main boathouse and an auxiliary boathouse. A second boathouse was often necessary because high cliffs made it nearly impossible to haul a boat wagon or beach cart to many areas. Auxiliary boathouses were equipped with boats and beach apparatus. (Point Reyes National Seashore)

Bolinas Bay Lifeboat Station replaced an earlier life-saving station which was burned. This California station was Coast Guard-built in 1917 in response to the Hanalei wreck. It is a Chatham-style station, a Life-Saving Service design. This station is now the biology station for the College of Marin. (U.S. Coast Guard)

house and keepers' dwelling were damaged beyond repair and the town was in ruins. Everywhere, "The lifesaving crews affected themselves of good account throughout the terrible scenes."[13]

Besides earthquakes, Pacific Coast surfmen faced exceptionally dangerous bars at harbor entrances. In the Pacific Northwest, Cape Disappointment and Point Adams Life-Saving Stations at the mouth of the Columbia River were constantly among those stations included in the *Annual Report* listings of *Disasters Involving the Loss of Life.* The fearsome waves on the commercial fishing grounds at the Columbia's mouth annually took a terrible toll of those who went down to the sea in small sailing boats. "The men who engage in fishing in this locality are a venturesome class," the Life-Saving Service wrote, "taking risks in these treacherous waters which frequently result in capsize and sometimes terminate fatally. When the sea and weather permit fishing, the grounds, which extend over four or five miles, are alive with fishing craft, manned in most cases by two men—a net puller and a boat puller. On such occasions the crew of the Cape Disappointment Life-Saving Station are usually in attendance upon the fishing fleet in a power lifeboat, ready to undertake a rescue or to give timely warning of sudden weather changes, the fishermen themselves being so occupied with their work that they frequently disregard signs of approaching danger until it is too late...[14] The danger at the Columbia River mouth would continue throughout the span of the Life-Saving Service.

On the morning of January 7, 1913 the Associated Oil Company's tanker *Rosecrans* was approaching the Columbia River entrance. The Columbia River entrance has been called the Graveyard of the Pacific and over 2,000 vessels and 1,500 lives are reported to have been lost in the area.[15] Entering these waters, the tanker encountered 60 to 70 mile-an-hour winds, heavy seas and thick, rainy weather. After passing Tillamook Rock lighthouse, the ship's officers became confused as to her position and she stranded on Peacock Spit, off the Washington side of the Columbia River entrance. Huge waves immediately began smashing the tanker, breaking her up and smothering her with seas which ripped away all the ship's lifeboats. Upon stranding the captain ordered his wireless operator to send an S.O.S. message. It did not specify the ship's position and ended with "Water has washed in the cabins—I can't stay much longer—hel—."[16]

On the north side of the Columbia River mouth in Washington, Cape Disappointment Life-Saving Station's lookout tower stood atop the headland overlooking the river entrance. The surfman in the tower spotted the *Rosecrans*, barely visible in the fog. He alerted Keeper Alfred Rimer who rushed up the hill from the station to the tower to appraise the situation. Within minutes, Rimer had the Cape Disappointment motor lifeboat *Tenacious* underway to the rescue. At first Rimer tried to power the

Point Bonita Life-Saving Station was a guardian of the Golden Gate. Located in the soaring Marin Headlands its crews watched over shores with cliffs hundreds of feet high. This station was a modified Port Huron-type with an octagonal lookout tower. The main boathouse was far below at the foot of high California cliffs. (U.S. Coast Guard)

Arena Cove Life-Saving Station at Point Arena, California. This is a modified Port Huron-type station which is located in a picturesque canyon. It was built without the octagonal tower typical of Port Huron-type stations because high hills necessitated a cliff-top lookout tower. Today Arena Cove is Coast Guard House, a bed and breakfast inn. (Robert J. Lee)

Danger of the surfman's occupation is evident as a lifeboat crosses a treacherous bar. Even larger breakers loom ahead. Coquille River, Oregon, Life-Saving Station crew shown here lost three of their own under conditions like these. (U.S. Coast Guard)

motor lifeboat around Cape Disappointment to the tanker, but after an hour of futile attempts he realized that the "furious gale and strong flood tide" were too much for his power lifeboat. Rimer then hailed a tug and asked to be towed over the bar, but the tugboat captain refused because the river entrance was too dangerous.[17]

Across the storm-blown channel on the south shore of the Columbia River at Oregon's Point Adams Life-Saving Station, Keeper Oscar S. Wicklund and his surfmen set out in the motor lifeboat *Dreadnaught* for the *Rosecrans.* Discovering the wreck, Keeper Wicklund found the oil tanker already destroyed. "All that could be seen was the mast sticking up with three men clinging to it. I did not have much hope of reaching the vessel, but thought it would encourage those men in the rigging if they saw the lifeboat constantly trying to reach them. I made two attempts but our (motor lifeboat) was constantly submerged and we were forced to return."[18]

The Cape Disappointment and Point Adams power lifeboats met back at Cape Disappointment station. Uppermost in the minds of the keepers were the three sailors desperately clinging to the mast. Realizing that little time remained, both USLSS motor lifeboats boats then shoved off for another rescue attempt. The Cape Disappointment motor lifeboat *Tenacious* led the way, running at full speed and taking a damaging pounding. *Tenacious* developed a bad leak and, although the engine kept running, the lifeboat's speed could no longer be controlled.

The *Tenacious* was in trouble. Undaunted, Keeper Rimer went into the huge breakers to try to save the three sailors. The first attempt to get close failed and the lifeboat ran out to await another opportunity to approach the tanker. While standing off the tanker, the power lifeboat "got into a run of tremendously heavy breakers. Their engine stopped and their boat, swept along helplessly, turned turtle."[19]

During this capsizing, Keeper Rimer and two surfmen were thrown from the power lifeboat. The keeper reported that "after a few moments we all managed by the greatest effort to get on board again, but found the boat and engine room full of water. We, nevertheless, manned the oars and tried our best to get back to the wreck."[20]

Keeper Rimer described the Pacific as a "seething cauldron" with confused seas moving in every direction. "One time Captain Wicklund's (Point Adams power lifeboat) was headed into a sea which appeared to be forty feet high. It struck the *Dreadnaught* and I thought he was gone. I started to go to his assistance, but when I looked again I found he was all right."[21]

Facing waves up to 40-foot high and with the Cape Disappointment power lifeboat now disabled, Point Adams' power lifeboat *Dreadnaught* moved in to try to save the three sailors. Breakers around the sunken tanker seemed impassable. Keeper Wicklund "circled five times and got as near the vessel as I dared each time, signaling the sailors to jump, but they would not do it. As we got near the

Humboldt Bay Life-Saving Station answered calls on one of the most dangerous harbor entrances in California. Location just inside harbor entrance allowed marine railway to be erected for launching heavy lifeboats. A modified 1875-type station. (Garner and Thora Churchill photo in Shanks collection)

The peaceful scene is deceptive as Coquille River Life-Saving Station was considered a rough station due to a hazardous river entrance. A Marquette-type station in southwest Oregon. Most Oregon stations were built in the Marquette-style. (U.S. Coast Guard)

Cape Arago Life-Saving Station was reached by a platform suspended from high cable (barely visible at left). Note rugged coast, countless rocks and high cliffs faced by surfmen at this 1875-type station near Coos Bay, Oregon. (U.S. Coast Guard)

Coos Bay Life-Saving Station replaced Cape Arago station because it was closer to the harbor entrance and in more protected waters. Dangerous rescues on the Coos Bay bar, however, continued. Coos Bay was one of four Marquette-style stations in Oregon. (U.S. Coast Guard)

Coos Bay surfmen with English-type lifeboat and "witch's hat" boathouse. (Coos-Curry Museum)

Yaquina Bay Life-Saving Station near Newport, Oregon. A beautiful scene with a Fort Point-type "witch's hat" boathouse and Marquette-style station built in 1895. (Lincoln County Historical Society)

In an unusual move the Life-Saving Service used abandoned Yaquina Bay lighthouse as a full-fledged life-saving station from 1908 to 1915. Note USLSS sign above the entrance. (Lincoln County Historical Society)

wreck the fifth time, a terrific sea struck our boat, turning it almost end over end and washing five (surfmen) overboard, including myself." By grabbing lifelines all but one surfman were hauled back into the motor lifeboat. Fortunately, the crew found the missing surfman and pulled him safely on board, too.[22]

At this point, the Cape Disappointment power lifeboat signaled for assistance and the Point Adams crew took them in tow. A tug, the *Fearless*, was standing by in calmer waters and the disabled USLSS *Tenacious* was towed to the tug.[23]

The Point Adams crew returned to the wreck and entered the breakers. This time one of the sailors got up his courage and jumped. Another sailor followed him into the sea. Both were picked up alive and pulled on board the power lifeboat. The third man was dead.

Sea conditions were still so bad there was no thought of returning to shore. The Columbia River bar could not be crossed. The Cape Disappointment power lifeboat *Tenacious* was in critical condition, its bottom split and its air compartments filled with water. Everyone was taken off the power lifeboat and an attempt was made to tow her. But big seas simply rolled the Cape Disappointment boat over and over until she disappeared.

With everyone now on board Point Adams' *Dreadnaught*, she ran for the *Columbia River Lightship* which was moored outside the breaking bar. It was very difficult for everyone to climb up the side of the rolling lightship, but it was finally safely accomplished.[24] The *Tenacious* was moored astern the lightship for a time, but the storm tore her loose. Neither USLSS power lifeboats

were ever seen again.

Miraculously, one other sailor from the *Rosecrans* had survived. A seaman clinging to wreckage was washed ashore five miles north of the wreck. He was taken to the Klipsan Beach Life-Saving Station and cared for. Thus, out of an oil tanker crew of 35, just three survived. If it had not been for the Life-Saving Service surfmen, at least two and perhaps all three sailors would not have survived.

The Point Adams and Cape Disappointment surfmen had lost both of their new power lifeboats, had faced 40-foot high waves and repeatedly risked their lives. The Life-Saving Service report stated that "rarely have crews of the service worked against more distressing odds or exhibited more indomitable spirit." The Oregon State Legislature commended by name every life-saver who took part in the rescue. Each of the Cape Disappointment and Point Adams keepers and surfmen received the gold life-saving medal, with an almost unprecedented total of sixteen gold medals awarded.[25]

If the Columbia River bar was said to be the Pacific Coast's worst maritime graveyard, California's San Francisco Bay approaches and the Redwood Coast were rivals for that notorious title. The location of the largest storm waves ever recorded in America, the Redwood Coast, extends from the Golden Gate north to the Oregon state line and had become by 1900 the domain of the steam schooner.[26]

The steam schooner was typically a wooden steamer with its superstructure usually at the stern. Built to haul lumber and passengers, they were predominantly a West Coast type vessel of Scandinavian origin.[27] Steam schoo-

Tillamook Bay Life-Saving Station was of an architectural type unique to West Coast. This rare 1908 Petersons Point-style station is now a private residence at Barview, Oregon. It is the only surviving example of this type of station. (U.S. Coast Guard)

Umpqua River Life-Saving Station on the north side of river entrance at Winchester Bay, Oregon. Note Marquette-style station house and Fort Point-type "witch's hat" boathouse. The dangerous Umpqua River entrance was the scene of many capsizings and strandings. (Coast Guard Museum Northwest)

Grays Harbor crew conducted breeches buoy drills beside Grays Harbor lighthouse. Crew is harnessed to beach cart ready to pull. Keeper Charles Jacobsen is at right. (U.S. Coast Guard)

ners plied the "dog hole" ports of the Redwood Coast, rugged, unprotected coves where redwood and Douglas fir lumber was loaded from high cliffs by chutes and cables. Redwood Coast steam schooners had an amazingly high mortality rate on a dangerous shore with only two safe harbors in hundreds of miles.[28]

The *Hanalei* was one of these steam schooners. In the winter of 1914 she had loaded passengers, railroad ties and shingles at Humboldt Bay and sailed south for San Francisco. Fog was the worst hazard to navigation on the California coast, and *Hanalei* had encountered winter fog at the great coastal promontory of Point Reyes. The fog wasn't as bad as it could have been and those on the *Hanalei* could recognize Point Reyes lighthouse halfway up the 600-foot high headland. After rounding the light, the *Hanalei* altered her course toward San Francisco. Shortly after noon on gloomy November 23, 1914 the steamer saw breakers appear ahead "and before anything could be done to avert disaster the vessel ran hard and fast on the reefs off Bolinas Point," about three miles "northward of the end of Duxbury Reef" off Bolinas Bay.[29]

Wireless distress calls were immediately sent out for assistance but, as the captain was unsure of his position, an erroneous position was given. The radio message incorrectly reported that the *Hanalei* was on Duxbury Reef, yet the Life-Saving Service responded promptly, sending out its motor lifeboats, the *Majestic* from Point Bonita Life-Saving Station in Marin County and the *Defender* from Fort Point Life-Saving Station in San Francisco.[30] The Revenue Cutter *McCullough* also had picked up the S.O.S. message and joined the other rescue vessels rushing toward Duxbury Reef. The weather was foggy with a light westerly wind and a very heavy Pacific swell.[31]

The two motor lifeboats reached Duxbury Reef that afternoon. The fog had worsened and was "now almost impenetrable." Other vessels had arrived to aid in the search and in the dense fog were blowing their whistles continuously to avoid ramming each other. All the whistle blowing made it impossible for rescuers to determine which, if any, of the whistle blasts came from the *Hanalei*. Finally, after much searching and despite great risk, Point Bonita's power lifeboat *Majestic* and Fort Point's power lifeboat *Defender* entered the breakers. They passed through the crashing waves and ran close to shore actually inside the surf line.

This was an extremely dangerous course but one by

Grays Harbor Life-Saving Station served a major Washington port. Crew stands in front of rare Peterson's Point-type station designed by Victor Mendleheff and built in 1898. Grays Harbor was originally called Petersons Point station and this was the prototype of the design. (Shanks collection)

Cape Disappointment Life-Saving on the Washington side of the Columbia River entrance was probably listed in USLSS Annual Reports *more often than any other station for disasters involving loss of life. Crew stands in front of this rare Niagara-style station. Today, because of heavy surf here the Coast Guard has established its National Motor Lifeboat School at Cape Disappointment where all the qualified surfmen in the country are trained. (Coast Guard Museum Northwest)*

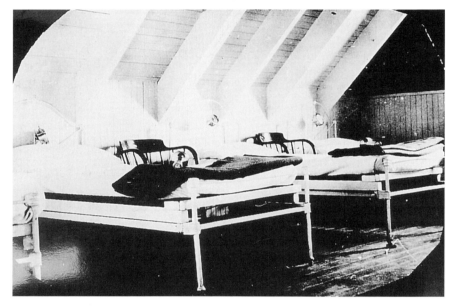

Sleeping quarters upstairs at Cape Disappointment Life-Saving Station. Crew here won Congressional gold life-saving medals for 1913 Rosecrans *rescue. (U.S. Coast Guard)*

Klipsan Beach Life-Saving Station (formerly Ilwaco Beach) guarded a sandy beach many miles long, a rarity on the rocky Pacific Coast. Marquette-style station was built in 1891 on southwest Washington coast. (Howard Underhill)

which the surfmen found the *Hanalei*. She was seen to be listing at almost a 45 degree angle with her deck exposed to the full force of the heavy swells, which were steadily pounding the steam schooner to pieces. The passengers and crew could be seen gathered on the upper side huddled behind the superstructure near the stern.

The two motor lifeboats tried to reach the calmer lee side of the wreck to take off survivors. The *Majestic* attempted to go around the bow and the *Defender* around the stern, but the heavy swells "broke into high, short-footed and angry surf, in which it was difficult for any type of boat to live."[32]

Danger was magnified by the questionable reliability of early lifeboat motors. Although highly seaworthy, early motor lifeboats operating under such extreme conditions often worked poorly and could quit at the worst possible moment. Both power lifeboats made two approaches to the ship and both were forced back because the heavy surf caused engine problems.

Fort Point's surfmen then went in for a third attempt. Their power lifeboat was unequal to the breakers, however, and the *Defender* capsized, throwing Keeper John S. Clark and Surfman John Stoll into the sea. The seas were so fast-moving and violent that upon reaching the surface, Keeper Clark found that he was already 40 feet away from the *Defender*. Clark realized that the *Defender* was now in danger of suffering the same fate as the steam schooner. Remaining in the crashing breakers with Stoll, the keeper ordered the surfmen still on the *Defender* to head for calmer water. Keeper Clark and Surfman Stoll were abandoned in the Pacific.

Keeper Clark advised Surfman Stoll to swim for the *Hanalei* while he tried to reach shore. Someone had to get ashore and call San Francisco for a Lyle gun and breeches buoy. Leaving Stoll to swim to the ship, Keeper Clark set out toward the beach. He faced "boiling surf," jagged rocks covered with slime, and strong currents. His three attempts to gain the shore failed and he was swept so far out sea he actually circled the *Hanalei*. For two and a half hours Keeper Clark swam, trying to reach Bolinas beach. In one of the most "heroic struggles in the line of duty" in Life-Saving Service history, Keeper Clark finally reached the beach unconscious but alive, and was pulled ashore by local West Marin residents.[33]

"After the capsize of the *Defender*, darkness, a dense fog and increasing seas prevented anything more from being accomplished by the boats until daylight." Both motor lifeboats spent the night along side the Revenue Cutter *McCulloch* off Bolinas Bay.[34]

The Life-Saving Service district office in San Francisco was worried. That evening a truck was obtained from a San Francisco newspaper and Golden Gate Park Life-Saving Station surfmen, under Keeper Norman Nelson,

climbed in with their beach apparatus. The truckload of surfmen crossed San Francisco Bay by Northwestern Pacific ferryboat and landed on the north shore at Sausalito. To reach the coast required driving one of the most steep, crooked and narrow dirt roads in the state. The life-savers had to traverse soaring Mount Tamalpais' flanks, slowed by very rough roads that threw the surfmen about and by dense patches of dark fog. At times, the truck had to be backed up grades too steep for the gasoline to reach the engine from the fuel tank in any other way. Alternately driving forward and backwards, Keeper Nelson and his crew made it to Bolinas Bay at 2 a.m.

The Golden Gate Park surfmen set up the Lyle gun atop the bluff and fired lines from the Lyle gun. None of the projectiles reached the *Hanalei*. Large bonfires were built on the beach to give those on the steam schooner hope.

The sea became more violent during the night. At 3:30 a.m. crashing timbers could be heard, indicating that the steam schooner was completely breaking up. "For a distance of 200 yards off the beach, extending for a mile on either side of the wreck, the water was literally covered with grinding, tossing material, consisting of portions of the wrecked vessel and her cargo of railroad ties and shingles, in the midst of which the surviving passengers and crew were battling for their lives." The railroad ties became battering rams in the surf and dodging them was a matter of life or death.[35]

Keeper Nelson rushed his men down along the beach and set the Lyle gun up again. He fired, hoping to get a line across the wreckage while it floated and provide the people a chance to reach shore alive. Shot after shot was fired, sending life-lines across the water toward the struggling survivors.

"Joining hands and forming a living chain the (Golden Gate Park surfmen) rushed into the water wherever a human form was seen struggling, sometimes beaten back by the force of the surf or battered by floating wreckage, sometimes entirely submerged, and again taking desperate risks by crawling over the larger portions of flotsam in the surf, they valiantly held to their work until every soul had been saved that could be reached. Out of the 30 persons hauled up on the beach only one was lost." With the coming of daylight and the cessation of shore rescue work, Golden Gate Park Life-Saving Station's surfmen "were found to be in a pitiable condition, their clothing stripped to tatters and their bodies covered with bruises and cuts from head to foot." The flying, cutting wreckage had taken a toll on those brave enough to enter the sea.

While the Golden Gate Park surfman dressed their wounds on the beach, dawn broke and the surfmen in the motor lifeboats went back into action. Fort Point's *Defender* was in no condition for further rescue work, but Point Bonita's *Majestic* was ready. Point Bonita Keeper

Neah Bay Life-Saving Station in Washington, an 1875-type station. Located at Neah Bay on the Makaw Indian Reservation, many surfmen here were Native Americans. The Neah Bay stations went through three name changes: Neah Bay became Waaddah Island and it in turn became Baaddah Point, all Indian names. With each change a new station was built. When older stations were retired, they became Indian homes. (U.S. Coast Guard)

Waaddah Island Life-Saving Station at Neah Bay, Washington. After many years of service, Neah Bay Life-Saving Station was discontinued in December 1890. After several terrible shipwrecks in the area, this new station was established at nearby Waaddah Island in 1908. The station was moved to the mainland within two years to be part of Baaddah Point Life-Saving Station. The move was prompted by the drowning of two surfmen, on November 19, 1908 as they attempted to row the station dory from their motor lifeboat mooring to the station launchway during very rough seas. The dory capsized and the two surfmen were lost. The Life-Saving Service had enough of treacherous Waaddah Island and relocated the station on the mainland at Baaddah Point. The station was moved ashore and stood alongside a new station, shown below. (U.S. Coast Guard Academy)

The Life-Saving Service later built a new station at Neah Bay. This is the 1910 Baaddah Point (Neah Bay) Life-Saving Station with motor lifeboats on launchway. This station conducted its rescues at the entrance to Washington's Strait of Juan de Fuca. (U.S. Coast Guard)

Nome Life-Saving Station was Alaska's lone station. Keeper Thomas A. Ross sometimes went on rescues using a dog team and sled. This one-of-a-kind station was destroyed in a violent 1913 storm. (Anchorage Historical & Fine Arts Museum)

Port Orford Lifeboat Station in southern Oregon was one of the early stations established by the Coast Guard. The Pacific Coast was so short of stations at the end of the Life-Saving Service era that the Coast Guard had to build many new stations. Surfmen had to climb down a 300-foot headland on a zig-zag stairway to reach their boathouse on Nelly Cove. Port Orford represents the Coast Guard transition period-type of architecture. This station is preserved as Port Orford Heads Wayside State Park in Port Orford, Oregon. (U.S. Coast Guard)

Fort Point Lifeboat Station in San Francisco was a first step in early Coast Guard architecture. Probably designed by Albert Mendleheff, this circa 1919 station was the beginning of the Coast Guard transition period architecture from about 1919 through the mid-1930s. Note the large launchway with power boats. The station today is part of Golden Gate National Recreation Area. (Howard Underhill)

Point Reyes Life-Saving Station suffered heavy loss of surfmen. Three men died in surfboat drills in huge breakers while a fourth died of work related disease. Their graves rest in the "Surfmen's Cemetery" in California's Point Reyes National Seashore. Grave at right reads: "In memory of George Larson. Surfman of the Point Reyes Life-Saving Station killed in the accidental capsizing of the surfboat while at practice drill. March 1, 1893. Aged 27 years. Died at his post of duty." (Shanks collection)

The Life-Saving Service was an extremely dangerous career. Grave in San Francisco has this inscription: "In memory of Charles Henry, Keeper of the Fort Point Life-Saving Station, drowned Feb. 21, 1891, aged 41 years. In making heroic effort to rescue others in peril he was washed out of the Life-Boat. Erected by the officers and crews of the 12th Life-Saving District." Keeper Henry was swept from his position at the steering oar while going to the rescue of the Elizabeth. *(Shanks collection)*

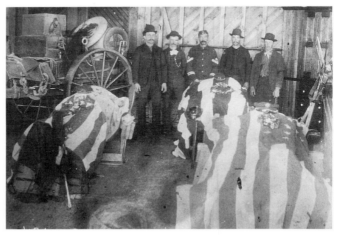

"They had to go out, but they did not have to come in." Coquille River Keeper Edward M. Nelson and Surfmen Billy Green and Jimmie Sumner were lost during the April 12, 1892 capsizing of their surfboat by giant waves. Photo taken inside the Coquille River Life-Saving Station boathouse in Oregon. (Bandon Historical Society)

Joseph Nutter, with his own surfmen, and two more from Fort Point, shoved off for the wreck scene. They had no knowledge of Golden Gate Park Station's rescue work that night, only a desire to help save lives. "In the growing light of the early morning, with a heavy fog made more dense…by smoke from the bonfires, the keeper, with great skill and daring, maneuvered the *Majestic* in toward the beach through the outlying reefs, over which a tremendous sea was breaking."[37]

The view in the foggy dawn was shocking. The *Hanalei* had disappeared. The people were nowhere to be seen. There was an oil soaked mass of wreckage. There were also the bodies, too many bodies. But here and there were living souls, most suffering so from the cold water that they could not even wave for help. The *Majestic* moved from one person to the next, the surfmen bending over the side to pull in the living and the dead.

Suddenly two more struggling survivors were seen, both about to go under. Surfman Michael Maxwell leaped overboard into the oily sea and swam to them, supporting and encouraging them both until the *Majestic* got them safely on board. The search went on until thirteen survivors were aboard Point Bonita's power lifeboat. All were taken to the *McCulloch* to be cared for.

Thirteen persons were saved by the Point Bonita surfmen by motor lifeboat and twenty-nine by the Golden Gate Park surfmen on shore. One other person was rescued by employees of the local wireless station, bringing the total to 43 survivors. The *McCulloch* then set out at full speed for San Francisco with the survivors, many in very poor condition. Upon making port, doctors and nurses rushed aboard to aid the victims.[38]

In its very first annual report, the new U.S. Coast Guard wrote, "It is doubtful if in the annals of shipwreck any was ever before reported as having occurred within the scope of the Coast Guard establishment which was attended by so many dramatic incidents and spectacular features… There certainly could not be a shipwreck in which the individual examples of heroism, self-sacrifice, and humanitarian service on the part of the rescuers could be more numerous and more praiseworthy… Taken altogether this was the most thrilling wreck encountered by the Coast Guard during the entire (1914-1915 fiscal) year."[39] Keeper John S. Clark of Fort Point Life-Saving Station and Keeper Joseph L. Nutter and Surfman Michael Maxwell, both of Point Bonita Life-Saving Station, were awarded gold life-saving medals.[40] They had to go out and they did not have to come in. Mercifully, these surfmen all returned home alive.

There was a huge public outcry that the burned Bolinas Bay Life-Saving Station be rebuilt.[41] In 1917 the Coast Guard built the Bolinas Bay Lifeboat Station and Duxbury Reef and Bolinas Point once again had their own rescue station.[42]

THE LAST YEARS

In 1915 the civilian Life-Saving Service was merged with the military Revenue Cutter Service to create the modern Coast Guard. The USLSS could look back on 43 years of proud service to humanity. During its existence the Life-Saving Service saved over 150,000 lives and had annually saved property that exceeded the cost of maintaining the entire national system. The USLSS was one of the best investments the American people ever made. When looked at in terms of both social good and economic benefit, this was an example of government workers at their best.

It has been said that by 1915 the Life-Saving Service "was growing old" and that there were "keepers in their seventies manning the customary sweep oar while the strokes were manned by men in their sixties."[43] This was not really the problem. As the *1914 Annual Report of the Life-Saving Service* points out rather "the veteran surfmen of the service—those whose annual enlistment cover periods running back 20 or 30 years, and whose experience and skill have been the mainstay of the corps—have been rapidly falling out of the ranks, and the service has been compelled" to replace them with less experienced and less capable men.[44] The problem was not one of aging veterans, but of declining numbers of such men.

The new Coast Guard militarized the Life-Saving Service to some degree, but at least as late as 1939 the lifeboat stations were operated much as the Life-Saving Service had done. A man could still enlist to serve at a particular station and many of the station keepers and older surfmen had been trained by the Life-Saving Service. The drills, boats and equipment were still fundamentally unchanged. Pulling boats were still used at some stations at least as late as 1940.[45]

The Coast Guard's lasting monuments of the period from the 1920s through the early 1940s were the magnificent neocolonial lifeboat stations constructed during the period. These represented the highest achievement in Coast Guard architecture, one not equalled to this day. These often red roofed, gleaming white buildings symbolized the best of the Coast Guard and are national treasures. Some have been preserved in national parks, as museums and for other uses; some are still active as lifeboat stations and deserve to be the pride of the Coast Guard.[46]

World War II changed the lifeboat stations and made them more military in character. During the 1950s Coast Guard architecture declined in grandeur and lost its distinctive features. Sadly, most Coast Guard stations built since the 1950s are architecturally indistinguishable from other functional structures. This unnecessary turn of events paralleled the period when many Coast Guard lighthouses were allowed to decay.

By the 1950s the breeches buoy was rarely used, replaced by helicopters. Wooden 36-foot motor lifeboats were almost completely replaced by steel 44-foot motor lifeboats by the 1970s. Yet in the 1970s it was still possible, despite Coast Guard rotation policies, for a Coast Guardsman to spend most or all of his career at lifeboat stations. The 13th Coast Guard District comprising Washington and Oregon developed a reputation as the homeland of the most traditional lifeboatmen, some of whom were still active in the 1990s. Women became motor lifeboat coxswain and surfmen by the 1980s and achieved a fine record.

The spirit of the Life-Saving Service still lives. It can be witnessed at Coast Guard stations on the Pacific and Atlantic Coasts and on the Great Lakes. True lifeboat stations still exist. Coast Guard men and women still operate the motor lifeboats in rescues requiring courage and skill, as in the days of the Life-Saving Service. The name "surfman" remains an honored one, though today's surfman may also be a woman. The surfmen still have to go out and they still know that they may not come back. The heroes are still on duty.

Life-Saving Stations of the Pacific Coast

Life-Saving Station of Alaska

Station	Location
Nome	On the beach at Nome

Life-Saving Stations of California

Humboldt Bay	North Spit, near Eureka
Arena Cove	At Arena Cove, west of town of Point Arena[47]
Point Reyes	On Point Reyes Beach 3½ miles north of lighthouse
Point Bonita	Bonita Cove at light station near Sausalito
Fort Point	East of fort ¾ mile, San Francisco
Golden Gate Park	On Ocean Beach in Golden Gate Park, San Francisco
Southside	On Ocean Beach end of Sloat Blvd., San Francisco

Life-Saving Stations of Oregon

Point Adams	Mouth of Columbia River, Hammond
Tillamook Bay	Barview, north of Tillamook
Yaquina Bay	Newport
Umpqua River	North side river entrance, Winchester Bay
Coos Bay	North side, Coos Bay entrance
Coquille River	Bandon

Life-Saving Stations of Washington

Baaddah Point	Neah Bay
Grays Harbor	South of Grays Harbor Lighthouse, Westport
Willapa Bay	Near North Cove, Willapa Bay
Klipsan Beach	13 miles north of Cape Disappointment
Cape Disappointment	Baker's Bay, Ilwaco

NAME CHANGES: Most Washington stations had name changes: Grays Harbor station was once called Petersons Point; Klipsan Beach station was formerly called Ilwaco Beach; Willapa Bay station was called Shoalwater Bay and, informally, North Cove. Baaddah Point station was called Neah Bay and Waaddah Island. After the Coast Guard took over Baaddah Point station, it again became Neah Bay. Cape Arago, Oregon, was replaced by Coos Bay.

DISCONTINUED STATION: Bolinas Bay station at Bolinas, California, was burned April 15, 1885. It was rebuilt by the Coast Guard in 1917 using USLSS plans. UNBUILT STATION: For years the USLSS "Annual Reports" listed a proposed station at Point Conception, Calif. This station was never built, but in the late 1930s, the USCG built a station close by at Point Arguello. ADDITIONAL STATIONS: Pacific Coast construction of stations necessarily continued long after the USLSS ended in 1915. Classic traditional lifeboat stations built by the Coast Guard included: Point Arguello, Santa Barbara County, California; Bolinas Bay, Bolinas, California; Port Orford, Oregon; Siuslaw River, Florence, Oregon; and Quillayute River, at La Push, Washington. Bolinas Bay and Siuslaw River stations were built using USLSS plans. Although not established until later and architecturally untraditional, the 1953 Depoe Bay Lifeboat Station in Oregon and the 1963 Bodega Bay Lifeboat Station in California did classic lifeboat rescue work. Numerous other late design Coast Guard stations have been built, particularly in California and Washington.

Life-Saving Stations of the Pacific Coast

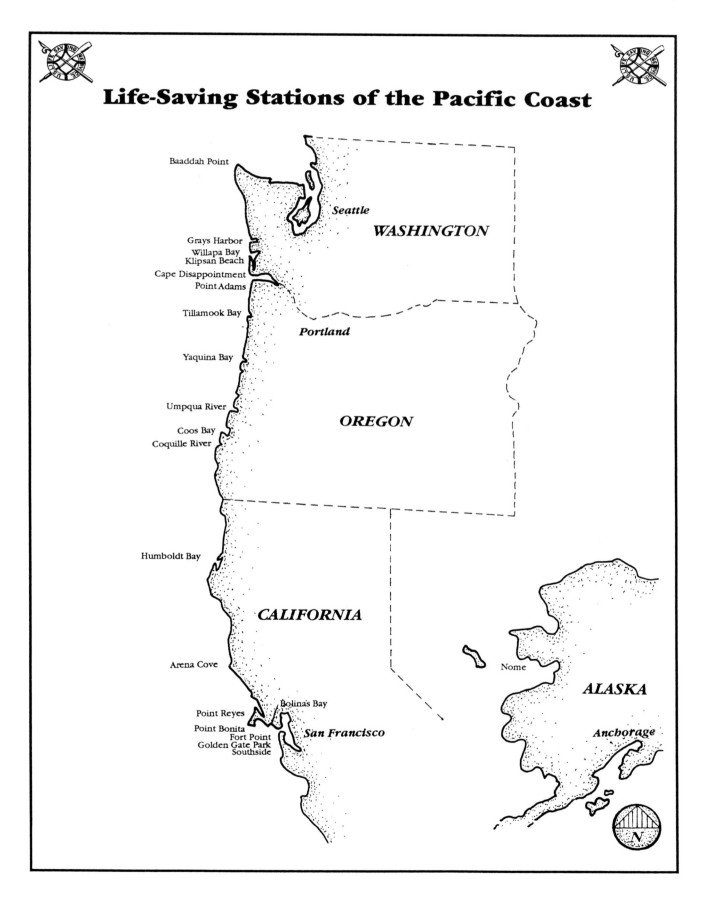

WASHINGTON

Baaddah Point

Seattle

Grays Harbor
Willapa Bay
Klipsan Beach
Cape Disappointment
Point Adams

Tillamook Bay

Portland

Yaquina Bay

OREGON

Umpqua River

Coos Bay
Coquille River

Humboldt Bay

CALIFORNIA

Nome

ALASKA

Arena Cove

Bolinas Bay

Point Reyes
Point Bonita
Fort Point
Golden Gate Park
Southside

San Francisco

Anchorage

Bayhead Life-Saving Station in New Jersey was one of the nation's most elegant stations. Note the elaborate lookout tower. (Wick York)

Chapter 17
The Architecture of the U.S. Life-Saving Stations
Wick York

EARLY STATION DESIGNS: 1848-1855

Created for the purpose of rescuing victims from coastal shipwrecks, the United States Life-Saving Service built a closely-knit network of stations along all maritime coasts of the United States to house the lifesavers and their equipment. Although the history of coastal lifesaving in this country goes back to the Colonial period, the first rescue stations were not built until the early nineteenth century. Various private organizations, supported in part by ship owners and insurance underwriters, formed to lobby the government for better aids to navigation and to provide relief to victims in the event of a shipwreck. Their efforts concentrated around the major ports of Boston, New York and Philadelphia, and in the remote areas along the approaches to these cities. Cape Cod, Long Island and New Jersey had few harbors to offer refuge during a storm and their long unbroken stretches of offshore sandbars were extremely hazardous to shipping.

Listed among these organizations were the Boston Marine Society, the Merrimac Humane Society, The New York Life-Saving Benevolent Association and the New York Shipwreck Society.[1] But the oldest and most well-known was the Massachusetts Humane Society. A volunteer group formed in 1786 and incorporated in 1791, and the Society became the first organization created solely to save the lives of shipwrecked mariners. Although its efforts were financed primarily by private contributions, it did receive some additional support from the state and federal government.

The Society first began its work by building unmanned shelter huts (Houses of Refuge) on desolate sections of the Massachusetts coast offering relief to shipwrecked crews able to make it to shore on their own. To assist crews in the event of a grounding along the dangerous coast of Cape Cod, the *American Coast Pilot* published in 1804 a description of the section between Race Point and Chatham, describing in detail "the spots on which the Trustees of the Humane Society have erected huts, and

other places where shipwrecked Seamen may look for shelter."[2]

The first House of Refuge was built on Lovell's Island in Boston Harbor during 1789 and additional ones were soon erected along other sections of the Massachusetts coast. It is believed that all the huts constructed were alike, sharing similar features with those described below:

"The six huts...are all of one size and shape. Each hut stands on piles, is 8 feet long, 8 feet wide, and 7 feet high; a sliding door is on the south, a sliding shutter on the west, and a pole, rising 15 feet above the top of the building, on the east. Within it is supplied straw or hay, and is further accommodated with a bench."[3]

Outfitted with a wood stove and some supplies of food and clothing, each hut cost about $40.00 to build and equip.[4] Like many simple coastal structures built during this period, they were probably roofed and sheathed entirely with wood shingles.

The Society attempted to keep the huts in reasonable condition by appointing a nearby resident to occasionally look after each one. The *Coast Pilot* described a typical caretaking arrangement. "To prevent any accident from happening to it, or to the other hut near Peaked Hill, the Trustees have secured the attention of several gentlemen. Dr. Thaddeus Brown and Capt. Thomas Smalley, of Provincetown, have been engaged to inspect both huts, to see that they were supplied with straw or hay in the autumn, that the doors and windows were kept shut, and that repairs were made when necessary."[5]

The first lifeboat station designed solely to house a surfboat and other rescue apparatus was built by the Society in 1807 at Cohasset. Although no formal description has been found, it was probably a simple frame building one-story high and only slightly longer than its thirty foot surfboat. Gradually the Society extended its lifesaving efforts to other areas of the Massachusetts coast so that by 1872 there were seventy-six lifeboat stations and eight

The Spermaceti Cove Life-Saving Station was the first American government life-saving station. This simple 1848-type station was the grandparent of all the Coast Guard stations of today. It now stands at Twin Lights State Historic Site in Highlands, New Jersey. (U.S. Coast Guard)

An 1855-type life-saving station in New York or New Jersey. Notice that, although still a simple structure, it is larger and more substantial than the 1848-type station shown above. (Richard Boonisar)

Cold Spring Life-Saving Station in New Jersey. This 1855-type station shows the facade, trim and windows typical of the 1855 stations. (U.S. Coast Guard)

shelter huts. (See page 6 for illustrations of a Massachusetts Humane Society station and a House of Refuge.)

The stations operated under the supervision of a paid trained keeper who drilled a volunteer crew in surfboat handling and various lifesaving techniques. Each crew member was paid for attendance at drills and for every rescue at which he assisted. As an added incentive, medals and other rewards were often given for outstanding acts of heroism.

Although the Humane Society succeeded in reducing the number of casualties from maritime disasters along the Massachusetts coast, the need for a national network of lifesavers was apparent. The extremely unreliable and poor conditions of United States coastal navigational aids accounted for numerous shipwrecks and stranded crews. Eighteen forty-eight marks the first steps toward a national system. In August of that year, Representative William A. Newell of New Jersey secured an appropriation of $10,000 to provide "surfboats, rockets and carronades, and other necessary apparatus for the better protection of life and property from shipwrecks on the Coast of New Jersey between Sandy Hook and Little Egg Harbor."[6] Prior to this date the only Congressional appropriation made for lifesaving efforts was an 1837 authorization for naval vessels, and later Treasury Department cutters, to cruise the coast during severe weather assisting distressed ships. Ten years later $5,000 was provided "for furnishing the lighthouses on the Atlantic coast with the means of rendering assistance to shipwrecked mariners."[7] That latter expenditure remained unused and was eventually given to the Massachusetts Humane Society to build and equip additional stations.

The Newell Act provided funds for the building of eight unmanned New Jersey life-saving stations, the first at Spermaceti Cove, on Sandy Hook.[8] The expenditure was made under the supervision of the Secretary of the Treasury, who in turn, directed Captain Douglas Ottinger of the Department's Revenue Marine Division to find suitable locations for each station and to oversee their construction. All eight were little more than crude one-and-a-half story frame boathouses, 16 feet wide by 28 feet long. The single room on the first floor housed the surfboat and other rescue equipment while a small loft above was used for storage. On the outside two or three layers of shingles covered the walls and roof and each station was painted or white washed.[9] (See page 212 for photo.)

Numerous additional appropriations were made during the six years following the passage of the Newell Act. In 1849 Congress approved $20,000 for construction of eight more stations along the outer shores of Long Island between Montauk Point and Coney Island, and two on Long Island Sound. Six more were placed in New Jersey extending coverage along that coast southward to Cape May. Construction of these sixteen new stations, all similar to the first eight, was also overseen by the Treasury Department. Edward Watts, a civil engineer from Washington, D.C., supervised the building of those on Long Island while Lieutenant John McGown of the Revenue Marine was appointed for the New Jersey section.[10]

During the 1850s the Service was enlarged and extended to other maritime coasts. In 1850 three additional Long Island stations and one at Watch Hill, Rhode Island, were built all under the supervision of Lieutenant Joseph Noyes.[11] That same year twenty-six lifeboats were placed along the coast of North and South Carolina, Georgia, Florida and Texas. During 1854 the first expenditure affecting lifesaving efforts on the Great Lakes was appropriated with $12,500 provided to purchase forty-seven lifeboats, and nearly half were stationed on Lake Michigan.[12]

Also in 1854 it was decided to construct fourteen additional stations on Long Island and a similar number in New Jersey. Most of the twenty-eight were built in between pre-existing ones, thus decreasing by one half the previous distance of approximately ten miles between stations. To carry this out the Treasury Department appointed J.C. Schillinger to supervise the building of those on Long Island while Samuel C. Dunham oversaw the New Jersey stations.[13] Slightly larger than the earlier stations, measuring 17 feet wide by 36 feet long, the walls of these new boathouses were covered with cedar boards rather than shingles.[14]

Although no architectural drawings of the early lifeboat stations in New Jersey or Long Island have been discovered, the similarity in appearance of all the stations suggests they were built from two or three closely related plans. One was probably drawn for the first eight completed in 1849 and a second similar but slightly larger plan used for the sixteen stations established later that year. It seems likely that the basic design was modified again to meet the needs of the more spacious 1855 stations. (See page 212 for photos.)

It has not been determined who might have drawn the station plans. Those officers of the Revenue Marine appointed to supervise the expenditure of funds and the construction of stations are not believed to have had any architectural skills. Little is known about Schillinger or Dunham but it is possible that Edward Watts, trained as a civil engineer and supervisor of construction for the 1849 stations, may have been involved in their design.[15]

Because the Supervising Architect of the Treasury Department was not established until 1853, the plans could not have been drawn by that office. Prior to this date the Secretary of the Treasury would usually appoint a local commission to oversee the construction of a specific public building such as a custom house or a courthouse. The commission, in turn, appointed a local architect to design the structure.[16] However, the situation differed for lifesaving stations in that standardized plans were drawn from which numerous buildings of the same type were constructed. It seems likely that the Secretary may have instead appointed an architect or engineer to work directly with the officers of the Revenue Marine who were responsible for overseeing the operation of the lifesaving system.

By the close of 1855 a total of fifty-six stations had been established between Cape May, New Jersey, and Watch Hill, Rhode Island. Additional boathouses of the Massachusetts Humane Society extended the network of lifesavers from Cape Cod to the New Hampshire border, thus providing a measure of protection to shipping around and between the major ports of Philadelphia, New York and Boston. While the number of stations had risen dramatically since 1849, there were still many problems plaguing the system which contributed to great loss of life from maritime disasters.

The government's complete lack of control over daily operations of the Service and the reliance on volunteers to man the stations were two major shortcomings. Although a local resident or benevolent society was initially appointed to look after the building and maintain its equipment, most overseers soon lost interest. No funds were provided for repairs and over time the stations began to suffer from neglect and the equipment became unfit for use. Furthermore, unpaid and poorly trained crews were often difficult to gather at a time when the situation demanded quick and well coordinated action. In sparsely populated areas response time remained particularly slow.

In 1853 an attempt was made to bring more order and effectiveness to the Service. A paid superintendent was appointed for the Atlantic and Great Lake coasts, and for the first time paid keepers took charge of the stations. However, this proved only moderately successful as many of the keepers were political appointees with few skills in training crews or directing rescue efforts. It was not until 1869 that surfmen were offered pay as well but then only at alternate stations and only during the severe winter months.

The Reorganization of 1871 and the Designs of Francis W. Chandler

A number of fatal shipwrecks along the Atlantic coast during the winter of 1870-71 demonstrated a lack of protection from an inefficient Service in need of greater organization and more stations. As a result of the public outcry which followed the news of the disasters, Congress appropriated funds for paid crews to live at stations for such periods as deemed necessary.

That winter Sumner I. Kimball was appointed head of the Revenue Marine Division.[17] To better assess the present state and needs of the Service, Kimball ordered a thorough investigation of every station, its equipment and crews.

The 1871 red house-type stations were larger than the 1848-1855 stations and had a ventilator on the roof. Loveladies Island Life-Saving Station, New Jersey. (National Archives)

RED HOUSE-TYPE STATIONS

The investigation found that stations had been located too far apart for neighboring crews to be of assistance during a disaster. Steps were taken to build additional stations in between older ones so that each would be no more than an average of three to five miles from the next. To bring this about eighteen new stations were ordered for New Jersey and Long Island while the existing ones underwent enlargement. These new stations represented the first building activity since 1855 and were the first ones designed to accommodate a live-in keeper and crew of six plus any rescue victims.

In New Jersey the original plans called for the construction of twelve new two-story houses, and the modification of all the existing twenty-eight stations. However, because of previous bad experiences in altering a few boathouses on Long Island, the refurbishing plans were changed, and new buildings were instead constructed at most of the old station sites. It is believed that the number of new buildings totaled thirty-seven. The earlier structures were disposed of, their parts often going into the new buildings.[18]

On Long Island, six stations, similar to those in New Jersey, were constructed at newly established sites while seventeen older ones, instead of being merely remodeled, were entirely rebuilt at their original locations. The rebuilt stations followed a similar design as the New Jersey ones.

In 1872 the Service was extended to the coasts of Rhode Island and Massachusetts. Stations at Narragansett Pier and Block Island were established while nine built on Cape Cod supplemented the efforts of the Massachusetts Humane Society. With the exception of the station at Narragansett Pier, all ten resembled those constructed the previous year on the coast of Long Island and New Jersey.

The new stations, all constructed from a set of standardized drawings, were nearly twice as large as the earlier boathouses. Shingled on their roofs and sides, they were often referred to as Red Houses as many were painted that color.[19] The 1872 *Annual Report of the Revenue Marine Bureau* contains a detailed description:

"All these houses have been constructed under plans and specifications carefully prepared with a view to durability, and affording proper accommodations for the apparatus and the means of providing comfortable protection to the crews and relief to those who may be rescued from shipwreck. They are 42 feet long by 18 wide, and each contains a lower and an attic story. Each story is divided into two apartments. The boats, a wagon, and other heavy apparatus occupy the large apartment below, while the smaller one is a living room for the crew, provided with conveniences for cooking. Above, one room is for the small articles of apparatus, and the other is provided with several cot-beds and suitable bedding."[20]

The completion in early 1873 of these stations brought the total number established to eighty-two, a third of which had been placed in new locations. The effects of Kimball's reorganization had not only resulted in increased building activity but also a dramatic drop in the number of lives lost from shipwrecks. During the two years following his appointment as Chief of the Revenue Marine Bureau there was only one fatality from a total of seventy-five disasters. Again in the *1872 Annual Report* Kimball wrote proudly of the successes of the newly revitalized Service and of his future goals.

"The results of the few years of its existence, and particularly those of the past year, demonstrate the usefulness of the Life-Saving Service. The great things it cannot fail to accomplish in the future will force it permanently upon the notice of the public, and it is destined to stand in the front rank of philanthropic institutions of the country. Without reference to its humane aspect, its importance to the interests of commerce alone render its extension to all very dangerous portions of our coast only a question of time; but there are some localities upon which disasters are so frequent as to call loudly for immediate attention, and to make delay until public sentiment compels action almost criminal."[21]

The extension of the Service was soon to come as Kimball lobbied Congress for funds to build stations on all hazardous sections of the United States coast. In 1873, $100,000 was appropriated to extend lifesaving activities to the states of Maine, New Hampshire, Virginia and North Carolina with the construction of twenty-three newly designed stations.

The 1870s saw a flowering in life-saving station architecture and produced some of the most charming structures. This was an 1874-type station, a style found only on the East Coast. Note the distinctive facade. Little Kinnakeet Life-Saving Station, North Carolina. (North Carolina Department of Cultural Resources)

1874-TYPE STATIONS

Like the 1871-Red House type stations, all twenty-three 1874-type stations appropriated in 1873, plus two more built later, were also built from a set of standardized plans. But unlike earlier stations, consideration was given not only to the functionalism of the design, but to stylistic detailing as well. In one of the few remarks on the appearance of stations, the Secretary of the Treasury's *Annual Report* for 1878 noted "these new stations were built on an enlarged and improved plan, some regard for architectural taste also being had."[22]

The design combined the elements of two architectural styles; Carpenter Gothic and the Stick Style. Inspired by the heavily detailed picturesque stone churches and public buildings constructed in England and the United States during the first half of the nineteenth century, Carpenter Gothic was a uniquely American style based on a strong carpentry tradition and a plentiful supply of high quality timber. It was a style readily distinguished by the frequent use of board and batten siding and an abundance of intricately sawn and carved wooden ornaments, all made possible largely by the introduction of the steam powered scroll saw. (See page 220 for photo.)

By the 1870s Carpenter Gothic had declined in popularity. Evolving from it was another style of construction also commonly carried out in wood frame residences; the Stick Style. In keeping with the belief that architecture should be "truthful," its main characteristic was the expression of the structure's inner frame through exterior ornamentation. Such buildings were highlighted by functional appearing wood bracketing in the roof gables and eaves, diagonal boards applied over horizontal or vertical siding and the occasional use of side buttresses. All elements worked to symbolize the structural skeleton within.

The 1875-type Pointe aux Barques Life-Saving Station on Lake Huron in Michigan. The 1875-type stations were built on both seacoasts and on the Great Lakes. Pointe aux Barques was the station of Keeper Jerome Kiah, lone survivor of a disastrous 1879 rescue attempt. Note the lighthouse adjoining station. Pointe aux Barques Life-Saving Station has been preserved at the Huron City Museum at Huron City, Michigan. (U.S. Coast Guard)

Grande Pointe au Sable Life-Saving Station on Lake Michigan. One of twenty 1875-type stations, Grande Pointe au Sable lost Keeper James Flynn and two surfmen in the 1886 A.J. Dewey rescue attempt. Note the unusual lookout tower atop the station. (U.S. Coast Guard)

Indian River Inlet Life-Saving Station was an 1875-type station on the Delaware coast. This aerial view shows the problems stations faced from shifting sands and high water as several feet of sand cover the entire reservation. The station was later moved and still stands today. (National Archives)

Slightly larger than the Red Houses, measuring 19 feet wide by 43 feet long and a story and a half high, the 1874-type stations featured an ornate exterior treatment, particularly in the use of scroll work detailing beneath the eaves. While each station closely resembled one another, there were some individual variations. Most exterior finishes combined Stick Style diagonal boarding at all four corners applied over a continuous run of beaded vertical siding at the first floor level. A more intricately cut Carpenter Gothic board and batten siding was used above. However, a few stations were instead sheathed entirely with shingles. While all stations featured decorative scroll work and bracketing beneath the gable and side eaves, on some stations it was more extensive than on others. At least one station did not have the dolphin motif and projecting stick work normally found at the outer extremes of the roof gables beneath the peak. On most buildings of this type, three or four buttresses, designed to provide added support against strong winds, were used on each side, but a few stations had none at all. Finally, all had a center roof observation platform where a constant watch of the coast was kept during the day. While most decks were built directly above the ridge pole a few were recessed about a foot below the peak into a hole cut out of the roof.

Although only a single set of specifications was issued for this type of station, most of the differences may be attributed to the presence of two remarkably similar plans. Why both plans were drawn is unclear as they were so alike. Regional styles, builder preferences and conditions of a particular site may also have accounted for a few additional differences.

The building program which started during the Reorganization of 1871 and continued with the construction of twenty-three stations in 1874, gathered greater momentum in the second half of the decade. An act passed on June 20, 1874 provided funds for an additional fifty-one stations to be built on the Atlantic coast and all Great Lakes except Superior.

In a letter dated December 27, 1874, Alfred B. Mullett, Supervising Architect of the Treasury Department discussed a request of Sumner Kimball that an architect from Mullett's office be appointed to design a station for Lakes Michigan and Erie. Mullett proposed that Frank W. Chandler, then Assistant Supervising Architect, be given this project.[23]

Francis Ward Chandler (1844-1926) began his career studying architecture at the Massachusetts Institute of Technology and as a student between 1864 and 1867 worked in the office of Ware and Van Brunt. This Boston firm, noted for their design of Memorial Hall in Cambridge (1870-78), was considered to be one of the leading proponents of high Victorian Gothic architecture in America. Leaving Boston in 1867 for two years of architectural studies in Paris, Chandler returned to M.I.T. in 1869 taking the position of assistant professor of architecture. This appointment lasted only one year for in 1871 Chandler joined Mullett's office in Washington.[24]

1875-TYPE STATIONS

Although Chandler did not sign the plans for the Great Lakes station design, a bill he submitted confirms his completion of the drawings during the winter of 1875, shortly after leaving Mullett's office.[25] It appears that Chandler's work actually consisted of two nearly identical plans. One of the plans from which at least sixteen stations of this type have been found, were built on the Atlantic and Great Lake coasts (except Lake Superior), and closely resembled the 1874-type stations. Having similar interior arrangements, the 1874-type and Chandler's 1875-type design were of like dimensions and massing

Grand Haven Life-Saving Station, an 1875-type clipped gable station on Lake Michigan. Clipped gable refers to the roof slanting down from its ridge, as seen just below the lookout tower. The eleven 1875 clipped gable-type stations were all on the Great Lakes. (Michigan State Archives)

Saint Joseph Life-Saving Station on Lake Michigan. This 1875-type clipped gable station clearly shows the clipped gable roof slanting down from the lookout tower. Note the lovely architectural details including a balcony above the boatroom doors. (Shanks collection)

and sheathed with the same vertical siding and exterior corner braces. Most of the detailing differed only slightly. Whereas the exterior corner braces on the 1874-type stations crossed each other in the shape of an "X," those on the 1875-type formed a diamond pattern. Both designs used battens to cover the joints between the siding above the second floor level, however, the 1875-type lacked the intricate scroll work found at the lower end of the 1874-

type siding. A simpler semicircular pattern was instead used. (See page 216 for photos.)

Other less subtle differences were more apparent. While each had bracketing beneath the eaves of the sides and gable ends, the stickwork in the peak of the 1875 stations was more angular than the curved wishbone shape of the 1874 design. All 1875 stations had a more elaborate roof deck with two separate lookout platforms, one in the center and one over the boatroom door, connected by a narrow walkway. Directly beneath the center platform on either side of the roof peak were two sets of windows, probably for observation in bad weather and to provide lighting for the upper story. A final decorative detail was the bracketed gable hood above the two side doors towards the rear of the station which provided shelter from the rain.

Chandler drew a slightly modified plan of his 1875-type from which at least four stations in California, Oregon and Washington were built between 1877 and 1878. These stations did not have the open lookout deck found on the original design, the exterior diagonal stickwork on the sides was slightly different, and each had a roof dormer. (See Pacific Coast chapter for photos.)

1875-TYPE CLIPPED GABLE STATIONS

A modified plan of the 1875-type was carried out in at least eleven stations built on Lakes Erie and Michigan during 1875-77. Slightly wider and shorter, the most visible differences between the two designs focused on the gable end treatment. Absent from the modified plan was the roof observation deck and the stickwork found in the peak of the 1875-type. Instead, a clipped gable terminated the front end, providing protection from the weather to an open gallery below from where the lookout was kept. (Later, enclosed lookout towers were added at some of these stations.) Also missing were the exterior diagonal corners braces. Otherwise, much of the detailing was similar, with two hooded doors, the same vertical siding, also battened on the second floor level, and bracketing beneath the eaves.

The fact that Kimball had requested the drawings for the 1875-type station from the Office of Supervising Architect suggests the 1874-type and possibly the Red House-type may have also been designed in this office. Although no documentation has been found verifying the architect of these two earlier designs, the strong similarity between the 1874 and 1875-type plans indicates Chandler may have been responsible for both.

HOUSES OF REFUGE

Florida's Houses of Refuge were fifteen feet wide by thirty-seven feet long with three apartments on the first floor and an upper story loft. Each house could accommodate twenty-five survivors with provisions for ten days.[26] They were, "two story structures of a style common in the

South, with broad gabled roofs, an ample verandah 8 feet wide on three sides of the structure, and large chimneys in the rear, built outside the wall. The houses are of pine, raised about six feet from the ground on light wood posts, and the roofs shingled with cypress. Instead of glass, the windows are fitted with wire-gauze mosquito netting."[27]

Unlike life-saving stations, all Houses of Refuge were alike, built from the same set of standardized plans. Chandler is credited with this design from which ten Houses of Refuge were completed during 1875-1885 in Florida.[28] Only two traditional style life-saving stations were built in Florida; the Jupiter Inlet Station on the east coast, and the Santa Rosa Station off Pensacola on the west coast.

Chandler left Washington during the winter of 1875 returning once again to Boston. There he joined in partnership with Edward C. Cabot to establish the firm of Cabot and Chandler, and during the late 1870s and 1880s designed numerous Queen Anne Style residences in and around that city. In 1888 he went back to M.I.T. for a third time as chairman of its Department of Architecture, staying until 1911. Chandler was also distinguished by his appointment as a fellow of the American Institute of Architects in 1889.[29] (See Florida chapter for photos.)

The Work of J. Lake Parkinson: First Life-Saving Service Architect

In July of 1875, shortly after Chandler's departure from Washington, J. Lake Parkinson was appointed Assistant Superintendent for Construction for lifesaving stations, a job where he also acted as architect.[30] Unlike Chandler who had worked in the Office of Supervising Architect of the Treasury Department, Parkinson's position came directly under the Life-Saving Service. It is not known how the decision was made to retain an architect within the Service but it appears to have been a result of the rapidly growing network of stations.

Not only were more stations put into service, but the varying requirements of different locations and crews could not be satisfied with only a few design types. While five plans had been drawn since the Reorganization of 1871 (Red Houses, 1874 and 1875-types, 1875-type with Clipped Gable, and Houses of Refuge), more would be needed to meet future expansion. Besides new designs, repairs and improvements to the 157 stations in service or appropriated by the mid-1875 were beginning to generate an additional workload. Kimball probably felt it would be more efficient and he could have a greater influence on station design if the architect worked directly under him.

Parkinson's early work received favorable acknowledgment in the Service's 1877 *Annual Report:* "The buildings which have recently been completed for lifesaving and life-boat stations at various points upon the Pacific coast, Lake Erie, Lake Superior, and Lake Michigan have

been designed by Mr. J.L. Parkinson, architect. The complete life-saving station exhibit at the Centennial Exposition, and since erected at Cape May, NJ, was also designed by him. These plans have been especially marked by architectural taste and adaptability to the requirements of the service, and call for suitable recognition and acknowledgment."[31]

1876-TYPE STATIONS

Twenty-six of Parkinson's 1876-type stations have been found on the Atlantic coast. These were built between 1875 and 1881, and may have been his first plan. This appears to have been influenced by previous designs as it closely resembled the 1874 and 1875-type stations in massing and layout. Much of the detailing was also similar, especially its open roof deck, gable end stickwork and the same second floor vertical battened siding as used in the 1875-type station. (See photos page 220.)

Parkinson reworked some of the earlier detailing in new ways while introducing a few ideas of his own. An overall covering of shingles at the first floor replaced the exterior vertical boarding and corner braces. The design was also toned down with the removal of bracketing beneath the eaves and gable overhang. A detail which became a characteristic feature on nearly all of Parkinson's designs, he rearranged the gable end stickwork with a simpler collar brace and king post terminated by a dropped pendant. A Gothically inspired redesigned roof deck surrounded by a railing with finials was located at the front of the building instead of in the center as found on earlier stations. The addition of two dormers placed in the middle of each side of the roof involved a final change.

Parkinson drew a more elaborately detailed plan of his 1876-type for a single station built on the grounds of the Philadelphia Centennial Exposition of 1876. The station featured characteristic Stick Style detailing in its abundance of diagonal braces applied over a beaded vertical first floor siding. However, a few subtle yet architecturally significant new elements were introduced. Decorative fish scale shingles between the first and second floor siding and scalloped edged bottoms of the lower sheathing boards hinted of Queen Anne influences and the beginnings of a departure from Carpenter Gothic and Stick Style station designs. An elaborate balcony over the boat room doors was found only on this particular station.

The station's highly ornate design spoke for the image which the Service wished to convey at the Centennial. Only five years after the Reorganization of 1871 and still struggling to gain Congressional support for the further extension, Kimball realized the value which national and international recognition at the Centennial would bring his organization. Open to the Fair's visitors and fully outfitted as if ready for action, the station was examined by numerous representatives of other life-saving institutions.

There were twenty-six 1876-type stations, all on the Atlantic Coast. Popes Island Life-Saving featured a type of lookout tower common in Virginia. (U.S. Coast Guard)

An 1876-type life-saving station in North Carolina, possibly Creeds Hill, with another style of lookout tower. Surfmen stand with their surfboat and lifecar. (National Archives)

Gull Shoal Life-Saving Station in North Carolina with the early open platform lookout. Keeper and six surfmen were a typical crew size for these 1876-type stations. (North Carolina Department of Cultural Resources)

Green Run Inlet Life-Saving Station in Maryland. This was an 1874-type station, one of twenty-five built during 1874-75. Note how its facade differs from the 1876-type stations. (U.S. Coast Guard)

After the close of the Exposition, the station was moved to Cape May, New Jersey, where it was put into service.

1876 LAKE SUPERIOR-TYPE STATIONS

Parkinson's next design was carried out in the first four stations established on Lake Superior during 1876. All were constructed on Michigan's Upper Peninsula in what was one of the most isolated areas on the Great Lakes. The setting around the Crisps Station typified this region: "We found Station No. 10 in an even wilder-looking place than the last. Tall somber fir and pine-trees in gloomy ranks reared their plumed heads beside the silent lakes four miles away. The station-house and the two or three cabins standing in the clearing beside it had a lonesome look on the edge of the endless forest. There are no habitations in this region beside the stations."[32]

As might be expected, finding a crew to man these stations in such remote settings was difficult. The keeper at Deer Park (Sucker River) had his hands full just maintaining discipline: "One of his first crews had jumped him on the beach one night, and intended to hang him, but he got 'the drop' on the crowd, and drove them up the beach and back to duty at the muzzle of their own revolver."[33]

Parkinson's 1876 Lake Superior design was more Gothically inspired than his earlier work, having a picturesque cottage-like feeling. The building abounded with numerous arched details including a steeply pitched gable roof topped by pointed ridge cresting and angular stickwork in the peak. The cross axial plan also marked the first departure from the previous rectangular layouts. One wing housed the lifeboat while a living room occu-

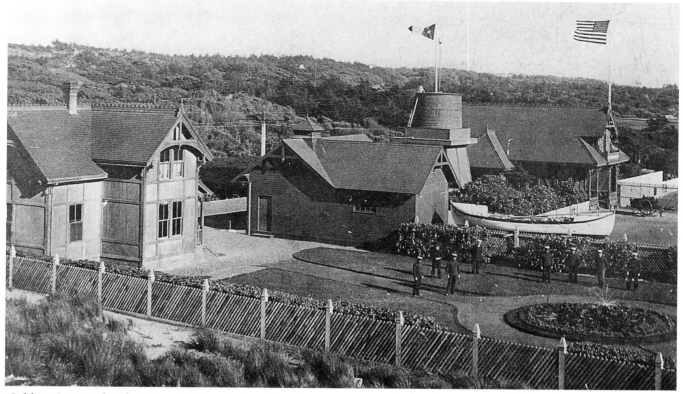

Golden Gate Park Life-Saving Station in San Francisco was a one-of-a-kind station with buildings designed by architects J. Lake Parkinson and John G. Pelton. The three-story station house/kitchen building at left shows a strong relationship to the 1876 Lake Superior-type stations with its facade and roof-top trim. The lifeboat-house/stable is at center while the main station-surfboat house is at right flying the American flag. The three-story station house was later moved to 47th and Cabrillo Streets in San Francisco where it stands today. (Howard Underhill)

Kenosha Life-Saving Station in Wisconsin was another one-of-a-kind design by architect J. Lake Parkinson. Note the double-bay boatroom and facade. (Nautical Research Center)

pied the other. Sleeping quarters were located above. (See page 168 for photos.)

ONE-OF-A-KIND STATIONS

Parkinson produced a number of designs from which only one or two stations were built. A small Gothic cottage established in 1877 at Grosse Point in Evanston, Illinois, featured some ornate Gothic Revival and Victorian Gothic detailing. A row of brackets entirely surrounding the eaves supported an overpowering hipped roof covered with horizontal bands of contrasting colored slate. An octagonal chimney pot and iron cresting with finials at each end topped the roof peak.

Two unique stations built in 1877—one in Buffalo, New York, and the other in San Francisco, California—shared similar elements. The smaller one-story Buffalo station was only large enough to accommodate the lifeboat and rescue equipment; the crew lived in separate quarters nearby. Heavily detailed wooden ornamentation abounded throughout. Diagonal braces over vertical siding surrounded the station, brackets supported a roof overhang at each corner, a king post and collar tie motif decorated the ends of all four gables and a paneled railing, broken by sharply pointed posts, ran along the ridge. Parkinson's other 1877 design, San Francisco's Golden Gate Park Station, used vertical and scallop-edged shingle sid-

A good example of how a station could be modified. Ludington, Michigan, Life-Saving Station was one of five 1879-type stations. By the time this photo was taken it had a lookout tower and wing (at right) added to the original structure in 1884. The modification is a tribute to the architect as the station looks very attractive. (U.S. Coast Guard)

ing, diagonal braces, bracketed eaves, gable and stickwork, and iron crested roof to create a spectacle of Gothic and Stick Style cottage architecture. At the north end of the Golden Gate Park Station was a three-story residence used as quarters and kitchen, which Parkinson is also believed to have designed. It is similar to the 1876-type stations and was probably designed in the 1870s. (See page 190 for Golden Gate Park station photo.)

Parkinson is known to have designed at least two other one-of-a-kind stations, both built on Lake Michigan in 1879. A station and small one-story boat house south of Milwaukee at Kenosha, Wisconsin, were more plainly detailed than many of his others. (See page 221.) Their steep pitched roof, dormers and ridge cresting, gave the buildings a top-heavy feeling. The one-and-a-half story Manistee, Michigan station featured his standardized king post and collar tie gable stickwork design on the front of the building with elaborate scroll cut brackets supporting a flagpole. (See page 14 for Manistee station photo.)

1879-TYPE and 1880-TYPE STATIONS

Five stations built from the same plan in 1879 on Lake Michigan and Lake Huron may also have been Parkinson's design. Although no original drawings for these stations have been found, the similarity of their gable stickwork to that of his other stations suggest the hand of the same architect. The design for the 1880-type stations in Texas was probably Parkinson's next plan. The stations shared similar layout, massing and detailing to his 1876 and 1879 plans, but were distinguished by a narrow, enclosed lookout tower. The 1880-type stations were built with rooftop open deck lookout platforms which were later replaced by narrow rooftop lookout towers. (See page 158.)

1882-TYPE STATIONS

An unsigned drawing for at least twenty-three stations built on the Atlantic coast between 1882 and 1891 was probably Parkinson's work as well. If so, this appears to be his last design before leaving the Service. The plan shares similar layout, massing, and detailing as Parkinson's 1876 station. Topped by a large lookout tower which sat on the roof towards the boat ramp end of the building, this was the first known use of an enclosed tower replacing the open deck of earlier stations. A large dormer protruded through the roof on each side with its base beginning slightly above the second floor level. Both the dormer and tower had the same pitched roof line, long overhanging eaves and peak stickwork as that of the front and rear gables. The tower was also identical to that used on the alteration plan of Parkinson's 1879 station.

On June 18, 1878, an act was passed to formally create the Life-Saving Service as an independent agency of the Treasury Department, with Sumner Kimball appointed as General Superintendent having overall administrative responsibilities. Although the Act separated the Service from the Revenue Marine, ties between the two organizations would remain strong as two Revenue Marine officers acted as Superintendents of Construction and Inspectors of Stations. (See page 223 for photo.)

CONSTRUCTION OF STATIONS

Inspectors were detailed to visit each station once a quarter to see that they were well maintained, properly equipped and that the crews were drilled and disciplined. Superintendents of Construction supervised the building of new stations and the repairs and additions to existing ones to insure that plans and specifications were followed.

Oak Island Life-Saving Station in North Carolina was a handsome example of an 1882-type station. Most 1882-type stations had this style lookout tower and facade. (North Carolina Department of Cultural Resources)

Paramore Beach Life-Saving Station in Virginia was a classic 1882-type station boasting the distinctive 1882-type lookout tower. (U.S. Coast Guard)

Lewes Life-Saving Station at the southeast entrance to Delaware Bay was an 1882-type station. Note how the lookout tower has been turned to parallel the roof-top. (U.S. Coast Guard)

Coskata Life-Saving Station and surfboat. An 1882-type station on Nantucket Island. In 1895 the Coskata crew won six life-saving medals for the H.P. Kirkham rescue. (Nantucket Life-Saving Museum)

Metomkin Inlet Life-Saving Station, Virginia. An 1882-type station with crew and surfboat. (U.S. Coast Guard)

Rare John G. Pelton design for keeper's dwelling at Willapa Bay (Shoalwater Bay) Life-Saving Station, Washington. Pelton dwelling is at left, original station at far right. This was the first station on the Pacific Coast. (Coast Guard Museum Northwest)

Keepers and crews often performed minor repairs.

Prior to the start of construction, advertisements were placed in local newspapers notifying private contractors of the Service's intention to build a station in that area. Builders requested from the Treasury Department a set of plans and specifications from which they then submitted a formal proposal, stating their cost and time of completion. Once a contract was awarded, a Superintendent of Construction would visit the site and send back to Washington progress reports and bills for labor, materials and traveling expenses. Occasionally some rather strong disagreements arose between the contractor and the Superintendent of Construction concerning the quality of work, as the following report to Kimball reveals:

"I have the honor to forward samples of the 'clear flooring' as laid in the Manistee [Michigan] Station and condemned and removed by my orders…I send them for your personal inspection and as partial refutation of at least one of the vile charges which I have heard were made against me. I respectfully ask that the specimens…be retained in your office until the charges made against me are withdrawn."[34]

One of the duties of the Superintendent of Construction as stated in the 1884 and 1899 *Revised Regulations of the U.S. Life-Saving Service* was to prepare plans and specifications for new stations and to make repairs to old ones. While Parkinson was actually an Assistant Superintendent of Construction, he is believed to be the only architect employed by the Service during his tenure. Both he and his successor designed stations and supervised their building.

Between 1848 and 1855, a total of fifty-six unmanned and poorly maintained boathouses had been built on the shores of New Jersey and Long Island. By 1871 most of these had either been destroyed, fallen into complete disrepair or were otherwise inoperable. However, the building program which followed the Reorganization of 1871 and continued up until the Act of 1878 resulted in 148 new stations and the planning of 37 additional ones. Of the established stations, 116 had been placed on the Atlantic coast, 30 on the Great Lakes, 2 on the Pacific and coverage was soon to be extended to the Gulf of Mexico. Except for 16 volunteer Great Lakes stations, all were complete lifesaving stations, manned by paid crews during their active season (September 1 to May 1).

Plans By Independent Architects: Pelz, Pelton and McKim, Mead and White

DEAL-TYPE STATIONS

No station designs drawn after the 1882-type have been attributed to Parkinson and it is believed that he left the Service a year or two after its completion. In 1882 Paul J. Pelz (1841-1918) submitted plans for four stations of the same design to be built at Atlantic City, Deal and Bay Head, New Jersey, and at Brenton Point in Newport, Rhode Island. (See pages 61, 74, 94, and 210.) Well known for his design for the Library of Congress in Washington, D.C., (completed in 1897) Pelz came to that city to work for the U.S. Lighthouse Board. As the Board's chief draftsman between 1872 and 1877, he designed numerous lighthouses, including Spectacle Reef Light on Lake Huron, considered to be one of the best examples of monolithic

Hither Plain Life-Saving Station on Long Island, New York was a fine example of an expanded red house-type enlarged during the 1887-88 expansion program under architect Albert Bibb. During conversion, Bibb added a lookout tower, built lean-tos on station sides and reshingled. (U.S. Coast Guard)

Side view of modified red house-type. Nauset Life-Saving Station on Cape Cod, Massachusetts. (Cape Cod National Seashore)

Front view of modified red house design. Crew stands proudly in front of Pamet River Life-Saving Station on Cape Cod. In later years porch at left was enclosed. (Cape Cod National Seashore)

stone masonry in the United States.[35]

Although Pelz's station plan used elements found in earlier design such as multiple sheathing materials, exterior diagonal braces and tall lookout towers, the overall feeling was more in the Queen Anne Style. Growing out of the Gothic Revival and Stick Style, Queen Anne buildings were characterized by asymmetrical massing and the use of a variety of forms, textures, materials and colors. The station's 56 foot tower was topped with ornamental ironwork, massive cross-gable roof which ended in a large projecting bay window and the application of both clap-

boards and scallop-edged shingles for siding typified this style. The September 15, 1885, issue of *American Architecture and Building News*, a popular architectural periodical of the late nineteenth century, featured the Bay Head station, complete with a tower clock provided by the local community.

KEEPER'S RESIDENCES FOR GOLDEN GATE PARK, CALIFORNIA AND WILLAPA BAY, WASHINGTON

In 1884 architect John G. Pelton of San Francisco designed a small Queen Anne Style keeper's residence next

New Shoreham Life-Saving Station on Block Island was a Bibb #2-type station in Rhode Island. (Shanks collection)

Hereford Inlet Life-Saving Station in New Jersey was one of the Bibb #2-type stations, all found in the Northeast. (Shanks collection)

A Bibb #2-type station showing the side and front view. Maddaket Life-Saving Station on Massachusetts' Nantucket Island. Note spacious porch. (U.S. Coast Guard)

Long Beach Life-Saving Station, Long Island, New York. Note the easily identifiable residential appearance, boatroom and lookout tower of the Bibb #2-type stations. (U.S. Coast Guard)

Block Island Life-Saving Station, Rhode Island. Crew stands in front of their Bibb #2-type station with unusually low lookout tower. (Robert Downie)

Snow at Pentwater Life-Saving Station on Lake Michigan. This was one of eleven Bibb #3-type stations, a style unique to the Great Lakes. (National Archives)

South Haven Life-Saving Station on Lake Michigan was a Bibb #3-type. This front view shows the steep roof and distinctive lookout tower and boatroom with launchway. Great Lakes stations usually had a marine railway to launch lifeboats. (Shanks collection)

Milwaukee Life-Saving Station was a Bibb #3-type station with "witch's hat" roof-top lookout. Note the storm warning tower at left. (Great Lakes Marine Historical Collection of the Milwaukee Public Library)

Fort Point-type stations were a Pacific Coast type found only in California and Oregon and only built in 1889. Fort Point Life-Saving Station shown on March 23, 1990 which was the last day a USLSS station was in active service as a Coast Guard station on the Pacific Coast. Typical of Fort Point stations, a "witch's hat" boathouse can be seen at right. (Ralph Shanks)

The Fort Point-type boathouse ("witch's hat" boathouse) originated at Fort Point in San Francisco. It was such a successful and pleasing design that it was used at all or nearly all Marquette-style stations as well. Klipsan Beach Life-Saving Station, Washington. (Shanks collection)

to Parkinson's Golden Gate Park Station of 1879. While little is known about Pelton, it is believed this was his only commission for the Service. Built in 1880, the cottage's unusual facade treatment focused on two large semicircular arches, one on either side of a center doorway. One arch over a window to the left was filled in with scallop-edged shingles while the other was open, forming the outer wall of a partially enclosed verandah to the right. Delicate circular cut-out patterns dotted the facade at various places and a scroll-cut railing surrounded the apex of the hipped roof. A residence of this same design was also built at the Willapa Bay Station in Washington. (See pages 190,221, and 224 for photos.)

Bois Blanc Life-Saving Station was a Marquette-type station on Lake Huron. Although two of the Marquette-types stations were found on the East Coast, this design was built primarily on the Great Lakes and Pacific Coast. (U.S. Coast Guard)

South Manitou Island Life-Saving Station on Lake Michigan was a Marquette-style station with three gables, as opposed to Bois Blanc's single gable. Marquette-style stations had freestanding, detached lookout towers and separate Fort Point-style boathouses. (U.S. Coast Guard)

NARRAGANSETT PIER, RHODE ISLAND STATION—ONE-OF-A-KIND

An unusual one-of-a-kind station designed by the well-known New York architectural firm of McKim, Mead and White, was built at Narragansett, Rhode Island, in 1888. Loosely based on a typical English stone lifesaving station, it is one of only two known masonry stations in this country. Its heavily rusticated granite block construction harmonized with the nearby Casino Towers of 1886, which they also designed. (See page 60 for photo.)

Neither Pelz, Pelton, nor McKim, Mead and White worked as Life-Saving Service architects but were instead commissioned for only one or two designs. It is not clear why they were hired for such limited projects but perhaps the areas where these stations were to be built was a factor. Most of the five communities where their designs were built were wealthy summer resorts with lavish and fashionable contemporary architecture. It may have been felt that these stations would be more compatible with their particular surroundings if designed by more well-known architects. Further research is needed to determine what, if any, significance lies in the fact that all three architects were commissioned between the end of Parkinson's term and before that of his successor.

This reasoning behind the building of one-of-a-kind stations also seemed to apply to those designed by Life-Saving Service architects. Most occupied small lots in more populated towns or summer resorts; only a few of these were placed in remote locations.

The Designs of Albert B. Bibb

In 1885 plans were drawn for the repair and alteration of twenty stations on Long Island and nine on Cape Cod, all designed as 1871 Red Houses. The ones on Long Island had been originally constructed in 1871 as replacements for some of the earlier 1849 and 1854 boathouses;

the Cape Cod stations built during 1872 accompanied the extension of the Life-Saving Service to the Massachusetts coast. Due to an increase in maritime traffic along these shores and a corresponding increase in the number of shipwrecks during the early 1880s, the stations were to be enlarged to accommodate additional rescue equipment.

The architect commissioned to design the alterations was Albert Buruley Bibb. Born in 1853 at Washington, D.C., Bibb attended Georgetown College prior to taking a position as a file clerk in the Sixth and Fourth auditors' Offices of the Treasury Department between 1872 and 1876.[36] How and when he became a draftsman for the Service is not known, but by 1885 he was working as architect in its Office of Construction.

Bibb may have begun working with the Service as an Inspector of Stations. A colorful account of a trip to various Great Lake stations written by him in 1882, *The Life-Savers on the Great Lakes*, follows the route of an inspector.[37] Although he does not reveal why or in what capacity the trip was made, it is possible that Bibb was an inspector at the time of its writing. If so, he would have gotten a firsthand exposure to many different station types.

1887-78 ALTERATIONS OF 1871 RED HOUSES

Bibb's 1885 alteration design, which was carried out in 1887 and 1888, called for a complete remodeling of the original 1871-72 stations in a contemporary architectural mode, the Shingle Style. Influenced by the Queen Anne Style that preceded it, the Shingle Style was first popularized on the East Coast by Boston architects William Ralph Emerson and Henry Hobson Richardson. It was inspired by a renewed interest in colonial architecture, particularly the shingle sided houses of coastal towns, and represented a reaction against the structural expressionism of the Stick Style. Instead, the building's frame became totally concealed in an overall covering of wood shingles from roof

Jackson Park Life-Saving Station in Chicago was built as a proud USLSS exhibit at 1893 Chicago World's Colombian Exposition. This heavily modified Quonochontaug-style station was more than an exhibit. It performed actual rescues during the world's fair and later continued to serve as an important life-saving station. (Shanks collection)

Core Bank Life-Saving Station in North Carolina was a classic Quonochontaug-type station. Note small lookout tower which blends into the roof, spacious porch and gable window at left. (U.S. Coast Guard)

Front view of Currituck Beach Life-Saving Station, a fine Quonochontuaug-type station. Surfboat is on boatroom ramp at this busy North Carolina station. (Shanks collection)

to foundation. Wide sweeping roofs with narrow eaves were dominant characteristics as these Shingle Style buildings took on a more horizontal massing. Although the style was popular in summer resorts for fashionable residences, its association with the sea also made it appropriate for life-saving stations. (See page 225 for photo.)

Bibb is noteworthy in that his alteration plan was such a successful statement of the Shingle Style. By adding a storage lean-to on either side of the original boathouse and extending the main roof over each addition in a sweeping unbroken line from peak to eave, Bibb converted what originally had been a vertical structure into a low, horizontally massed building. Rows of long horizontal windows and the application of scallop-shaped and straight-edged shingles over the entire exterior surface completed the transition.

Bibb designed alterations for the enlargements of many other stations as well. Using techniques of adding side lean-tos, extending the roof line, reshingling the exterior and replacing the lookout platform with a hipped cupola, he proved equally successful in turning an elaborate Stick Style station into a convincing Shingle Style building.

In other instances, Bibb's changes more closely reflected the buildings' original detailing as exemplified by his 1887 alteration of the station at Erie, Pennsylvania. His design for a new ell included sheathing, brackets, gable stickwork and doorways similar to that found on the building's original section. Only the lookout and dormer were totally new elements.

Alteration and enlargement of older stations was not a new practice. Almost from the time of construction, changes were made to provide additional space for the crew and rescue equipment. Side lean-tos were frequently added to fill the need. If a lifeboat was required at a station that had up to that time only used a surfboat, a separate boathouse would often be constructed at the water's edge. Cupolas, which gradually replaced the open roof decks on the older station, were usually of the same style as those being used on the latest station design of the period.

Many stations which had been previously enlarged to capacity later proved too small to accommodate the growing demands for more space. In such cases, a new station building would be ordered for the grounds. When the two stood on the same site, often side by side, the earlier building was often used for storage of equipment and an additional surfboat. The *1884 USLSS Annual Report* describes the ongoing process of rebuilding and enlargement:

"The appropriations have been sufficient to permit the rebuilding of two stations on the coast of New Jersey, one at Barnegat City and one at Chadwick's, and also the much-needed repair and improvement of several others.

Twenty-two of these were upon the same coast. They were built at a time when means were limited, and were never as commodious as they should have been. The addition of new apparatus to the station equipment and the employment of another man on each crew, involving the necessity of ampler and more comfortable quarters for the men, made it expedient to enlarge them, and this has been done in each instance of the number specified."[38]

BIBB #2-TYPE STATIONS

The first new design type since Parkinson's 1882 plan was carried out in at least twenty-two stations built on the Atlantic coast, and one on the Gulf Coast, between 1887 and 1892. Referred to as Bibb #2, the plan had a more toned down feeling than previous designs, looking like a cottage residence. (No plans for what would be called a Bibb #1-type station have been found to date.) The steep gable roof contained two hipped dormers while a lookout tower, like those added to Bibb's earlier alterations, topped an intersecting hipped roof. Queen Anne detailing, included clapboarding on the first floor, straight-edged shingles on the gables and roof, small-paned windows, molded four panel exterior doors and turned porch columns. (See page 226 for photo.)

BIBB #3-TYPE STATIONS

Bibb's next design, the Bibb#3-type station, was comprised of a gable dwelling placed parallel to the shore with a semi-detached hipped roof boathouse. (See pages 176 and 227 for photos.) For an unknown reason the dwelling had an open roof deck, while an enclosed lookout tower with a steeply pitched hipped roof and long overhanging eaves sat on top of the boatroom. At least eleven stations of this type were known to have been built on Lake Michigan between 1886 and 1893.

CAPE ELIZABETH, MAINE STATION—
ONE-OF-A-KIND

In 1887 Bibb designed a unique Shingle Style station for Cape Elizabeth, Maine. (See page 18 for photo.) Painted light green with a red roof, a two-and-a-half story lookout tower projected from the station's side. It featured Bibb's characteristic treatments; a mixture of clapboarding and textured shingles, windows with transoms, panel doors and turned porch columns.

CUTTYHUNK ISLAND, MASSACHUSETTS STATION—
ONE-OF-A-KIND

In 1889 Bibb designed another one-of-a-kind Shingle Style station; this one at Cuttyhunk Island, Massachusetts. It looked more like a large summer cottage than a rescue station with three round arched doorways, each with a dormer above, which pierced the first floor facade. A sharply pointed, eight-sided lookout cupola topped a large roof, and the entire building was sheathed in shingles. (See page 62 for photo.).

Duluth Life-Saving Station in Minnesota was the prototype of the Duluth-type stations. The tall rectangular lookout with an almost pagoda-like roof made the 28 Duluth-type stations unmistakable. (U.S. Coast Guard)

Wood End Life-Saving Station on Cape Cod in Massachusetts was a typical Duluth-type station. The Duluth-type station was built only on the East Coast and Great Lakes. Wood End answered many rescue calls during hurricanes and snow storms. (Richard Boonisar)

FORT POINT-TYPE STATIONS

Bibb designed a plan from which three stations on the West Coast were built in 1889. This was an precedent setting design because for what was probably the first time, the station did not contain an integral boathouse. Instead, the functions of housing the crew and rescue equipment became divided into two separate buildings; a dwelling and a boathouse. The plan permitted greater flexibility by allowing each building to be located in the most advantageous spot. The boathouse could be placed at the water's edge while the dwelling was usually set back from the shore on land less susceptible to coastal erosion.

The gambrel roof dwelling featured three large dormers on the front. The center dormer opened on to a balconied roof of a porch over the front door. The one-story, two bay boathouse that accompanied this type was a gothically inspired structure of board and batten siding and a steep hipped roof with long overhanging eaves. A sharply pointed round "witch's hat" cupola ventilator sat on top of the building. This was the Fort Point-type boathouse and it was used both with the Fort Point-type stations and on the Marquette-type stations. (See pages 186, 190, 192, and 228 for photos.)

MARQUETTE-TYPE STATIONS

The Marquette-type, named for the location of the first station built from this plan in 1890, is believed to be Bibb's final work for the Service. Although the original drawings are unsigned, the use of numerous characteristic Bibb details, and the fact that the drawings predate Bibb's successor, suggest his hand. Elements similar to those found on the Cape Elizabeth and Bibb #2 stations included clapboarding on the first floor, decorative shingles on the porch sides and gables, turned porch columns with brackets supporting a shed roof, transom windows and four panel doors. A Fort Point-type boathouse was usually built for Marquette stations. Thirteen stations of this design are known to have been built between 1890 and 1902. (See page 229 for photo.)

Although it has not been determined exactly when Bibb left the Service, it was probably during 1890 as his successor began working the following year. By the time of his departure, the number of stations in operation had grown to 232, but the total number built was actually closer to 335 as over 100 stations had been rebuilt at previously established sites, replacing earlier ones. During the six

Lake View Beach Life-Saving Station at Port Huron, Michigan was the prototype of the Port Huron-type stations. Note the octagonal three-story lookout tower dominating the station facade. Rescue boats were kept in a detached boathouse. (National Archives)

While keeper and surfmen relax in front of Two Rivers Life-Saving in Wisconsin, a lookout stands watch in the octagonal tower. A Port Huron-type station on Lake Michigan. (U.S. Coast Guard)

years of Bibb's employment as architect (considered to be between 1885 and 1890), 80 stations were constructed; 46 at new sites and 32 at old ones, while 112 underwent repairs. Bibb did not design all of these, however. Some stations of Parkinson's designs as well as two other by architects working outside the Service were constructed during these years just as Bibb stations continued to be built after his departure. While future research will most likely reveal additional numbers, it is known that at least twenty-two Bibb #2, ten Bibb #3, three Fort Point-types, thireen Marquette-types and two one-of-a-kind stations

were built from his plans. He also designed alterations for numerous older stations, including the 1885 enlargement of 29 Long Island and Cape Cod 1871 Red House-types.

THE YEARS OF GEORGE R. TOLMAN: 1892-1896

On January 2, 1891, George Russell Tolman succeeded Bibb as Life-Saving Service architect.[39] Born in Boston in 1848, Tolman entered into a partnership with George F. Moffette during the 1870s. Under the name of Moffette and Tolman, this Boston firm designed both residences

The Jersey Pattern was well named since all but two of the stations of this type were built in New Jersey. This design was a variation on the Port Huron plan. Both types had tall octagonal lookout towers, but the Jersey Pattern contained an integral boatroom. Corson Inlet Life-Saving, New Jersey. (U.S. Coast Guard)

Cleveland Life-Saving Station on Lake Erie was a modified Jersey Pattern station. This Ohio station was built on the jetty at the harbor entrance. It was the only Jersey Pattern station with a detached boathouse, seen to the right of the main station-house. (U.S. Coast Guard)

and commercial buildings, including the 1876 Victorian Gothic Charlestown (Massachusetts) Savings Bank, still standing in Thompson Square. Tolman was also skilled as a water-colorist, illustrating in 1877 the Rev. Edward G. Porter's *Rambles in Old Boston, New England.* Prior to taking his position with the Service, Tolman worked for the Treasury Department as draftsman in two short-term jobs. He resigned from the first at the Kittery, Maine, Navy Yard but completed a temporary position in 1889, designing the Marine Barracks for the Norfolk Navy Yard in Virginia. His brother, Albert J. Tolman, also served as draftsman for the Treasury Department working in the Office of Supervising Architect.

QUONOCHONTAUG-TYPE STATION

Tolman began his career with the Life-Saving Service designing a station in 1892 for Quonochontaug at

Charlestown, Rhode Island. At least twenty-one were built from this plan through 1908. Covered entirely with shingles this sparsely detailed one-and-a-half story building featured a single gable roof pierced by a small dormer on each side and a large hipped roof tower at one end. A covered verandah, extending completely along one side and half of the adjacent two sides, was an early addition to many stations of this design. (See page 230 for photo.)

Tolman's plan had a similarity of massing and feeling to the Bibb #2 station which may have been more than coincidental. Except for a 10-foot wide boatroom in Tolman's design, the crew areas in both plans were nearly identical in interior layout and dimensions. The only other real difference besides the larger boatroom of the Quonochontaug station was the addition of a side pantry and vestibule on Bibb's drawing.

Muskegon Life-Saving Station was one of two examples of the rare Racine-type. This handsome Lake Michigan station had a rectangular four-story lookout tower and detached boathouse. This station still stands at the Muskegon, Michigan harbor entrance. (Shanks collection)

A modified plan of the Quonochontaug station was included in the Government exhibit at the Chicago World's Columbian Exposition of 1893. Planned in recognition of the four hundredth anniversary of the discovery of America by Columbus, the "White City" that arose on the fairgrounds was composed of classically inspired monumental structures. The exhibition of the latest lifesaving station at the fair symbolized the public recognition which the Service sought. The station proved to be a popular attraction particularly for foreigners interested in the methods of the most extensive and only government supported lifesaving system in the world.[40] The *1893 Annual Report* proudly noted its appeal:

"The station which Congress in the act authorizing the World's Columbian Exposition directed to be placed on exhibition on grounds to be allotted for the purpose, fully equipped with the apparatus, furniture, and appliances used in the Life-Saving Service, and subsequently provided should be continued as a permanent station, was duly established, equipped, manned, and during the fair was visited by extraordinary numbers of our own citizens and foreigners, and examined with marked interest by the representative kindred institutions of other countries. The triweekly drills illustrating the methods of rescue were a special attraction, and never failed to gather upon the lake shore enormous crowds of interested spectators. While thus satisfactorily serving its original purpose, it had opportunity also, on several occasions, to prove its practical utility by effecting rescues from actual shipwrecks which occurred within the scope of its operations."[41]

The Exposition station was named the Jackson Park Life-Saving Station, and Tolman altered the basic Quonochontaug plan by adding a cross gable roof and replacing the first floor shingles with clapboards, which gave the station a look similar to Bibb's #2 design. The station was also enlarged with the addition of a third bay to the boatroom. More elaborately ornamented than others of its type, a back portico and a roof balustrade containing the inscription "U.S. Life-Saving Station" were a few of the more noticeable changes.[42]

The Southern Pattern was used only at four North Carolina stations, including Fort Macon Life-Saving Station, shown here. Note verandah, dormer windows and stocky lookout tower of the Southern Pattern. (North Carolina Department of Cultural Resources)

Chicamacomico-type stations were constructed only in North Carolina from 1911-13. Poyners Hill Life-Saving Station, North Carolina. (U.S. Coast Guard)

NIAGARA-TYPE STATIONS

Tolman's next design was carried out in at least two stations: Niagara, New York (1893) and Cape Disappointment, Washington (1897). It featured a long wrap around porch as used on his Quonochontaug design, a gable roof with a clip at each end, dormer on the roof and back with sided clapboards on the first floor and shingle on the second floor. These stations had detached lookout towers.

DULUTH-TYPE STATIONS

In 1893 Tolman designed a second station referred to as the Duluth-type. Like his first plan, most Duluth stations had an overall covering of shingles, although clapboards were occasionally applied at the first floor level. However, the design reflected more a mixture of styles and shapes, combining the massing of the Shingle Style with the Colonial Revival detailing.

By the 1890s the Colonial Revival Style was beginning to gain greater acceptance. Reflecting a desire to revive the classical feeling of Georgian and Federal Style buildings, the style employed such elements as porticoes, frontpiece entrances, Palladian and fanlight windows and large gambrel roofs. Often, the colonial features were oversized or exaggerated out of proportion with other parts of the structure. (See page 232 for photo.)

The rectangular plan of the first floor of the Duluth-type was divided into two sections with an interior layout similar to that of the Quonochontaug and Bibb #2-type stations. To one side of the building a large gable roof, clipped at both ends, topped a keeper's room, office, kitchen and mess room with sleeping quarters above. A one-story, two bay boatroom occupied the other side. Rising between the building's two sections along the front was a four-story, hipped roof lookout tower with its top floor cantilevered in stockade-like fashion. A series of different sized, small paned sashes and a semicircular fanlight window in the boatroom gable added Colonial Re-

vival detailing. At least twenty-eight stations of this type were built between 1894 and 1908.

GAY HEAD, MASSACHUSETTS STATION— ONE-OF-A-KIND

Tolman drew a unique design for a station at Gay Head on Martha's Vineyard, Massachusetts, which shared many features of the Duluth plan. (See page 62 for photo.) Slightly changing his earlier drawing, Tolman created a flush facade by relocating the front porch to the rear, and pushing the tower back into the front wall, shortening it one-story in the process. Clipped at both ends, the long sweeping gable roof extended down to the first floor on the front and out over the porch to the rear. The boatroom was removed entirely and placed in a separate building. Perched high above the ocean on a cliff, the structure appeared as one of the most striking Shingle Style stations built.

On July 16, 1896, Tolman was dismissed from the Service over a personal matter. In a letter to his lawyer, Tolman stated he had been relieved of his position for taking a sudden and unapproved leave of absence to escape a warrant for his recommitment to jail.[43] Unfortunately, nothing in his personnel file explains why he was jailed.

Tolman's letter gives an insight into the workings of his office which helps to clear up some of the confusion surrounding where stations were designed. The 1884 and 1896 *Revised Regulations of the U.S. Life-Saving Service* states that one job of Superintendents of Construction was to prepare plans and specifications. As Superintendents were officers of the Revenue Marine Bureau, this suggested that stations would have been designed at the Bureau's headquarters in New York City, rather than at the Treasury Department in Washington, where the Life-Saving Service was located. In practice, however, the position of Superintendent involved supervising the construc-

Rockaway Point Life-Saving Station at the entrance to New York harbor was a Lorain-type station. It featured Colonial Revival architecture, an enclosed porch and a square three-story lookout tower. (U.S. Coast Guard)

Cook and surfman take a break at Wachapreague Life-Saving Station, a Lorain-type station in Virginia. (National Archives)

Lorain Life-Saving Station in Ohio was the 1910 prototype of the Lorain class of stations. Lorain was an important Lake Erie port. (Shanks collection)

Tiana Life-Saving Station on Long Island, New York, among the wind-blown dunes and beach grass. This rear perspective of the Lorain-type station shows the five hipped roof dormer windows. (U.S. Coast Guard)

tion of stations, not designing them.

Tolman served during a period when many of the older stations needed replacement rather than repair. Although his six-and-one-half year term was shorter than that of any other architect, fifty-four of his stations are known to have been built. If he had stayed longer, Tolman's influence on Service architecture would perhaps have been even greater than that left by his Quonochontaug, Niagara, Duluth and Gay Head stations. Nevertheless, the honor of designing a building for the World's Columbian Exposition was an accomplishment few architects of Tolman's day could claim.

Victor Mendleheff: Last Life-Saving Service Architect

Tolman was succeeded by Victor Mendleheff. Unfortunately virtually nothing has been found on Mendleheff's background prior to joining the Service. His personnel records are missing from Treasury Department files and

no references to his works are known to have appeared in any architectural or biographical publications. While in the Service, however, he was the most prolific of all its architects, staying the longest and producing the most designs.

PETERSONS POINT-TYPE STATIONS

Mendleheff's early work involved the drawing of two types and four one-of-a-kind stations, all of which shared similar design themes. Probably the first of these plans was carried out for a station at Petersons Point (Grays Harbor) in Washington (1897), and at Tillamook Bay in Oregon (1908). (See pages 199 and 201 for photos.) These two-story Colonial Revival dwellings employed many of the classical elements which Mendleheff used throughout his early designs; a Tuscan columned entry, six-over-two double hung windows, a fanlight window with a keystone in each gable, an octagonal high peaked lookout tower and chimneys with flared tops. One of only a few known gambrel roof stations, it featured a well-balanced

Green Hill Life-Saving Station in Rhode Island was one of only three Isles of Shoals-type stations, both built in New England. Architect Victor Mendleheff simply took his Port Huron plan and replaced the octagonal tower with the square one show here. (U.S. Coast Guard)

facade. On the first story a paneled doorway opening to a covered porch was flanked on either side by a double hung window. Above, two shed roof dormers straddled a three-sided section of a shortened octagonal tower. The fenestration at one end reflected that of the other; two stories of equally spaced six-over-two double hung sashes beneath a peak fanlight.

PORT HURON-TYPE STATIONS

The Port Huron-type, named for the Michigan location of the first station of its design (Lake View Beach Station), incorporated some of the Petersons Point details in a reworked treatment. Classically inspired, a massive octagonal three-story tower projecting from the center of the facade dominated the station. A two-story bay window, closely resembling a five sided section of the tower, was built on the rear, while another similarly shaped one-story bay window was found to one side. Tuscan columns supported a covered porch on the tower's left side and a front portico to the right, both with a hipped dormer above. All windows were double hung six-over-two

sashes except for the two gable end fanlights and the large single panes in each of the tower's eight lookouts. Nine of these Colonial Revival stations, all entirely shingled, are known to have been constructed between 1898 and 1908. (See page 235 for photo.)

Mendleheff altered slightly the massing and changed the placement of a few key elements of the Port Huron plan to create his design for the 1898 station at Damariscove Island, Maine. In this case, he lengthened the facade with the addition of an integral boatroom while changing the gable roof to a long hip and added a side columned entrance porch.

A design for the 1899 station at Point Bonita, California reworked the Port Huron theme in a slightly different way. The dwelling featured the same single gable roof with hipped dormers. The porch to the left of the tower was filled in and a new entry in a one-story, hipped roof forward projecting ell replaced the portico on the right. A balconied porch added a second entrance on the left side

Bodie Island Life-Saving Station, an 1876-type station in North Carolina. This historic station is now a part of Cape Hatteras National Seashore. (Outer Banks History Center)

Creeds Hill Life-Saving Station in North Carolina was representative of most Chatham-style stations in that it had a detached lookout tower rather than rooftop top cupola. (U.S. Coast Guard)

Victor Mendleheff's most widely used plans were his Chatham-type stations. These stations were built beginning in 1914 and the Coast Guard constructed stations at least through 1929 using this design. Chatham stations were built on both coasts and on the Great Lakes. Chatham Life-Saving Station, Massachusetts, the prototype for the design. (U.S. Coast Guard)

Siuslaw River Life-Saving Station at Florence, Oregon was a Chatham-type station. In later years its cupola was removed. Siuslaw River was built by the Coast Guard using Life-Saving Service plans drawn by Victor Mendleheff. (U.S. Coast Guard)

Hatteras Inlet Life-Saving Station in North Carolina was one of the few Chatham-type stations with a rooftop cupola lookout. This station was destroyed by sea encroachment. (Cape Hatteras National Seashore)

Point Reyes Lifeboat Station was unusual among Chatham-type stations because it featured an interior boatroom. Even when modified, the Chatham plan was barely large enough to accommodate 36-foot motor lifeboats. Note the Class H motor lifeboat on the launchway. This station is preserved at Point Reyes National Seashore complete with 36-foot motor lifeboat Number 36542 in the boatroom. (Point Reyes National Seashore)

of the facade while the rear bay window became shortened from two stories to one. (See page 195 for photo.)

JERSEY PATTERN STATIONS

The Jersey Pattern of 1898, another variation of the Port Huron design, was carried out in nine stations built along the New Jersey coast and one at Hampton Beach, New Hampshire, during the following two years. Like the Damariscove Island plan, the Jersey Pattern also contained

an integral hipped roof boatroom to the right of the tower. The covered porch found on the left side of the Port Huron's facade was shortened for the Jersey Pattern and extended forward under a newly added gable roof. The Port Huron's side and rear bay windows were left off the plan. (See pages 102-103 and 234 for photos.)

The 1900 Cleveland, Ohio station appeared to be a shorter modification of the Jersey Pattern. With a detached hipped roof boatroom, separated from the dwelling, the gable roof over the front porch of the Jersey Pattern was, in this case, moved around to the rear of the building.

NAHANT, MASSACHUSETTS STATION— ONE-OF-A-KIND

Although it is not known who designed the station at Nahant, Massachusetts, it was probably the work of Mendleheff. With a tower different in shape and placement from that used on the Port Huron-type and Jersey Pattern, the Nahant Station nevertheless employed many of Mendleheff's familiar elements in a new manner. At the center of the balanced facade was a two bay boatroom flanked on either side by a covered entry porch. A long hipped roof, broken in the center by a steep intersecting cross gable over the boatroom, contained six hipped dormers. Nearly all windows were six-over-two double hung sashes. Only the semi-detached square tower, rising four stories at one end, differed significantly from other characteristic Mendleheff treatments. (See page 62 for photo.) Constructed in 1899, the original plans called for the establishment of another station of this design at Gloucester, Massachusetts. However, a Tolman designed Duluth station was built there the following year.

OLD CHICAGO-TYPE STATIONS

The 1903 Old Chicago Station appears also to be the work of Mendleheff. This rambling Shingle Style structure with Colonial Revival detailing featured a long hipped roof terminated by a broad cross gable at one end and a hipped four-story tower at the other. Typical Mendleheff details included wide hipped dormers, six-over-two sashes and an overall covering of shingles.

Like many early stations, the original one at Chicago was no longer adequate for the needs of such an important port. The station's history of numerous changes was not uncommon: "The station which is to be replaced at Chicago was originally a boathouse only, which was afterwards converted into a temporary life-saving station, to be used until a proper location could be secured and a new building erected. Plans and specifications for the new building have been completed, and proposals are about to be invited."[44]

A second station of this type, but slightly smaller than the one at Chicago, was built in Buffalo, New York during the same year. (See page 180 for photos of both stations.)

RACINE-TYPE STATIONS

Mendleheff's next plan was carried out in at least two stations built on Lake Michigan between 1903 and 1905. A four-story square hipped tower, similar to that found on the Nahant and Old Chicago Stations, rises from the center of the Racine-type, projecting forward from the facade

for half of its width. Two shed dormers on the single gable roof straddle the tower. Like all of Mendleheff's other stations, the buildings were totally sheathed with shingles. (See page 182 and 235 for photos.)

SOUTHERN PATTERN STATIONS

Mendleheff introduced some new design ideas for four North Carolina stations carried out in the Bungalow Style. Popular from the turn of the century until the 1940s, bungalows were typically simple one-story houses covered entirely with unpainted shingles. Many featured a low, gently pitched broad gabled roof with rafters, ridge beams and purlins extending beyond the walls and roof. Like other simple but functional houses, the Bungalow was often modified for its particular location.

The Southern Pattern station appeared markedly different from much of Mendleheff's earlier work. Attached to one side of this square one-story shingled dwelling was his characteristic three-story hipped tower. But what distinguished this plan from others was its adaptation for the warm climate of the southern Atlantic beaches. The hipped roofs over the station, tower and four dormers all had long overhanging eaves to shade the sun while a verandah surrounded the quarters of the building. (See page 235 for photo.)

JACKSON PARK, ILLINOIS STATION— ONE-OF-A-KIND

Another unique Mendleheff design constructed at Chicago's Jackson Park during 1908 replaced the Columbian Exposition station of 1893. Larger than any of his previous buildings, the plan reworked many familiar details into a rambling Shingle Style structure. The low pitch of its long hipped roof and the wide overhanging eaves of the short tower, along with dormers borrowed from the Southern Pattern, all combined to give this one-and-a-half story station a horizontal massing typical of its style. (See page 180 for photo.)

CHICAMACOMICO-TYPE STATIONS

Mendleheff's 1910 plan for a station at Chicamacomico, North Carolina, was reminiscent of the Quonochontaug-type. Windows of similar size and shape, paneled exterior doors, a complete covering of shingles and, most noticeably, a nearly identical lookout tower suggest the strong influence of Tolman's earlier design. Only the front portico and double dormer on one side appear as new ideas. Three other stations of this type are known to have been built during the following three years, all in North Carolina. (See page 236 for photo.)

LORAIN-TYPE STATIONS

In a treatment similar to that given the Port Huron theme, Mendleheff varied a Colonial Revival plan in a few slightly different configurations. The simplest of these designs was drawn in 1910 for a station at Lorain, Ohio. It featured a tower at one end of the facade like that used on the Southern Pattern beside two hipped roof center dormers. An enclosed entry porch, closely resembling that of the Petersons Point Station, extended across three quarters of the front and around part of one side. A similar shorter porch was found to the rear. In a plan of the same year for Wachapreague, Virginia, Mendleheff balanced the facade more evenly by adding a boatroom to the left. In this case he also moved the front porch to the right side and placed the tower in the facade's center. At least eleven stations of this type are known to have been built. (See page 237 for photo.)

ISLES OF SHOALS-TYPE STATIONS

Elements of both the Southern Pattern and the Port Huron-type were combined for three stations; one built in 1910 at Isles of Shoals in Maine, one built at Green Hill, Rhode Island the following year and one constructed at Peaked Hill Bars, Cape Cod, Massachusetts. (The Peaked Hill Bars structure replaced an earlier red house-type structure.) From the basic Port Huron plan, Mendleheff simply removed the octagon tower and replaced it with one from the Lorain-type, flush with the facade. (See page 27 for photo.)

Like his predecessors, Mendleheff also designed modifications to earlier stations. One example was drawn in 1912 for the repair and alteration of the 1876-type, Cranberry Island Station in Maine. Improvements included the replacement of the original lookout deck with a four-story front tower, the addition of a dormer on one side of the roof and a new foundation. (See page 22 for photo.)

GULF-TYPE STATIONS

Mendleheff drew a plan for at least six stations built along the Gulf Coast in Texas and Louisiana between 1903 and 1923. These low one-story buildings were surrounded by a verandah on all four sides and were built on stilts so that hurricanes and flood waters could pass underneath them. The roofs were gable-on-hip, and a hipped-roof cupola with a lightning rod projected from the apex of the peak. (See pages 156 and 160 for photos.)

CHATHAM-TYPE STATIONS

The last design believed to be drawn for the Life-Saving Service is probably Mendleheff's work as well. The distinctive elements of this two-story, five bay plainly detailed dwelling included the same roof and cupola design found on many of his Gulf-type station designs, with six-over-two window sashes, and either a Tuscan Style columned portico or a three bay entrance porch. The first of the twenty-six known stations of this type was built in 1914 at Chatham, Massachusetts.

A modified Chatham-type station was built at Point Reyes, California, in 1927. It featured a two bay boatroom at one end of the first floor. A marine railway led from the boatroom to the Pacific for launching. (See page 239 for photo.)

The Organic Act: Transition from the Life-Saving Service to the Coast Guard

On January 28, 1915, Congress passed the Organic Act joining the Life-Saving Service with the Revenue Cutter Service to form the United States Coast Guard. A total of 279 stations were active, an all time high (some lists show up to 285 stations during earlier years but this number included discontinued and inactive stations).

Although the length of Mendleheff's term as architect is not known, it is believed he was not replaced by another designer during the transition period. Chatham stations continued to be built at least until 1929 and few new design types are known to have been produced by Coast Guard architects until the end of the 1920s. In fact, much of the work between 1915 and the late 1920s constituted repairs to existing stations rather than the designing of new ones.

Soon after the creation of the Coast Guard in 1915, consolidation of operations began to take place due to changes in shipping, navigation and rescue techniques. Commercial sailing ships were gradually replaced by motorized vessels and improvements in navigational aids greatly reduced the dangers of coastal shipping. With the advent of radio, a more reliable communication system was developed which could warn of hazardous weather conditions and help to determine more accurately a ship's position.

It was the change from rescue boats powered entirely by oars and sails to motorized lifeboats which had the most far-reaching effect on the need for fewer stations. Motor lifeboats allowed crews to cover a much larger area and equally important, "the power boat places the men at the scene of their labors physically fit to meet the demand likely to be made upon their endurance and skill."[45] Gradually, many of the remote outposts, especially on the East Coast, were deactivated as the need for a closely-knit network of rescue stations declined.

Today, at least 115 of the old life-saving stations still stand. They are monuments of a great maritime saga. They must be preserved and their history made known to all.

STATIONS OF THE U.S. LIFE-SAVING SERVICE

There were 279 active stations at the height of the Life-Saving Service in 1914. While several *USLSS Annual Reports* list up to 285 stations that figure includes inactive and discontinued stations. Some stations did have more than one station-house (main station building) during their career. Of all these structures, only about 115 are known to survive today. The toll has been high among our historic and beautiful life-saving stations.

In the following pages, Wick York provides us with a classification of life-saving stations by architectural type and construction date. The lists are probably not exhaustive and there may be other representatives of the various classes as yet unknown to the authors. He has listed stations geographically, usually from north to south and east to west. The specific locations of stations can be found in the state chapters.

The notation * indicates station still standing. A question mark indicates station reported standing but status unverified or possibly changed. Undoubtedly, additional stations remain.

U. S. LIFE-SAVING STATION DESIGN TYPES

Station Type	Construction Period	Location
1848-type	1848-49	NJ
1849-type	1849	NY, NJ
1850-type	1850	RI, NY
1855-type	1855	NY, NJ
1871 Red House-type	1871-73	MA, NY, NJ
1874-type	1874-75	ME, NH, MA, RI, VA, NC
1875-type	1875-79	RI, NY, NJ, DE, WA, OR, Lakes Ontario, Erie, Michigan, Huron
1875 Clipped Gable-type	1875-76	Lakes Ontario, Erie, Michigan
Houses of Refuge	1875-85	FL
1876-type	1875-81	ME, MA, RI, NY, NJ, DE, MD, VA, NC
1876 Lake Superior-type	1876	Lake Superior
1879-type	1879	Lakes Michigan and Huron
1880-type	1882-88	TX
1882-type	1882-94	ME, MA, NY, NJ, DE, MD, VA, NC, FL
Deal-type	1882-85	RI, NJ
Bibb #2-type	1886-92	NH, MA, RI, NY, NJ
Bibb #3-type	1885-93	Lake Michigan
Fort Point-type	1889	CA, OR
Marquette-type	1890-1905	ME, NC, CA, OR, WA, Lakes Superior, Michigan
Quonochontaug-type	1891-1908	MA, RI, NY, NJ, MD, VA, NC, FL, Lake Michigan
Niagara-type	1893-97	NY, WA
Duluth-type	1894-1908	ME, NH, MA, NY NJ, VA, NC, Lakes Superior, Michigan
Petersons Point-type	1898-1908	WA, OR
Port Huron-type	1898-1908	ME, RI, NY, NJ, CA, Lake Michigan
Jersey Pattern	1898-99	NH, NJ
Old Chicago-type	1903	Lakes Michigan, Ontario
Racine-type	1903-05	Lake Michigan
Southern Pattern	1904	NC
Chicamacomico-type	1911-13	NC
Lorain-type	1910-13	NY, VA, Lakes Erie, Superior
Isle of Shoals-type	1910-12	NH, RI
Gulf-type	1903-28	TX, LA
Chatham-type	1914-33 ?	ME, MA, NY, VA, NC, CA, OR, Lakes Ontario, Erie, Michigan, Superior
One of-a-Kind Designs	1887-1916	ME, NH, MA, RI, NJ, TX, CA, WA, Lakes Ontario, Erie, Huron, Michigan

STATION LISTS
THE 1840-50 EARLY STYLE STATIONS

1848-Type
Number of Stations: 8
Architect: Unknown
Plans Drawn: 1848

Built	Station
1848-49	Spermaceti Cove, NJ *
1848-49	Monmouth Beach, NJ
1848-49	Deal, NJ
1848-49	Spring Lake (Wreck Pond), NJ
1848-49	Chadwick, NJ
1849-49	Island Beach, NJ
1848-49	Harvey Cedars, NJ
1848-49	Bonds, NJ

1849-Type
Number of Stations: 16
Architect: Unknown
Plans Drawn: 1848 or 1849

1849	Fishers Island ?, NY
1849	Amagansett, NY
1849	Mecox (Bridgehampton), NY
1849	Quoque, NY
1849	Moriches, NY
1849	Bellport, NY
1849	Fire Island, NY
1849	Pt. Lookout (Long Beach, east end), NY
1849	Barren Island, NY
1849	Eatons Neck, NY
1849	Brigantine, NJ
1849	Atlantic City ?, NJ
1849	Great Egg, NJ
1849	Townsend Inlet, NJ
1849	Hereford Inlet, NJ
1849	Cape May, NJ

1850-Type
Number of Stations: 4
Architect: Unknown
Plans Drawn: 1850 ?

1850	Watch Hill, RI
1850	Southampton, NY
1850	Gilgo (Oak Island, west end), NY
1850	Coney Island, NY

1855-Type
Number of Stations: 28
Architect: Unknown
Plans Drawn: 1854 ?

1855	Montauk, NY
1855	Ditch Plain, NY
1855	Napeague, NY
1855	Georgica, NY
1855	Shinnecock, NY
1855	Potunk (Petunk), NY
1855	Smiths Point, NY
1855	Blue Point, NY
1855	Lone Hill, NY
1855	Point of Woods, NY
1855	Oak Island, NY
1855	Jones Beach, NY
1855	Rockaway Point, NY
1855	Sheepshead Bay, NY
1855	Sandy Hook, NJ
1855	Long Branch, NJ
1855	Squan Beach, NJ
1855	Toms River, NJ
1855	Forked River, NJ
1855	Barnegat, NJ
1855	Ship Bottom, NJ
1855	Little Egg, NJ
1855	Absecon ?, NJ
1855	Great Egg, NJ
1855	Corson's Inlet, NJ
1855	Stone Harbor (Tathams), NJ
1855	Holly Beach (Turtle Gut), NJ
1855	Cold Spring, NJ

1870-1880 STYLE STATIONS

1871 Red Houses
Number of Stations: 71
Architect: Unknown
Plans Drawn: 1871

1872-73	Race Point, MA
1872-73	Peaked Hill Bars, MA
1872-73	Highland, MA
1872-73	Pamet River, MA *
1872-73	Cahoons Hollow, MA
1872-73	Nauset, MA
1872-73	Orleans, MA
1872-73	Chatham, MA
1872-73	Monomoy, MA
1872-73	Block Island, RI
1871	Hither Plain, NY
1872 ?	Shinnecock, NY
1871	Tiana (Tyana), NY
1872 ?	Quoque ?, NY
1872 ?	Potunk (Petunk), NY
1872 ?	Moriches ?, NY
1871	Forge River, NY
1872	Smiths Point, NY
1872	Bellport, NY
1872	Blue Point, NY
1872	Lone Hill, NY *
1872	Point of Woods, NY
1872	Fire Island, NY
1872	Oak Island, NY *
1872	Gilgo (Oak Island, west end), NY
1871	Jones Beach, NY
1872	Zacks Inlet (Jones Beach, west end), NY
1871	Meadow Island, NY
1872	Point Lookout (Long Beach, east end), NY *

1872	Long Beach, west end, NY
1871	Far Rockaway (Hog Island, west end), NY
1872	Rockaway, NY
1872	Rockaway Point, NY
1872	Sandy Hook, NJ
1872	Spermaceti Cove, NJ
1872	Seabright, NJ
1872	Monmouth Beach, NJ
1872	Deal, NJ * ?
1871	Shark River, NJ
1872	Spring Lake (Wreck Pond), NJ
1872	Squan Beach, NJ
1872	Bayhead (Point Pleasant), NJ
1871	Mantoloking (Swan Point), NJ
1872	Chadwick, NJ
1872	Toms River, NJ
1872	Island Beach, NJ
1872	Cedar Creek, NJ
1871	Forked River, NJ
1872	South end, Island Beach, NJ
1872	Barnegat, NJ
1871	Loveladies Island, NJ *
1872	Harvey Cedars, NJ *
1872	Ship Bottom, NJ
1871	Long Beach, NJ
1872	Bonds, NJ
1872	Little Egg, NJ
1871	Little Beach, NJ
1872	Brigantine, NJ
1871	South Brigantine, NJ
1872	Atlantic City, NJ
1871	Absecon, NJ
1871	Great Egg, NJ *
1872	Ocean City (Beazleys), NJ
1871	Pecks Beach, NJ
1872	Corson's Inlet, NJ
1871	Sea Isle City (Ludlam's Beach), NJ
1872	Townsend Inlet, NJ
1872	Stone Harbor (Tathams), NJ
1872	Hereford Inlet, NJ
1871	Holly Beach (Turtle Gut), NJ
1872	Two Mile Beach, NJ

1874-Type
Number of Stations: 25
Architect: Unknown
Plans Drawn: 1873

1873-4	Quoddy Head, ME
1874	Cross Island, ME *
1874	Browney's Island, ME
1873-74	White Head, ME *
1873-74	Fletchers Neck (Biddeford Pool), ME *
1874	Rye Beach, NH *
1873-7	Plum Island, MA *
1874	Straitsmouth (Davis Neck), MA
1873-7	Gurnet, MA

1873-74	Manomet Point, MA *
1873-74	Surfside, MA *
1874	New Shoreham, RI *
1875-76	Green Run Inlet, MD
1875	Assateague Beach, VA
1875	Smith Island, VA
1874	Cape Henry, VA
1874	Dam Neck Mills, VA
1874	False Cape, VA
1874	Currituck Beach (Jones Hill), NC
1874	Caffeys Inlet, NC
1874	Kitty Hawk, NC *
1874	Nags Head, NC
1874	Oregon Inlet, NC
1874	Chicamacomico, NC *
1873-74	Little Kinnakeet, NC *

1875-Type
Number of Stations: 20
Architect: Francis W. Chandler
Plans Drawn: 1875

1876	Point Judith, RI
1877	Mecox, NY
1876	Eatons Neck, NY
1875-76	Big Sandy, NY
1878-79	Long Branch, NJ *
1878-79	Spring Lake (Wreck Pond), NJ
1876	Cape Henlopen, DE
1876	Indian River Inlet, DE *
1875-76	Erie (Presque Isle), PA
1875-76	Pointe aux Barques, MI *
1875-76	Tawas (Ottawa Point), MI *
1875-76	Sturgeon Point, MI
1875-76	Thunder Bay Island, MI
1875-76	Hammond (40-Mile Point), MI *
1875-76	Point Betsie (Point au Bec Scie), MI
1875-76	Grande Pointe au Sable, MI

1875-Type, Modified Design

1877	Willapa Bay (Shoalwater Bay), WA
1877	Neah Bay, WA
1878	Cape Arago (Coos Bay), OR
1878	Humboldt Bay, CA ?

1875-Type with Clipped Gable
Number of Stations: 11
Architect: Francis W. Chandler
Plans Drawn: 1875

1875-76	Oswego, NY
1875-76	Charlotte, NY
1875-76	Fairport, OH
1875-76	Cleveland, OH
1875-77	Marblehead, OH
1875-76	Beaver Island, MI *
1875-76	North Manitou Island, MI *
1875-77	Grand Haven, MI
1875-76	Saint Joseph, MI
1875-76	Two Rivers, WI
1877	Milwaukee, WI

Houses of Refuge
Number of Houses of Refuge: 10
Architect: Francis W. Chandler
Plans Drawn: 1875

1885	Bulow (Smiths Creek), FL
1885	Mosquito Lagoon, FL
1885	Chester Shoal, FL
1885	Cape Malabar, FL
1882-83	Bethel Creek (Indian River), FL
1885	Indian River Inlet, FL
1875-76	Gilbert's Bar, FL *
1875-76	Orange Grove, FL
1875-76	Fort Lauderdale, FL
1875-76	Biscayne Bay, FL

1876-Type
Number of Stations: 27
Architect: J. Lake Parkinson
Plans Drawn: 1875

1878	Cranberry Islands, ME *
1879	Fourth Cliff, MA
1879	Watch Hill, RI
1880-81	Amagansett, NY *
1878	Southampton, NY *
1878-79	Short Beach, NY
1880	Seabright, NJ *
1883-84	Lewes, DE
1878	Rehoboth Beach, DE *
1878	Ocean City, MD
1878	Popes Island, VA
1875	Hog Island, VA
1875	Cobb Island, VA
1878-79	Seatack (Virginia Beach), VA
1878-79	Little Island, VA
1878	Wash Woods (Deal's Island), NC
1878	Penneys Hill (Currituck Inlet), NC
1878	Poyners Hill, NC *
1878	Paul Gamiels Hill, NC
1878	Kill Devil Hills, NC *
1878-79	Bodie Island, NC *
1878-79	Pea Island, NC
1878	Gull Shoal (Cedar Hummock), NC
1878-79	Big Kinnakeet, NC
1878-79	Creeds Hill, NC
1878-79	Durants (Hatteras), NC *

1876-Type Modified Design

1876	Cape May, NJ (Philadelphia Centennial Station)
1877-78	Golden Gate Park, CA *

1876 Lake Superior-Type
Number of Stations: 4
Architect: J. Lake Parkinson
Plans Drawn: 1876

1876	Vermilion Point, MI *
1876	Crisps, MI
1876	Two Heart River, MI
1876	Deer Park, MI

1879-Type
Number of Stations: 5
Architect: J. Lake Parkinson
Plans Drawn: 1879

1881	Middle Island, MI
1881	Port Austin, MI *
1881	Harbor Beach, MI
1879	Ludington, MI
1879	Muskegon, MI

1880-Type
Number of Stations: 5
Architect: J. Lake Parkinson
Plans Drawn: 1879-80 ?

1882-83	Brazos, TX
1882-83	San Luis, TX
1887-88	Velasco, TX
1882-83	Saluria, TX
1882-83	Aransas, TX

1882-Type
Number of Stations: 26
Architect: J. Lake Parkinson
Plans Drawn: 1882 ?

1883	Hunniwells Beach, ME *
1882	High Head, MA
1883	Coskata, MA
1883	Muskeget, MA
1885	Ditch Plain, NY
1886	Georgica, NY
1884	Chadwick, NJ
1883-84	Barnegat, NJ
1883	South Brigantine, NJ
1885-86	Ocean City, NJ *
1883-84	Lewes, DE
1891	Fenwick Island, DE
1891	Ocean City, MD *
1883-84	North Beach, MD
1883-84	Wallops Beach, VA
1888-89	Metomkin Inlet, VA
1883-84	Parramore Beach, VA
1894	Smith Island, VA
1882	Cape Hatteras, NC
1882-83	Ocracoke, NC
1887	Cape Lookout, NC *
1881-92	Cape Fear, NC
1888-89	Oak Island, NC *
1884-85	Morris Island, SC
1885	Jupiter Inlet, FL
1885	Santa Rosa, FL

STATION-HOUSE STYLE STATIONS

Deal-Type
Number of Stations: 4
Architect: Paul J. Pelz
Plans Drawn: 1882

1884	Brenton Point, RI
1882-83	Deal, NJ
1884-85	Bayhead, NJ
1884	Atlantic City, NJ

Bibb #2-Type
Number of Stations: 22
Architect: Albert B. Bibb
Plans Drawn: 1886 ?

1887	Jerrys Point, NH
1889	Wallis Sands, NH
1890	Rye Beach, NH *
?	Newburyport (Plum Island), MA
1890-91	Plum Island (Knobbs Beach), MA
1887	North Scituate, MA *
1890	Point Allerton, MA *
1892	Gurnet, MA *
1890	Maddaket, MA
1888	Point Judith, RI
1888	New Shoreham, RI
1886	Block Island, RI *
1888-89	Napeague, NY
1890-91	Sandy Hook, NJ
1891	Seabright, NJ *
1886-87	Shark River, NJ
1887-88	Bonds, NJ *
1888	Great Egg, NJ
1888	Sea Isle City, NJ *
1886-87	Townsend Inlet, NJ *
1888-89	Hereford Inlet, NJ
1890-91	Cold Spring, NJ * ?

Bibb #3-Type
Number of Stations: 11
Architect: Albert B. Bibb
Plans Drawn: 1885 ?

1886-87	Frankfort, MI *
1886-87	Pentwater, MI
1886-87	White River, MI *
1885-86	Holland, MI
1887	South Haven, MI
1888-89	Michigan City, IN *
1888-89	South Chicago, IL
18??	Milwaukee, WI
1889	Sheboygan, WI *
1893	Kewaunee, WI *
1885	Sturgeon Bay Canal, WI *

1887-88 Alterations of 1871 Red Houses
(Note: This was an expansion of the existing red house structures. For original construction dates see 1871 Red House listing.)
Number of Stations: 29
Architect: Albert B. Bibb
Plans Drawn: 1885

1888	Race Point, MA
1888	Peaked Hill Bars, MA
1888	Pamet River, MA *
1888	Highland, MA
1888	Cahoons Hollow, MA
1888	Nauset, MA
1888	Orleans, MA
1888	Chatham, MA
1888	Monomoy, MA
1887	Hither Plain, NY

1887	Shinnecock, NY
1887	Tiana, NY *
1887	Quogue, NY *
1887	Potunk, NY
1887	Moriches, NY
1887	Forge River, NY
1887	Smiths Point, NY
1887	Bellport, NY
1887	Blue Point, NY
1887	Lone Hill, NY *
1887	Point of Woods, NY
1887	Fire Island, NY
1887	Oak Island, NY *
1887	Gilgo, NY
1887	Jones Beach, NY
1887	Zacks Inlet, NY
1887	Point Lookout, NY *
1887	Rockaway, NY
1887	Rockaway Point, NY

Fort Point-Type
Number of Stations: 3
Architect: Albert B. Bibb
Plans Drawn: 1889 ?

1889	Point Adams, OR (Boathouse only stands)
1889	Point Reyes, CA
1889	Fort Point, CA *

Marquette-Type
Number of Stations: 13
Architect: Albert B. Bibb
Plans Drawn: 1889 ?

1891	Burnt Island, ME *
1894	Sullivans Island, SC *
1891	Bois Blanc, MI *
1902	Portage (Ship Canal), MI *
1890	Marquette, MI *
1901	South Manitou Island, MI *
1901	Sleeping Bear Point, MI *
1891	Klipsan Beach (Ilwaco Beach), WA *
1895	Yaquina Bay, OR
1890	Umpqua River, OR
1890	Coos Bay, OR * (Boathouse only standing ?)
1890	Coquille River, OR
1894	Southside, CA

Quonochontaug-Type
Number of Stations: 21
Architect: George R. Tolman
Plans Drawn: 1891

1892-93	Brant Rock, MA
1894	Cahoons Hollow, MA *
1904	Monomoy Point, MA
1896-97	Muskeget, MA
1891	Quonochontaug, RI
1898	Sandy Point, RI
1902	Amagansett, NY *
1895	Spring Lake, NJ *
1896	Little Beach, NJ *
1897-98	Isle of Wight, MD

1904   Cape Henry, VA
1903   Virginia Beach, VA *
1897-98   Dam Neck Mills, VA
1897-98   False Cape, VA
1903   Currituck Beach, VA *
1897-98   Caffeys Inlet, NC *
1897-98   Oregon Inlet, NC *
1894   Portsmouth, NC *
1895   Core Bank, NC
1908   Santa Rosa, FL *
1892   Jackson Park, IL (modified)

Niagara-Type
Number of Stations: 2
Architect: George R. Tolman
Plans Drawn: 1892 ?
1893   Niagara, NY *
1897   Cape Disappointment, WA

Duluth-Type
Number of Stations: 28
Architect: George R. Tolman
Plans Drawn: 1893
1904   Fletchers Neck, ME *
1908   Portsmouth Harbor, ME (modified-type) *
1897   Salisbury Beach, MA
1900   Straitsmouth, MA *
1900   Gloucester, MA
1901   Manomet Point, MA (boatroom only stands) *
1896   Wood End, MA
1898   Old Harbor, MA *
1896   Rocky Point, NY *
1894   Spermaceti Cove, NJ *
1895   Monmouth Beach, NJ *
1902   Squan Beach, NJ *
1895   Chadwick, NJ
1907-08   Forked River, NJ *
1901   Harvey Cedars, NJ *
1907   Long Beach, NJ *
1896   Absecon, NJ *
1894   Avalon, NJ *
1894-95   Stone Harbor, NJ *
1896   Cape May, NJ
1907   Bethany Beach, DE
1897-8   Hog Island, VA
1900   Grand Marais, MI
1899   Charlevoix, MI
1904   Grande Pointe au Sable, MI
1895-6   Baileys Harbor, WI
1895-96   Plum Island, WI *
1894   Duluth, MN

Petersons Point-Type
Number of Stations: 2
Architect: Victor Mendleheff
Plans Drawn: 1897
1898   Petersons Point, WA
1908   Tillamook Bay, OR *

Port Huron-Type
Number of Stations: 9
Architect: Victor Mendelheff
Plans Drawn: 1897
1904   Great Wass Island, ME (Boathouse only stands)
1907-08   Watch Hill, RI
1904   Fishers Island, NY *
1903-04   Long Branch, NJ * ?
1897-98   Lake View Beach, MI
1907-08   Two Rivers, WI *
Port Huron-Type Modified Design
1897   Damariscove Island, ME *
1902   Arena Cove, CA *
1899   Point Bonita, CA

Jersey Pattern
Number of Stations: 11
Architect: Victor Mendleheff
Plans Drawn: 1898
1898   Hampton Beach, NH
1898   Mantoloking, NJ
1899   Toms River, NJ
1898   Island Beach, NJ *
1898   Ship Bottom, NJ
1899   Little Egg, NJ
1898-99   Brigantine, NJ *
1899   Pecks Beach, NJ
1899   Corson Inlet, NJ *
1899   Holly Beach, NJ
Jersey Pattern Modified Design
1900   Cleveland, OH

Old Chicago-Type
Number of Stations: 2
Architect: Victor Mendleheff
Plans Drawn: 1902 ?
1903   Buffalo, NY
1903   Old Chicago, IL

Racine-Type
Number of Stations: 2
Architect: Victor Mendleheff
Plans Drawn: 1903 ?
1904-05   Muskegon, MI *
1903   Racine, WI *

Southern Pattern
Number of Stations: 4
Architect: Victor Mendleheff
Plans Drawn: 1904 ?
1904   Little Kinnakeet, NC *
1904   Ocracoke, NC
1904   Fort Macon, NC
1904   Bogue Inlet, NC *
1911   Galveston, TX

Chicamacomico-Type
Number of Stations: 4
Architect: Victor Mendleheff
Plans Drawn: 1910
1913   Poyners Hill, NC

1911	Kitty Hawk, NC *
1912	Nags Head, NC
1911	Chicamacomico, NC *

Lorain-Type
Number of Stations: 12
Architect: Victor Mendleheff
Plans Drawn: 1910 ?

1910	Peaked Hill Bars, MA
1912	Tiana, NY *
1912	Quogue, NY *
1912	Potunk, NY
1912	Moriches, NY
1912	Smiths Point, NY
1913	Blue Point, NY *
1913	Rockaway, NY
1912-13	Rockaway Point, NY
1912	Wachapreague, VA
1910	Lorain, OH
1912	Eagle Harbor, MI

Isles of Shoals-Type
Number of Stations: 3
Architect: Victor Mendleheff
Plans Drawn: 1909

1910	Isles of Shoals, ME *
1911-12	Green Hill, RI
191 ?	Peaked Hills Bars, MA

Gulf-Type
Number of Stations: 7
Architect: Victor Mendleheff
Plans Drawn: Uncertain

1903-04 ?	Sabine, TX
1913	Brazos, TX
1916	San Luis, TX
1917	Velasco, TX
?	Saluria, TX
?	Aransas, TX
1918	Barataria, LA *

Chatham-Type
Number of Stations: 31
Architect: Victor Mendleheff
Plans Drawn: 1914

1918-19	Quoddy Head, ME *
1929	Cross Island, ME *
?	Cape Elizabeth, ME *
1929	Merrimac River, MA
?	Race Point, MA *
?	Highland, MA
?	Pamet River, MA *
?	Orleans, MA
1914	Chatham, MA
?	Coskata, MA *
1937	Galloo Island, NY *
1916	Point of Woods (cupola), NY *
1915-16	Oswego, NY
1922	Assateague Beach, VA *

1924	Little Island, VA *
1919	Wash Woods, NC *
1925	Bodie Island, NC *
1929	Big Kinnakeet, NC
1918	Creeds Hill, NC *
1917	Hatteras Inlet (cupola), NC
1916	Cape Lookout, NC *
1918	Cape Fear, NC * ?
1922	Marblehead, OH
1916	Point Betsie (cupola), MI *
1922	Whtiefish Point, MI *
1933	Munising, MI *
1917	Siuslaw River (cupola), OR
1934	Port Orford, OR *
1917	Bolinas Bay, CA *
1918	Golden Gate, CA

Chatham-Type Modified Design
| 1927 | Point Reyes, CA * |

ONE-OF-A-KIND STATIONS[57]

Designed by Albert B. Bibb
| 1887 | Cape Elizabeth, ME * |
| 1890 | Cuttyhunk, MA |

Designed by John G. Pelton
| 1885 ? | Cottage for Willapa Bay, WA |
| 1885 | Cottage for Golden Gate Park, CA |

Designed by McKim, Mead and White
| 1887-88 | Narragansett Pier, RI * |

Designed by Victor Mendleheff
1899	Nahant, MA *
1903	Long Branch, NJ *
1916	Mackinac Island, MI
1908	Jackson Park, IL *
1915	Milwaukee, WI *
1905	Nome, AK
1908	Waaddah Island, WA ?
1909-10	Baaddah Point, WA

Designed by J. Lake Parkinson
1876-77	Evanston (Grosse Point), IL
1877	Buffalo, NY
1879	Manistee, MI *
1879	Kenosha, WI
1877	Cape Disappointment, WA
1877-78	Golden Gate Park, CA *

Designed by George R. Tolman
| 1892-93 | Ashtabula, OH |
| 1895 | Gay Head, MA |

Floating Stations
| 1881, 1903, 1929 | Louisville, KY * (1929 vessel still afloat) |
| 1896 | City Point, MA |

Designed by R. S. Williamson (for Lighthouse Service)
| 1871 | Yaquina Bay, OR * (This was a lighthouse used by the USLSS as a full-fledged life-saving station during 1908-1915) |

Chapter 18
Footnotes

Chapter 1 - Introduction
1. Tom Hartman, *Guinness Book of Ships and Shipping Facts and Feats* gives the Chinese credit for the world's first life-saving service. However, the Chinese life-saving system is actually even older than *Guinness* indicates. Chinese life-saving dates back to at least 1708. See *Chinese Lifeboats, Etc.* by Inspector General of Customs, Shanghai. Published in Chinese and English, 1-60. This important book chronicles the world's first life-saving organizations.
2. *Chinese Lifeboats, Etc.*,1-60
3. Ibid.
4. Ibid., 4. See also Karl Baarslag, *Coast Guard to the Rescue*, 44-45.
5. Noel T. Methley in *The Life-Boat and Its Story* discusses British and Dutch life-saving organizations. See also *Lifeboats of the World* by E.W. Middleton for an account of these maritime rescue organizations.
6. Eric C. Fry, *Life-Boat Design and Development*, 13-19. Sir John Cameron Lamb details the roll of these early life-saving leaders. See his *The Life-Boat & Its Work* (London: Royal National Lifeboat Institution, 1911). Also see Methley.
7. This section is based on M.A. DeWolfe Howe, *The Humane Society of the Commonwealth of Massachusetts*, esp. pp. 5-6. See Howe for a detailed history of the Society.
8. Ibid., 234 and 246. The last active Massachusetts Human Society station was at Cohasset. It was closed in 1936. Personal communication by Richard Boonisar to Ralph Shanks, 1995.
9. *U.S. Life-Saving Service (USLSS) Annual Report, 1876*, 40-58. See also Robert F. Bennet *Surfboats, Rockets and Carronades* for a discussion of this period.
10. *USLSS Annual Report, 1876*, 42-44. The pioneer Spermaceti Cove station is often called "the first Coast Guard station."
11. *USLSS Annual Report, 1876*, 43-44 and Joseph Francis *History of Life-Saving Appliances*
12. Ellice Gonzalez, *Storms, Ships & Shipwrecks: The Life-Savers of Fire Island*, (Eastern National Park & Monument Association, New York City, 1982), 21
13. *USLSS Annual Report, 1876*, 46
14. Ibid., 48
15. Ibid., 46
16. Ibid., 48
17. Ibid., 48-51
18. Edwin Emory, *History of Sanford, Maine* contains *Sketch of the Life of Hon. S.I. Kimball.*
19. *USLSS Annual Report, 1882*, 46-47, discusses this period.
20. Stephen H. Evans, *The United States Coast Guard: 1790-1915*, 100
21. *USLSS Annual Report, 1876*, 66
22. Dennis L. Noble, *That Others Might Live*, (Anapolis: Naval Institute Press, 1994) 155

Chapter 2 Launching the Life-Saving Service
1. *USLSS Annual Report, 1878*, 53-54
2. Ibid., 53-61
3. Stephen H. Evans, *The United States Coast Guard: 1790-1915* (Menasha, WI: Banta, 1968), 103
4. *Register of the United States Life-Saving Service* (Washington: G.P.O., July 1, 1914)
5. Sumner Kimball, *Organization & Methods of the U.S. Life-Saving Service* (Washington: G.P.O., 1912), 11
6. See Frederick Stonehouse, *Wreck Ashore* (Duluth: Lake Superior Port Cities, 1994), 26. Also see: *USLSS Annual Report, 1906*, 19
7. Kimball, *Organization*, 11
8. J.W. Dalton, *Life Savers of Cape Cod* (Old Greenwich, CT: Chatham, 1902), 57-59, provides a good picture of District Superintendent Benjamin C. Sparrow's duties.
9. Kimball, *Organization*, 12-13. Also see *USLSS Lists of Persons Who Have Died By Reason of Injury or Disease Contracted in the Line of Duty* (Washington, G.P.O., 1914), 1-6
10. Kimball, *Organization*, 11-12

11. *USLSS Annual Report, 1876*, 53-55
12. Ibid.
13. Ibid.
14. Stonehouse, *Wreck Ashore*, 104-105
15. See *USLSS Annual Report, 1908*, 12-13
16. After the Coast Guard took over, the life-saving stations again became known as lifeboat stations. Surviving life-saving stations with only surfboats either had to be relocated or abandoned or have entirely new structures built because the Coast Guard required deep water and an absence of heavy surf to safely launch its heavy motor lifeboats and utility boats using marine railway-type launchways. Today, although a handful of Coast Guard station launchways survive for small boats, modern Coast Guard lifeboat stations keep their steel and aluminum motor lifeboats in the water. It makes sense then to distinguish between life-saving stations and lifeboat stations only in the later Coast Guard usage of the terms. In this book life-saving station is generally defined as all these USLSS stations except the Houses of Refuge. Lifeboat stations are those stations in use during the Coast Guard years and equipped with motor lifeboats and launchways. Some Coast Guard stations are still properly referred to as lifeboat stations today.
17. Regarding Far Rockaway station see *USLSS Annual Report, 1892*, 220. The Coast Guard continued to move its much larger lifeboat stations by barge at least into the 1950s. For example, in 1952 Massachusetts' Cuttyhunk lifeboat station was barged to Martha's Vineyard to become the Gay Head Lifeboat Station at Menemsha. In 1955 Long Island's Napeague lifeboat station was also barged to become Montauk lifeboat station. Both had better luck with their moves than Far Rockaway.
18. *USLSS Annual Report, 1897*, 32-33
19. *USLSS Annual Report, 1878*, 38-39. For Cobb Island and Pea Island see *USLSS Annual Report, 1880*, 28-29; for Bolinas Bay see *USLSS Annual Report, 1885*, 31 and Jack Mason *Last Stage for Bolinas* (Inverness, CA: North Shore, 1978), 54; for Salmon Creek see *USLSS Annual Report, 1886*, 58.
20. The *USLSS Annual Reports* have numerous examples of Sumner Kimball's pleas for funds for stations.
21. *USLSS Annual Report, 1879*, 46
22. By then it was too late. Most of the Point Conception and Point Arguello shipwrecks had already occurred in earlier years with no life-savers around. See: Charles Lockwood and H. C. Adamson, *Tragedy at Honda* (Philadelphia: Chilton, 1960) for details of Point Arguello's spectacular seven shipwrecks in one night. For an account of the Point Arguello Lifeboat Station see: David Gebhard and David Bricker, *The Former U.S. Coast Guard Lifeboat Station and Lookout Tower Point Arguello, California* (Santa Barbara: Univ. of Calif., 1980).
23. USLSS *Register of the U.S. Life-Saving Service*, July 1, 1914

Chapter 3 Maine and New Hampshire
1. Sumner Kimball, *Organization & Methods of the U.S. Life-Saving Service* (Washington: G.P.O., 1912), 5
2. *U.S. Coast Pilot: Atlantic Coast, Eastport to Cape Cod* (Washington: Dept. of Commerce, 1960), 37
3. Ibid., 164-165
4. *USLSS Annual Report, 1880*, 40-41
5. *USLSS Annual Report, 1905*, 12
6. *USLSS Annual Report, 1898*, 19-23
7. Ibid., 20
8. Ibid., 22
9. Ibid., 22
10. Ibid., 23
11. Ibid., 23
12 Station lists for all chapters are taken from the *Register of the United States Life-Saving Service* (Washington: G.P.O., July 1, 1914).
13. *USLSS Annual Report, 1907*, 18

Chapter 4 Surfmen and Keepers

1. USLSS *Revised Regulations* (Washington: G.P.O., 1884), 59-61. Stations and half-way houses eventually were equipped with telephones, beginning in 1884. About 1880, some stations also received horses to lighten surfmen's burdens. The horses were used primarily to help pull beach carts and boat carriages, but in some areas surfmen rode them on beach patrol. See Joe A. Mobley, *Ship Ashore* (Raleigh: North Carolina Division of Archives & History, 1994), 99.

    It is also important to note that patrol checks were primarily an East Coast custom. Patrol checks were used on the Great Lakes only at four Lake Superior stations (Stonehouse, *Wreck Ashore*, 64). On the Pacific coast, Ralph Shanks could only find documentation that they were used at the three San Francisco Life-Saving Stations. Given the widespread location of the Texas stations, checks probably were never used on the Gulf coast.

2. Kimball, *Organization*, 17-18

3. Ibid., 18

4. Kimball, *Organization*, 17-18; *Revised Regulations, Life-Saving Service*, 61-62; J.W. Dalton, *Life Savers of Cape Cod*, esp. 34-35, 51 and Frederick Stonehouse, *Wreck Ashore*, 63-65. Also from Ralph Shanks interview with Surfman Cornelius Sullivan, 1977.

5. Kimball, *Organization*, 18 and *Revised Regulations, Life-Saving Service*, 61-62. Also see Stonehouse, 67-75. Ralph Shanks 1995 interview with Arthur B. Barr, surfman at Galveston, San Luis and Saluria, Texas stations, 1923-1929.

6. Interviews with surfmen Garner Churchill (USCG ret.) and Samuel H. Mostovoy, USCG (ret.) 1977. Garner Churchill became keeper of Humboldt Bay, Calif., life-saving station during the early years of the Coast Guard. His crew was composed of both USLSS veterans and USCG personnel. Chief Churchill often studied the *USLSS Annual Reports* and wreck reports for insights into how to handle disasters at Humboldt Bay. His controversial response to the *Brooklyn* wreck in Nov. 1930 was based in part on his studies of USLSS accounts of what had happened at previous shipwrecks at Humboldt Bay. Keeper Churchill believed, based on his reading, that the *Brooklyn* wreckage would come ashore carrying survivors with it. It did not and it could have ended a career of a heroic keeper who had saved over 300 lives. Ralph Shanks interview with Garner Churchill, 1977. See: Ralph Shanks, *Lighthouses and Lifeboats on the Redwood Coast* (San Anselmo, CA: Costaño, 1978), 175-194 for an account of Churchill's career.

7. *USLSS Annual Reports*, various years. USLSS *Regulations* 1889, 58

8. *Harpers New Monthly* and *Frank Leslie's Popular Monthly* were but two mass circulation magazines of the period that helped build the "storm warrior" image. A popular British book, Rev. John Gilmore's *Storm Warriors* (London: MacMillan, 1885) also contributed to the adulation.

9. Kimball, *Organization*, 25

10. Newspaper clip file, Ralph Shanks

11. For example, Fort Point, Calif., Keeper Charles Henry was swept overboard while at his steering oar and drowned during the *Elizabeth* rescue in Feb. 1891. See *USLSS Annual Report, 1891*, 69-76

12. *USLSS Annual Report*, various years

13. Kimball, *Organization*, 30

14. *USLSS Annual Report, 1876*, 68-69

15. Ibid., 69

16. USLSS *Annual Report, 1904*, 47

17. See: *USLSS Annual Report, 1876*, 68-69; *USLSS Annual Report, 1909*, 24-28; Stonehouse, 39-41; and Dennis Noble, *That Others Might Live*, (Annapolis: Naval Institute, 1994), 56

18. *USLSS Annual Report, 1907*, 22

19. USLSS, *List of Persons Who Have Died By Reason of Injury or Disease Contracted in the Line Duty in the Life-Saving Since Origin of the Present System* (Washington: G.P.O., 1914). This is the most complete list of USLSS personnel lost in the line of duty and includes cause of death.

20. *USLSS Annual Report, 1905*, 12-13

21. See: Ralph Shanks, *Lighthouses and Lifeboats on the Redwood Coast*, 30, 179. Also Edward Canfield and Thomas Allen, *Life on a Lonely Shore* (Sault Sainte Marie: Lake Superior State Univ., 1991)

22. A.B. Bibb, *The Life-Savers on the Great Lakes* (F. Leslie's Pop. Monthly, April 1882), 391

23. USLSS *Revised Regulations*, 49-50

24. Additional work could be had during the "inactive season" especially on the Atlantic Coast where USLSS layoffs coincided with summer. See: Ellice Gonzalez, *Storms, Ships & Shipwrecks* (New York: Eastern Parks Assoc., 1982) for an excellent account of other employment by surfmen.

25. A.B. Bibb, 391

26. See: Edward Canfield and Thomas Allen, 37; Stonehouse, 77. Richard Boonisar has a photograph of a Pt. Allerton, Mass., keeper's wife praying, presumably for those at sea. Personal communication,

1993.

27. *USLSS Annual Report, 1889*, 65-66. Chief Samuel H. Mostovoy while keeper at Pt. Reyes Lifeboat Station during the early Coast Guard years stopped using the Lyle gun after it terrified two commercial fishermen he was rescuing. Interview with Ralph Shanks, 1977.

28. *USLSS Annual Report, 1889*, 66

29. Donald L. Canny and Barbara Voulgaris, *Uniforms of the U.S. Coast Guard* (Washington, USCG Historian's Office, Dec. 1990). Also see Robert Bennet *The Life-Saving Service at Sandy Hook* (Washington: USCG, 1976)

30. Kimball, *Organization*, 13-14

31. USLSS *Revised Regulations*, Surfman Arthur Barr interview with Ralph Shanks, 1995. Photos show surfmen in the water during capsize drill. Keepers could stay dry when surfboats were used in capsize drills but, because of their design, not when Dobbins lifeboats were being used.

32. *USLSS Annual Report, 1908*, 20-22 and Ralph Shanks, *Guardians of the Golden Gate* (Petaluma, CA: Costaño, 1990), 266

33. *USLSS Annual Report, 1884*, 54-56

34. Ibid., 54-57

35. Michael Whatley, *Marconi Wireless on Cape Cod* (Cape Cod National Seashore, 1987), 23-26

36. Mobley, 148-149

37. Bernard Nalty and Truman Strobridge, *The U.S. Coast Guard: Midwife at the Birth of the Airplane* (Aerospace Historian Sept. 1975), 139-142. Also clipping file at U.S. Coast Guard Historian's office.

38. Nalty and Strobridge, 141 and USCG Historian's clipping file

39. Ibid.

Chapter 5 Massachusetts and Rhode Island

1. *USLSS Annual Report, 1876*, 34-35

2. USLSS *Register of the U. S. Life-Saving Service* (GPO: Washington, 1914)

3. Sumner Kimball, *Joshua James* (Boston: American Unitarian Assoc., 1909), 52-55 Also see Karl Baarslag, *Coast Guard to the Rescue* (New York: Farrar & Rhinehart, 1937), 73-74

4. Kimball, *Joshua James*, 54-59

5. Ibid., 54-59

6. Ibid., 59-61

7. Ibid., 60-62

8. Ibid., 63-71

9. Ibid., 71-72

10. Ibid., 72. See also: *USLSS Annual Report, 1899*, 61-63; *USLSS Annual Report, 1909*, 314; M.A. DeWolfe Home, *The Humane Society of the Commonwealth of Massachusetts*, 328

11. Baarslag, 79 and Kimball *Joshua James*, 14

12. *USLSS Annual Report, 1899*, 13-14

13. Ibid., 26

14. Ibid.

15. Ibid., 29-30

16. Ibid., 30-31

17. Ibid., 30-33

18. *USLSS Annual Report, 1899*, 136 Also wreck files of the Massachusetts Humane Society, Boston, especially the wreck of the *Lucy Nichols*.

19. Ibid.

20. Ibid., 33

21. Ibid., 33-36

22. Ibid., 34

23. Ibid.

24. Ibid.

25. Ibid.

26. *USLSS Annual Report, 1902*, 13-14, 32-36, 42. See also J.W. Dalton *Life Savers of Cape Cod* (Old Greenwich, CT: Chatham, 1902), 126-141

27. Elmer F. Mayo saved Surfman Ellis in a very daring rescue. Captain Mayo was the son of the first keeper of the Chatham Life-Saving Station just north of Monomoy. Elmer Mayo had also served as a substitute surfman. For details see: J. W. Dalton, *The Life Savers of Cape Cod*, 132-141

28. Ibid., 36. Monomoy was not the only Cape Cod station to lose much of its crew. Peaked Hill Bars station lost Keeper David H. Atkins and Surfmen Elisha M. Taylor and Stephen F. Mayo on Nov. 30, 1880 while attempting to take ashore the crew of the stranded *C. E. Trumbull*. See *USLSS Annual Report, 1881*, 64-76

29. *USLSS Annual Report, 1902*, 14 and Baarslag, 80. Captain James is buried in the cemetery behind the Hull Lifesaving Museum in Hull, Massachusetts. The museum is located in the old Point Allerton USLSS station, his old station.

30. *USLSS Annual Report, 1902*, 14

Chapter 6 Equipment: Rockets, Mortars, Lifecars and More

1. Roy Clark, *Manby-Saver of Life at Sea* in Sea Breezes, Nov. 1954, 374-377. See also Noel T. Methley *The Lifeboat and its Story*, 281-299

2. Methley, 281-299
3. Methley, 296-297
4. Sumner Kimball, *Organization*, 25-27 and Methley, *The Lifeboat and its Story*, 296
5. M.A. DeWolfe Howe, *The Humane Society...of Massachusetts*, 234; Kimball, *Organization*, 25-27 and J.P. Barnett, *The Lifesaving Guns of David Lyle*, (South Bend: South Bend Replicas, 1976), 3-9
6. The Benicia Arsenal has been preserved. It had a fascinating career of its own. The U.S. Army camel barn was here during the period when camels were used to transport soldiers in the arid southwestern U.S. The Arsenal also supplied the first Pacific Coast fog signal, a cannon which was established at Point Bonita lighthouse in 1856. See: Ralph and Lisa Shanks, *Guardians of the Golden Gate: Lighthouses and Lifeboat Stations of San Francisco Bay* (Petaluma, CA: Costaño, 1990), 68-72.
7. Barnett, *The Lifesaving Guns of David Lyle*, 1-2
8. Ibid., 13
9. Kimball, *Organization*, 25
10. Barnett, 27 and 102-13; *USLSS Annual Report, 1878,* which contains David Lyle's *Report on Life-Saving Ordinance*, 45 and 219-375. See: Bernard C. Webber, *Chatham: The Lifeboatmen*, 98-101 for what may have been the last USCG Lyle gun rescue.
11. Joanna R. Nichols-Kyle, *The U.S. Life-Saving Service*, 358-359
12. Charles Ellms, *Shipwrecks and Disaster at Sea...With a Sketch of the various Expedients for Preserving the Lives of Mariners by the Aid of Life Boats, Life Preservers, Etc.* (New York, Bixby, 1844), 416-427; Methley, 281-299
13. See both books by Joseph Francis, *History of Life-Saving Appliances* (New York: Slater, 1885) and *Francis Metallic Lifeboats* (New York: William Bryant, 1852). *The Wreck and Rescue of the Schooner J.H. Hartzell* (Traverse City, MI: Brauer Productions, 1988) is a fine video of a reenacted USLSS lifecar rescue using authentic equipment.
14. See: Joseph Francis; Kimball, *Organization*, 27-28; *USLSS Annual Report, 1878*, 47. Also personnel communication from Richard Boonisar to Ralph Shanks, 1995
15. Kimball, *Organization*, 27-28
16. For detailed instructions for operating a breeches buoy see: USLSS *Beach Apparatus Drill* (G.P.O.: Washington, 1899).
17. Over the years there were at least seven different types of beach carts used by either the Life-Saving Service or the Coast Guard. Gradually horses and, later, tractors and trucks were used to pull the beach carts instead of men. Personal communications with Richard Boonisar, 1993-95 and with Samuel H. Mostovoy, USCG (ret.), 1977.
18. *USLSS Annual Report, 1878*, 47
19. C.S. Merriman of Iowa is not to be confused with Captain James H. Merryman, Life-Saving Service inspector, and another inventor of life-saving devices.
20. Paul Boyton, *The Story of Paul Boyton* (Milwaukee: Riverside, 1892), 105-106
21. *USLSS Annual Report, 1876*, 50. See also Paul Boyton, *The Story of Paul Boyton*
22. *USLSS Annual Report, 1878*, 12
23. Boyton, 105-108. See: Peter Lyon, *The Fearless Frogman* (*American Heritage* April 1960)
24. *USLSS Annual Report, 1876*, 50

Chapter 7 New Jersey and Rhode Island
1. *Register of the U.S. Life-Saving Service* (G.P.O., 1914)
2. Ibid.
3. Baarslag, *Coast Guard to the Rescue*, 52. New Jersey had a forty-second life-saving station, Bay Shore, located near Cape May City. By 1914 it was inactive.
4. *USLSS Annual Report, 1876*, 35-36
5. *USLSS Annual Report, 1904*, 28-31
6. Ibid., 29
7. Ibid.
8. Ibid.
9. Ibid., 29-30
10. Ibid., 10
11. Ibid.
12. Ibid.
13. Ibid., 30-31
14. Ibid., 31
15. *USLSS Annual Report, 1880*, 106-107
16. Ibid.
17. Ibid., 107
18. Ibid., 107-108
19. Ibid.
20. Ibid., 108-109
21. Ibid., 109-111
22. Ibid., 110
23. Ibid.

24. Ibid., 111-112
25. Ibid., 112-114
26. Ibid.
27. Ibid., 114-117.
28. *USLSS Annual Report, 1886*, 72-74
29. Ibid., 39-45
30. Ibid., 41
31. Ibid., 42
32. Ibid., 42-43
33. Ibid., 44-45

Chapter 8 Lifeboats and Surfboats
1. See: Eric Fry, *Lifeboat Design and Development* (London: David & Charles, 1975) and Methley, *The Life-Boat and its Story* for accounts of lifeboat development.
2. Imperial General of Customs, *Chinese Lifeboats, Etc.*, 1-60 and Baarslag, *Coast Guard to the Rescue*, 51
3. G.R.G. Worcester, *Sail and Sweep in China* (London: Science Museum, 1966), 8
4. E.W. Middleton, *Lifeboats of the World*, (New York: Arco, Publishing, 1978), 83 and Methley, *The Life-Boat and its Story*, 239
5. See: Methley and Baarslag
6. M.A. DeWolfe Howe, *The Humane Society of the Commonwealth of Massachusetts*, 108
7. Kimball, *Organization*, 21
8. *USLSS Annual Report*, various years
9. *USLSS Annual Report, 1899*, 18 and Kimball, *Organization*, 20-24. Also see William Wilkinson, *Surfboat Authority Sheds Light on Race Point Type* (*National Fisherman*, Nov. 1972) *USCG Annual Report, 1917* lists boat types by station, 68-72
10. Kimball, *Organization*, 22-23
11. *USLSS Annual Report, 1907*, 20-21. See also Frederick Stonehouse, *Wreck Ashore* (Duluth: Lake Superior Port Cities, 1994), 69-71
12. *USLSS Annual Report, 1910*, 20; 1911, 18-21; 1911, 12; 1914, 20-21; Kimball, *Organization*, 39; Methley, *The Life-Boat and its Story*, 199-200
13. William Wilkinson, *Nineteenth Century Coastal Lifeboats in the Collection of the Mariners Museum* (Washington: National Trust for Historic Preservation, 1976), 52-62
14. Kimball, *Organization*, 20-23. There was also a Richardson lifeboat.
15. Ibid., 24
16. Ibid., 20-24 and Methley, *The Life-Boat and its Story*, 190-205
17. Stonehouse, *Wreck Ashore*, 95-102
18. The entrance bars at Pacific Northwest rivers are still unsurpassed in difficulty for Coast Guard motor lifeboats. More USCG motor lifeboats have been capsized here over the years than anywhere else in the country. Ralph Shanks interviews with USCG motor lifeboat coxswains, 1971-1994.
19. David Porter Dobbins, *The Dobbins Life-Boat* (Buffalo, NY, 1886), 16-15 and 41-48; Stonehouse, 98-100
20. *USCG Annual Report*, 1917, 72; Stonehouse, 100-101
21. C.H. McLellen, *Twin Screw Lifeboat for the U.S. Life-Saving Service* (*Marine Engineering*, Jan. 1900), 25-26
22. Fry, *Lifeboat Design & Development*, 21-27 and USLSS *Annual Report, 1906*, 18
23. C.H. McLellen, *Evolution of the Lifeboat* (*Marine Engineering*, Jan. 1906), 7-11; Stonehouse, 93-95; and *USLSS Annual Reports*, various years
24. *USLSS Annual Report, 1900*, 421, 436-439. See also: McLellen, *Twin Screw Lifeboat for the USLSS*, 25-26 and Stonehouse, 108
25. *USLSS Annual Report, 1900*, 439
26. McLellen, *Evolution of the Lifeboat*, 7-10
27. *USLSS Annual Report, 1909*, 25
28. William Wilkinson, *The Standard 36-Foot Motor Lifeboat of the U.S. Life-Saving Service—1909* (Nautical Research Journal, Summer 1960), 46-49 and *USLSS Annual Report, 1914*, 20
29. Thomas E. Appleton, *Canada's First Motor Lifeboat* (Maritime Museum of British Columbia *Bulletin*, Spring 1976), 2-4
30. Thomas E, Appleton, *Usque Ad Mare: A History of the Canadian Coast Guard and Marine Services* (Ottawa: Dept. of Transport, 1968), 141-147
31. Wilkinson, *The Standard 36-Foot Motor Lifeboat of the USLSS*, 46. Motor lifeboats, probably 34-footers, were in use by the USLSS on the Pacific Coast beginning in 1905 at Cape Disappointment, Washington. Another very early 36-footer, the *Victory*, was used at Wood End station in Massachusetts.
32. *USLSS Annual Report, 1908*, 23-24
33. *USLSS Annual Report, 1914*, 20
34. Interview with Surfman Cornelius Sullivan by Ralph Shanks, 1977. See also Ralph Shanks, *Guardians of the Golden Gate: Lighthouses and Lifeboat Stations of San Francisco Bay* (Petaluma: Costaño, 1990), 117-127

35. Personal communication between T. Michael O'Brien and Ralph Shanks, Sept. 8, 1977.
36. Ibid.
37. Station records, U.S. Coast Guard Station Depoe Bay, Oregon. The last wooden motor lifeboat was affectionately known as *Woody* by the Depoe Bay crew. Ralph Shanks interview with crew in 1994. Both the first USLSS English pulling lifeboat in America and the last 36-foot Coast Guard motor lifeboat are on exhibit at Newport News, Virginia's Mariners Museum.

Chapter 9 Delaware, Maryland and Virginia
1. *USLSS Annual Report, 1876,* 36
2. *USLSS Annual Report, 1887,* 30-32
3. Ibid.
4. Ibid., 30-33
5. Ibid., 32
6. Ibid., 33
7. Ibid., 34-36
8. Ibid., 34-35
9. Ibid., 33-36
10. *USLSS Annual Report, 1892,* 35-36
11. Ibid., 36
12. Ibid.
13. Ibid., 37-39. See also: Richard and Julie Pouliot, *Shipwrecks on the Virginia Coast and the Men of the Life-Saving Service* (Centreville, MD: Tidewater), 1986

Chapter 10 Women and Minority People
1. See Martha Coston, *A Signal Success: The Work and Travels of Mrs. Martha J. Coston, An Autobiography* (Philadelphia: J. B. Lippencott, 1886). Also: Anne Boone, *Beauty and Brains to the Rescue of the Seafarer, U.S. Coast Guard Magazine,* Sept. 1932), 32-37
2. Martha Coston, *Signal Success,* 27-36
3. Ibid., 35-49
4. Ibid., 53
5. Ibid., 50-304
6. New York *Times,* Dec. 27, 1864
7. See: Coston Signal Company, *Coston's Telegraphic Night Signals* (New York: S. W. Green, 1880)
8. Martha Coston discusses in detail the opposition she faced from some naval officers in *Signal Success.*
9. *USLSS Annual Report, 1895,* 219
10. Anne Boone, *Beauty and Brains,* 35 and Dennis Noble, *That Others Might Live,* 164-165. Information regarding highway flares from Richard Boonisar, personal communication, 1995.
11. *USLSS Annual Report, 1914,* 153-154 and Richard and Julie Pouliot, *Shipwrecks of the Virginia Coast and the Men of the Life-Saving Service* (Centreville, MD: Tidewater, 1986), 42
12. Ralph Shanks, *Lighthouses and Lifeboats on the Redwood Coast* (San Anselmo, CA: Costaño, 1978), 30 and 179
13. Edward Canfield and Thomas Allen, *Life on a Lonely Shore,* 37. Also interview with Richard Boonisar, 1992
14. Jeannette Edwards Rattray, *Ship Ashore!* (New York: Coward-McCann, 1955), 94
15. *USLSS Annual Report, 1880,* 39-40
16. *USLSS Annual Report, 1895,* 86 and Joanna Nichols-Kyle, *The U.S. Life-Saving Service,* 359
17. Often called a lifeboat, photos show these vessels actually to be surfboats. For this wreck see: M. A. DeWolfe Howe, *Massachusetts Humane Society,* 238-241. Also see: George Hough, *Disaster on Devil's Bridge* for a detailed account, 71-73
18. *USLSS Annual Report, 1877,* 18 and Mark R. Harrington *Shinnecock Notes* (Journal of American Folklore, vol. 16, no. 60, 1903), 37-39
19. George Hough, *Disaster on Devil's Bridge,* 68-74
20. Ibid.
21. Ibid., 86
22. M.A. DeWolf Howe, *Massachusetts Humane Society,* 238-241
23. Dennis Noble, personal communication with Ralph Shanks, 1994.
24. *USLSS Annual Report, 1882,* 118-120
25. *USLSS Annual Report, 1890,* 57-58
26. A.B. Bibb, *The Life-Savers on the Great Lakes* (Frank Leslie's *Popular Monthly,* April 1882), 395. Thomas Allen personal communication, 1994
27. *USLSS Annual Report, 1905,* 47
28. *USLSS Annual Report, 1878,* 29-30
29. Dennis Noble, *That Others Might Live,* 51-54
30. John Tilly, *Out of Uniform: Civilians in the U.S. Coast Guard,* (Supplement to USCG Commandant's Bulletin, April 1994, 12-13) See also Noble, *That Others Might Live,* 51-54
32. *USLSS Annual Report, 1897,* 114-115. For more on Keeper Richard Etheridge see: Joe A. Mobley, *Ship Ashore!,* 94-98
33. David Stick, *Graveyard of the Atlantic,* 156. At least one Pacific Coast station had an African-American keeper; R. Shanks photo file.
34. David M. Santos, *Ties That Bind* (USCG Commandant's Bulletin Maga-
zine, Feb. 1994), 18-19

Chapter 11 North Carolina and South Carolina
1. See: David Stick, *Graveyard of the Atlantic* (Chapel Hill, NC: Univ. of North Carolina Press, 1987). Also Ralph Shanks interview with U.S. Coast Guard Station Hatteras Inlet crew, 1989 and 1994.
2. U.S. Department of Commerce, *U.S. Coast Pilot Atlantic Coast, Cape Henry to Key West* (Washington: G.P.O., 1948), 35
3. Ibid., 40-41
4. *USLSS Annual Report, 1876,* 11-14
5. *USLSS Annual Report, 1877,* 66-67
6. Ibid., 81-98
7. *Harpers New Monthly Magazine, The American Life-Saving Service,* Feb. 1882, 364
8. *USLSS Annual Report, 1900,* 21
9. Ibid., 20-25
10. Ibid., 22
11. Ibid.
12. Ibid.
13. Ibid.
14. Ibid., 23-25
15. Ibid., 25-28, 85-86. Also see: Joe A. Mobley, *Ship Ashore: The U.S. Life-Saving Service of Coastal North Carolina* (Raleigh: North Carolina Division of Archives & History, 1994)
16. Ibid., 38
17. Ibid., 38-39
18. Ibid., 39
19. Ibid., 39-40
20. Ibid., 40
21. *USLSS Annual Report, 1876-1883*

Chapter 12 Floating Life-Saving Stations
1. S. H. Harris, *Where the Breakers Roar* (Frank Leslie's *Popular Monthly,* vol. 28, no. 3, Sept. 1894), 283
2. In 1899 another Louisville surfman, Keeper Benjamin Cameron, won a gold medal for saving 108 people between 1875 and 1897. See: Dennis Noble, *That Others Might Live,* 51
3. *USLSS Annual Report, 1881,* 77 and USLSS *Annual Report, 1883,* 51
4. Sumner Kimball, *Organization,* 10
5. *USLSS Annual Report, 1882,* 182-183
6. Ibid., 184-185
7. Ibid., 185
8. *USLSS Annual Report, 1882,* 183-186
9. Kimball, *Organization,* 10 and USLSS *Annual Report, 1883,* 50-56
10. James P. Delgado and Candace Clifford, *Inventory of Preserved Vessels* (Washington: National Park Service, 1990), 176
11. *USLSS Annual Report, 1895,* 68
12. *USLSS Annual Report, 1896,* 54 and *USLSS Annual Report, 1897,* 18
13. The USLSS seemed to have an affinity for naming the rescue boats at its floating stations with words beginning with the letter "R."
14. J.W. Dalton, *The Life Savers of Cape Cod* reports a number of surfmen from City Point newly transferred to Cape Cod shore stations.
15. Personal communication from Richard Boonisar to Ralph Shanks, 1995.
16. In later years the Coast Guard established other floating stations indicating the continued usefulness of the concept. For example, National Archives Record Group 26, Boxes CGS 1 and 3, contain information on two floating Coast Guard stations established in 1963, one at Annapolis, Maryland, and the other at Fort Myers, Florida. The key advantage cited for both stations was mobility. Both were equipped with 30-foot utility boats and 16-foot trailerable boats for rescue work.

Chapter 13 Florida
1. *USLSS Annual Report, 1900,* 314
2. Ibid.
3. Sumner Kimball, *Organization,* 7
4. Ibid., 10
5. Ibid.
6. Ibid., 14
7. Janet Hutchinson, *House of Refuge* in *History of Martin County* (Port Salerno, FL: Florida Classics Library, 1987), 55-62
8. *USLSS Annual Report, 1886,* 49-53
9. Ibid., 50-51
10. Ibid., 50
11. *USLSS Annual Report, 1891,* 104
12. *USLSS Annual Report, 1905,* 30-32. Also see Hutchinson, *History of Martin County,* 60-61
13. *USLSS Annual Report, 1905,* 100 and Hutchinson, *History of Martin County,* 60-61

Chapter 14 Texas
1. *USLSS Annual Report, 1878,* 36
2. *USLSS Annual Report, 1880,* 27-28
3. Ralph Shanks photo collection

4. *USLSS Annual Report, 1900,* 17, 51-56
5. Ibid.
6. Ibid., 56
7. *USLSS Annual Report, 1910,* 28-29
8. Ibid., 28-33. It is also notable that a hurricane destroyed still another Gulf life-saving station. Santa Rosa Island Life-Saving Station near Pensacola, Florida, was swept away on September 27, 1906. The surfmen escaped in their surfboat, saving nine women and children in the process. Santa Rosa Island station stood on elevated land, but the hurricane was so powerful it "leveled the site almost to the sea and rendered it useless for further occupancy." A new USLSS station was later built nearby. See: USLSS *Annual Report, 1907,* 18-19.
9 *USLSS Annual Report, 1910,* 29-31
10. Ibid., 31-32
11. Ibid., 32-33
12. Ibid.
13. *USCG Annual Report, 1916,* 23-24
14. *USCG Annual Report, 1917,* 39. Also Ralph Shanks photo collection
15. Station plans on file at U.S. Coast Guard Historian's Office, Washington, D.C. and at the Nautical Research Center, Petaluma, California.

Chapter 15 Great Lakes
1. Sumner Kimball, *Organization,* 7-8
2. Ibid., 8
3. T. Michael O'Brien, *Guardians of the Eighth Sea* (Washington, G.P.O., 1979), 47
4. Ibid., 33-34
5. Edward Canfield and Thomas A. Allen, *Life on a Lonely Shore* (Sault Sainte Marie, MI: Lake Superior University Press, 1991), 25-36
6. See also Kendrick Kimball, *Strange Dream Foretold Shipwreck* (Grand Marais *Pilot & Pictured Rocks Review,* June 7, 1972); Detroit *News,* March 17, 1935; Frederick Stonehouse, *Wreck Ashore,* 80-81
7. Sumner Kimball, *Organization,* 9-10
8. Ibid., 9-10. See also: David P. Dobbins, *Dobbins Life-Boat Illustrated,* 25-40
9. *USLSS Annual Report, 1880,* 21-26, 38. Surfboats could be used at all stations.
10. *USLSS Annual Report, 1907,* 317-351; *USLSS Annual Report, 1906,* 319, 327. See also Dennis Noble, *That Others Might Live,* 80
11. *USLSS Annual Report, 1893,* 47-51
12. Ibid., 50-51
13. *USLSS Annual Report, 1890,* 218-223
14. Ibid., 219-221
15. Ibid., 220
16. Ibid.
17. Ibid., 221
18. Ibid., 222. See also Frederick Stonehouse's *Wreck Ashore* for additional information on the Evanston station.
19. *USLSS Annual Report, 1903,* 43-45 and 127-128
20. Louisville Life-Saving Station, a floating life-saving station, at the Falls of the Ohio River, Louisville, Kentucky, was administered along with the stations on Lakes Erie and Ontario. See the chapter on floating life-saving stations.
21. Darrel H. Smith and Fred W. Powell give a detailed listing of U.S. life-saving stations still in existence in 1928 as well as listing all stations built after the 1915 creation of the Coast Guard. See: Smith and Powell, *The Coast Guard: Its History, Activities & Organization* (Washington: Brookings Institute, 1929). Great Lakes stations are on pages 145-146.

Chapter 16 Pacific Coast
1. For details see Ralph Shanks' *Guardians of the Golden Gate: Lighthouses and Lifeboat Stations of San Francisco Bay,* especially the chapter on Point Bonita and his *Lighthouses & Lifeboats on the Redwood Coast,* especially the chapters on Trinidad Head and St. George Reef.
2. See Shanks, *Lighthouses and Lifeboats on the Redwood Coast,* especially pages 9, 109-120, 155-249. See also Shanks *Guardians of the Golden Gate,* 147 and 288.
3. The U.S. Lighthouse Service *Annual Report of the Lighthouse Board* (Washington: G.P.O., 1852-1939) provides detailed records of fog signal hours for all active American lighthouses. Northern California and Maine were the two most fogbound.
4. Coast Guard establishment of Pacific Coast Lifeboat Stations continued for five decades beyond 1915. For example, Bodega Bay, California, Lifeboat Station was not built until 1963. (Station files USCG Bodega Bay) Other late USCG lifeboat stations include Channel Islands station in southern California and Chetco River station at Brookings, Oregon.
5. *USLSS Annual Report, 1909,* 24. See: Shanks, *Lighthouses and Lifeboats on the Redwood Coast,* 45-70 for details on Farallon Islands Light Station.

6. Kimball, *Organization,* 7
7. Shanks, *Guardians of the Golden Gate,* 256-257
8. See Ernest L. Osborne and Victor West, *Men of Action* (Bandon, OR: Bandon Historical Society Press, 1981), 36-39, 47
9. *USLSS Annual Report, 1909,* 27-29
10. *USLSS Annual Report, 1914,* 66-74. In a 1979 interview with Ralph Shanks, Chief Garner Churchill, an early Coast Guard commanding officer at Humboldt Bay Lifeboat Station stated he had seen waves 70-feet high on the Humboldt Bay bar. A big derrick was in place on the jetty at the time allowing him an accurate mark to determine wave height. Pacific Coast waves were so large that when the Coast Guard looked to establish its National Motor Lifeboat School to train surfmen as motor lifeboat coxswains it selected Cape Disappointment, Washington, because of the exceptionally heavy surf conditions at the mouth of the Columbia River. Many 44-foot motor lifeboats were capsized during drills off "Cape D" in the 1960-1990 period.
11. *USCG Annual Report, 1917,* 72
12. *USLSS Annual Report, 1906,* 19-20
13. *USLSS Annual Report, 1906,* 19-20 and Shanks, *Guardians of Golden Gate,* 84-85 and 265-266. For Arena Cove, see *Lighthouses & Lifeboats on the Redwood Coast,* 75-78
14. *USLSS Annual Report, 1907,* 39-40
15. James Gibbs, *Pacific Graveyard* (Portland, OR: Binfords & Mort, 1973), 288
16. *USLSS Annual Report, 1913,* 66-74
17. Ibid., 70
18. Ibid., 71
19. Ibid., 71-73
20. Ibid.
21. Ibid., 71-73
22 Ibid., 71
23. Ibid., 72
24. Author Ralph Shanks had first hand experience climbing aboard the Columbia River lightship. When the *Relief Lightship* (WLV 605) was moored outside the Columbia River bar, he was on a 40-foot Coast Guard utility boat out of Cape Disappointment Lifeboat Station. They were bringing out relief crew members, food and mail. Their 40-foot Coast Guard boat tied up alongside the lightship and a Jacob's ladder was lowered down the side. As the lightship rolled, the utility boat would rise far up the Jacob's ladder. As he climbed the side of the lightship, Shanks had to climb as fast as he could to prevent his legs from being crushed by the 40-footer. The boat seemed to follow him right up the ladder.
25. *USLSS Annual Report, 1913,* 73. These sixteen gold medals were the largest number ever awarded on the Pacific coast and apparently the second largest single award of gold medals ever made to regular USLSS keepers and surfmen nationally. See: *USLSS Annual Report, 1908,* 303-340. The largest number of gold medals awarded seems to have been to seventeen surfmen and keepers on the Great Lakes from Portage and Eagle Harbor stations in Michigan for the November 1913 wreck of the *Waldo.* See: *USCG Annual Report, 1915,* 275-276. Eighteen gold medals were awarded at the Feb. 3, 1880 *Taulane* wreck in New Jersey, but six of the recipients were not surfmen. The New Jersey stations involved were Swan Point (Mantoloking) and Green Island (Chadwick). See: *USLSS Annual Report, 1880,* 115-120 and *USLSS Annual Report, 1908,* 307.
26. See Shanks, *Lighthouses & Lifeboats on the Redwood Coast,* 199-203. For steam schooners see: Jack McNairn and Jerry MacMullen, *Ships of the Redwood Coast* (Stanford: Stanford Univ. Press, 1970) and Walter A. Jackson, *The Doghole Schooners* (Volcano, CA: California Traveler, 1969).
27. Similar vessels were also found on the Great Lakes and in Scandinavian countries.
28. San Francisco and Humboldt Bays were the only protected harbors in 400 miles of coastline capable of handling large commercial vessels. The region's harbors are detailed in Shanks, *Lighthouses & Lifeboats on the Redwood Coast* and in McNairn and MacMullen, *Ships of the Redwood Coast.*
29. *USCG Annual Report, 1915,* 118-122
30. At that date, Point Reyes Life-Saving Station to the north of Bolinas Bay had not yet received a motor lifeboat and the distances involved were too great to cover by pulling lifeboat unless assisted by a tug.
31. *USCG Annual Report, 1915,* 118-119
32. Ibid.
33. Ibid., 119-120
34. Ibid. 120
35. Ibid., 120-121
36. Ibid.
37. Ibid., 121
38. Ibid., 121-122

39. *USCG Annual Report, 1915*, 9-10
40. Ibid., 276
41. Jack Mason, *Last Stage for Bolinas* (Inverness, CA: North Shore, 1973), 58
42. Wick York, *The Architecture of the U.S. Life-Saving Service* (Master's thesis, Boston University, 1983), 242
43. Dennis Noble, *That Others Might Live*, 14 and Robert Bennet, *The Lifesavers*, 63
44. *USLSS Annual Report, 1914*, 25
45 Ralph Shanks 1990 and 1978 interviews with early Coast Guardsmen Steve Toth, Commanding Officer Point Reyes Lifeboat Station and Garner Churchill, Commanding Officer Humboldt Bay Lifeboat Station. Also personal communication with Richard Boonisar, 1995.
46. New Coast Guard stations should be designed using the architectural styles of the Life-Saving Service and early Coast Guard. They are the true architectural styles of the Coast Guard. As then Coast Guard Commandant Admiral William Kime said upon visiting historic Fort Point Coast Guard Station, "This looks like a Coast Guard station!"
47. Arena Cove Life-Saving in California, has been mistakenly called Point Arena by a few historians. It was always Arena Cove, only the town and lighthouse were called Point Arena.

Chapter 17 Architecture

1. Robert F. Bennett, *Surfboats, Rockets and Carronades* (Washington: G.P.O., 1976), 7
2. Lawrence Furlong, *The American Coast Pilot* 4th ed. (Newburyport, MA: Edmund M. Blunt, 1804), 157
3. Ibid., 159
4. Karl Baarslag, *Coast Guard to the Rescue* (New York: Farrar & Rinehart, Inc., 1936), 50
5. Furlong, *Coast Pilot*, 157
6. Bennett, *Surfboats*, 2
7. W. D. O'Connor, *The United States Life-Saving Service*, Reprint from *Appleton's Annual Cyclopaedia of the Year 1878* (New York: D. Appleton and Company, 1889), 749. Hereafter cited as "U.S.L.S.S."
8. For the first eight stations and their locations see the list for the 1848-type in the Station List section. Hereafter, if the reader wishes to know which stations were built, their dates of construction or location of any particular type being discussed in the text refer to the corresponding Station List.
9. For a more detailed description of the stations built in New Jersey and on Long Island between 1849 and 1855 see Bennett, Surfboats, 35-37
10. Bennett, *Surfboats*, 27-28; and O'Connor, *U.S.L.S.S.*, 750
11. Ibid.
12. O'Connor, *U.S.L.S.S.*, 751; and T. Michael O'Brien, *Guardians of the Eighth Sea: A History of the U.S. Coast Guard on the Great Lakes* (Cleveland, OH: Ninth Coast Guard District, 1976), 33. Neither publication provides an architectural description or detailed location of any stations on the Great Lakes.
13. Bennett, *Surfboats*, 30-31; O'Connor *U.S.L.S.S.*, 751
14. Bennett, *Surfboats*, 35-37
15. The study of the architecture of the stations built between 1849-1855 has had to rely primarily upon photographs and descriptions as no plans are known to exist.
16. Darrell Hivnor Smith, *The Office of Supervising Architect of the Treasury: Its History, Activities and Organization,* Service Monographs of the United States Government No. 23 (Baltimore, MD: Institute for Government Research, The Johns Hopkins Press, 1923), 2-3
17. Damas Malone, ed., "Kimball, Sumner Increase," *Dictionary of American Biography* (New York: Charles Scribner's Sons, 1935), 379-380
18. J.W. Dalton, *The Life-Savers of Cape Cod* (Sandwich, MA: The Barta Press, 1902. Reprint, Old Greenwich, CT, The Chatham Press, [1968]), 28
19. *Regulations for the Government of the Life-Saving Service of the United States* (Washington: G.P.O., 1873)
20. Robert F. Bennett, *The Lifesaving Service at Sandy Hook Station: 1854-1915* (Washington, D.C.: Public Affairs Division, Historical Monograph Program, U.S. Coast Guard, 1976), 6
21. Ibid. It is not known when the term "Red House" originated.
22. *Annual Report of the Chief of the Revenue Marine Bureau* (Washington: G.P.O., 1872), 28
23. Ibid., 32
24. *Annual Report of the Secretary of the Treasury of the State of the Finances* (Washington: G.P.O, 1876), 840
25. Letter, A(lfred) B. Mullett, Supervising Architect of the Treasury, to (Chas. F. Conant?), Assistant Secretary, Dec. 21, 1874, Correspondence of the United States Life-Saving Service, Records of the U.S. Coast Guard, Record Group 26, Judicial, Fiscal and Social Branch, Civil Archives Division, The National Archives, Washington, D.C., Letters Received, 1874-1914. Hereafter cited as Correspondence of the Life-Saving Service.
26. Chandler, Francis Ward, *Who Was Who in America* (Chicago, IL: Marquis Who's Who, 1943), 211
27. Letter, J.H. Merryman, Superintendent of Construction, U.S. Life-Saving Service, to Sumner I. Kimball, General Superintendent, May 6, 1875, Correspondence of the Life-Saving Service.
28. Chandler, Francis Ward, *Who Was Who in America* (Chicago, IL: Marquis Who's Who, 1943), 210
29. O'Connor, *U.S.L.S.S.*, 756
30. Ibid
31. Ibid., 759
32. Sumner I. Kimball, *Organization and Methods of the United States Life-Saving Service* (Washington: G.P.O., 1890), 9
33. A. B. Bibb, *The Life-Saving Service on the Great Lakes,* Frank Leslie's Popular Monthly, Vol. 13 (April 1882), 390. Hereafter cited as *Great Lakes.*
34. O'Connor, *U.S.L.S.S.*, 757
35. Ibid., 759
36. Eleven Houses of Refuge and at least sixteen 1875-type and seven 1875-type with Clipped Gable stations are known to have been built from Chandler's three plans. While this number does not add up to the fifty-one stations appropriated by the Act of 1874, it is believed that future research will discover the actual number built was much closer to or equaled the number appropriated.
37. Bibb, *Great Lakes,* 387
38. Ibid., 391
39. Kimball, Organization and Methods, 18
40. J.L. Parkinson, Personnel Files, The National Archives, Washington, D.C., Records of the United States Treasury Department, Record Group 56, Judicial, Fiscal and Social Branch, Civil Archives Division, Applications and Recommendations for the Positions in the Washington, D.C., Office of the Treasury Department. Hereafter cited as Applications and Recommendations for Positions in the Treasury Department.
41. *USLSS Annual Report, 1877*, 69
42. Bibb, *Great Lakes*, 395
43. Ibid., 398.
44. Letter, J.L. Parkinson, Architect, Life-Saving Service, to S(umner) I. Kimball, General Superintendent, Nov. 28, 1879, Correspondence of the Life-Saving Service.
45. Damas Malone, ed., "Pelz, Paul Johannes," *Dictionary of American Biography* (New York: Charles Scribner's Sons, 1935), 411-412
46. Albert B. Bibb, Personnel Records, Applications and Recommendations for Positions in the Treasury Department.
47. Bibb, *Great Lakes*
48. *USLSS Annual Report, 1884,* 58
49. George R. Tolman, Personnel Records, Applications and Recommendations for Positions in the Treasury Department.
50. Although many other countries with maritime coasts had lifesaving organizations all were volunteer or privately supported. These groups frequently sought advice from officers of the Live-Saving Service concerning organizational structure and innovations in rescue techniques.
51. *USLSS Annual Report, 1893*, 61
52. The Life-Saving Service had exhibits at other expositions beside the World's Columbian and Philadelphia Centennial Expositions. Because those stations constructed were built only for the fairs and did not continue in service after the close of the expositions they are not dealt with in this book. In all cases, except for the previously mentioned two, the stations were designed specifically for their respective expositions and were not the same types as any of those built for the Service. Stations and/or exhibits were erected for the following other expositions: Trans-Mississippi International Exposition, Omaha, NE, 1898 (exhibit only, no station); Pan American Exposition, Buffalo, NY, 1901; Louisiana Purchase Exposition, St. Louis, MO, 1904; Lewis and Clark Centennial Exposition, Portland, OR 1905; Jamestown Ter-Centennial Exposition, Norfolk, VA, 1907; Alaska-Yukon Pacific Exposition, 1909, Seattle, WA; Panama-Pacific Exposition, San Francisco, CA, 1916; Panama-California Exposition, San Diego, CA, 1916 (exhibit only, no station); and the Panama-National Exposition, Canal Zone, Panama, 1916 (exhibit only, no station).
53. George R. Tolman, Personnel Records, Applications for Positions in the Treasury Department
54. *USLSS Annual Report*, 1903, 51
55. *USLSS Annual Report, 1917*, 36
56. Ibid.
57. A third station at Neah Bay, Washington, Baaddah Point may be a one-of-a-kind station. Further study, however, may show it to be of the same type as Harbor Beach, Michigan.

Bibliography

The authors have spent two decades independently researching this book. Primary sources consulted include interviews with retired surfmen and keepers, architectural plans, photos and records of the USLSS, USCG and Massachusetts Humane Society. Station primary source material plans are on file at the National Archives, U.S. Coast Guard Historian's Office, U.S. Coast Guard Academy, U.S. Coast Guard Civil Engineering Offices or at the Nautical Research Center of Petaluma, California (where Eoin Colin MacKenzie has restored many plans). See the acknowledgment section for photo sources. The Ralph Shanks photographic collection includes pictures of 272 of the 279 USLSS stations active in 1914.

Anonymous, "Along Our Jersey Shore" (Harper's New Monthly, Feb. 1878)

Appleton, Thomas L., "Usque Ad Mare: A History of the Canadian Coast Guard and Marine Services" (Ottawa: Department of Transport, 1968)

_____, "Canada's First Motor Lifeboat" (Maritime Museum of British Columbia "Bulletin," Spring 1976, 2-4)

Baarslag, Karl, "Coast Guard to the Rescue" (New York: Farrar & Rinehart, 1937)

Barnett, J.P., "The Lifesaving Guns of David Lyle" (South Bend, IN: South Bend Replicas, 1976)

Bennet, Robert F., "The Lifesavers: For Those in Peril on the Sea" (Annapolis, MD: Naval Institute, "Proceedings," March 1976, 54-63)

_____, "The Life-Saving Service at Sandy Hook" (Washington: U.S. Coast Guard, 1976)

_____, "Surfboats, Rockets and Carronades" (Washington: G.P.O., 1976) Volunteer era life-saving history

Beston, Henry, "The Outermost House" (New York: Viking, 1976) Includes accounts of Cape Cod life-savers

Bibb, A.B., "The Life-Savers on the Great Lakes" (Frank Leslie's "Popular Monthly" magazine, April 1882)

Biggs, Howard, "Sound of Maroons" (Lavenham, Suffolk, U.K.: Terence Dalton, 1977) English life-saving including women launchers.

Boone, Anne, "Beauty and Brains to the Rescue of the Seafarer" (U.S. Coast Guard Magazine, vol. 5, no. 11, Sept. 1932, 32-37) Martha Coston

Boyton, Paul, "The Story of Paul Boyton: The Lone Voyager of Over 25,000 Miles in a Rubber Suit" (Milwaukee: Riverside Printing Co., 1892)

Canfield, Edward J. and Thomas A. Allan, "Life on a Lonely Shore: A History of the Vermilion Point Life-Saving Station" (Sault Sainte Marie, MI: Lake Superior State Univ. Press, 1991)

Canny, Donald L. and Barbara Voulgaris, "Uniforms of the U.S. Coast Guard" (Washington: Coast Guard Historian's Office, Dec. 1990)

Clark, Roy, "Manby—Saver of Life at Sea" (U.K., "Sea Breezes," Nov. 1954, 374-377) Also "Sea Breezes" March 1955

Coston, Martha, "A Signal Success: The Work and Travels of Mrs. Martha J. Coston: An Autobiography" (Philadelphia: J. B. Lippencott, 1886)

Coston Signal Company, "Coston's Telegraphic Night Signals" (New York: S.W. Green, 1880)

Couch, Danny, Noah Price & Shawn Gray, "A History of the U.S. Life-Saving Service on Hatteras Island" (Buxton, NC: Cape Hatteras School, "Sea Chest," Winter 1977)

Crowner, Gerald E. "The South Manitou Story" (Mio, MI: Futura Printing, 1982) South Manitou Island Life-Saving Station, MI

Dalton, J.W., "The Life Savers of Cape Cod" (Old Greenwich, CT: Chatham Press, 1902)

Delgado, James P. and Candace Clifford, "Inventory of Preserved Historic Vessels" (Washington: National Park Service, 1990)

Delgado, James P. and Stephen Haller, "Shipwrecks at the Golden Gate" (San Francisco: Lexikos, 1989)

Dobbins, David Porter, "Dobbins Life-Boat Illustrated" (Buffalo, NY: Matthews, Northrup & Co., 1886)

Ellms, Charles, "Shipwreck and Disasters at Sea . . .With a Sketch of the Various Expedients for Preserving the Lives of Mariners by the Aid of Life Boats, Life Preservers, Etc." (New York: Robert P. Bixby & Co., 1844)

Emory, Edwin, "History of Sanford, Maine" (Fall River, MA: Privately printed, 1901) Contains "Sketch of the Life of Hon. S.I. Kimball"

Evans, Stephen H., "The United States Coast Guard: 1790-1915" (Menasha, WI: George Banta Co., 1968)

Francis, Joseph, "History of Life-Saving Appliances" (New York: E.D. Slater, 1885) Francis lifecars and lifeboats

"Francis Metallic Lifeboat Company" (New York: William Bryant & Co., 1852)

Fry, Eric C., "Lifeboat Design & Development" (London: David & Charles, 1975)

Gebhard, David and David Bricker, "The Former U.S. Coast Guard Lifeboat Station and Lookout Tower at Point Arguello, California" (Santa Barbara: Univ. of California, Santa Barbara 1980)

Giambarba, Paul, "Surfmen & Lifesavers" (Centerville, MA: Scrimshaw, 1967)

Gibbs, James A., "Shipwrecks of the Pacific Coast" (Portland, OR: Binfords & Mort, 1971)

_____, "Pacific Graveyard" (Portland, Oregon: Binfords & Mort, 1973)

Gilmore, Rev. John, "Storm Warriors" (London: MacMillan, 1885)

Gonzalez, Ellice, "Storms, Ships & Shipwrecks: The Life-Savers of Fire Island" (New York: Eastern National Park and Monument Assoc., 1982)

Guthorn, Peter J., "The Sea Bright Skiff and Other Shore Boats" (Exton, PA: Schiffer, 1982) Origins of surfboats

Hartman, Tom, "Guinness Book of Ships and Shipping Facts & Feats" (Middlesex, U.K.: Guinness)

Hitchcock, Henry-Russell, "Architecture: Nineteenth and Twentieth Centuries" (Middlesex, England: Penguin, 1958)

Hough, George A., Jr. "Disaster on Devil's Bridge" (Mystic, CT: The Marine Historical Association, 1963) Includes Gay Head surfmen

Howe, Mark Antony DeWolfe, "The Humane Society of the Commonwealth of Massachusetts" (Boston: The Massachusetts Humane Society, 1918)

Humane Society of the Commonwealth of Massachusetts, "Annual Reports" (Boston, Nathan Swayer & Son, various years)

Hurley, George and Suzanne, "Shipwrecks & Rescues" (Norfolk: Donning, 1984) Delaware, Maryland & Virginia stations

Hutchinson, Janet, "House of Refuge" in "History of Martin County," (Port Salerno, FL: Florida Classics Library, 1987, 55-62) Gilbert's Bar House of Refuge

Inspector General of Customs, "Chinese Lifeboats, Etc." (Shanghai, China: The Statistical Department of the Inspectorate General of Customs, 1893) 18th and 19th Century history of Chinese life-saving stations

Jackson, Walter, "The Doghole Schooners" (Volcano, CA: California Traveler, 1969)

Johnson, Erwin J., "Guardians of the Sea: The History of the United States Coast Guard, 1915 to the Present" (Annapolis, MD: Naval Institute Press, 1987)

Kimball, Sumner I., "Organization & Methods of the United States Life-Saving Service" (Washington: G.P.O., 1912)

_____, "Joshua James" (Boston: American Unitarian Association, 1909)

Lamb, Sir John Cameron, "The Life-Boat and its Work" (London: Royal National Lifeboat Instution, 1911)

Lamb, M.J., "The American Life-Saving Service" (Harper's New Monthly magazine, Feb. 1882)

Law, Rev. William Hanistock, "The Life Savers on the Great Lakes" (Detroit: Pohl, 1906)

Lenik, Edward J., "The Truro Halfway House, Cape Cod, Massachusetts" ("Historical Archaeology," Vol. VI, 1972, 77-86)

Lincoln, Joseph C., "Rugged Water" (New York: D. Appleton, 1924) Novel based on Cape Cod life-saving

Livingston, Dewey and Steven Burke, "The History and Architecture of the Point Reyes Lifeboat Station" (Point Reyes, CA: Point Reyes National Seashore, 1991)

Lockwood, Charles A. and Hans Christian Adamson, "Tragedy at Honda" (Philadelphia: Chilton, 1960) Seven Navy destroyers wreck at Pt. Arguello, CA

Lombard, Asa Cobb Paine, Jr., "East of Cape Cod" (New Bedford, MA: Reynolds-DeWitt, 1976)

Lyon, Peter, "The Fearless Frogman" ("American Heritage," Vol. 11, No. 3, April 1960) Paul Boyton and the life-dress

MacNeill, Ben Dixon, "The Hatterasman" (Winston-Salem, NC: John F. Blair, 1958) Cape Hatteras region life-saving

Mason, Jack, "Point Reyes: The Solemn Land" (Inverness, CA: North Shore, 1972)

_____, "Last Stage for Bolinas," (Inverness, CA: North Shore, 1973)

Maxam, Oliver M., "The Life-Saving Stations of the U.S. Coast Guard" ("U.S. Naval Institute Proceedings," May 1929)

McLellen, Charles H., "Twin Screw Lifeboat for the U.S. Life-Saving Service" ("Marine Engineering" Jan. 1900, 25-26)

_____, "The U.S. Life-Saving Service Self-Bailing Water Ballast Surfboat" ("Marine Engineering" March 1901, 94-99)

_____, "The Evolution of the Lifeboat" ("Marine Engineering," Jan. 1906, 7-11)

McNairn, Jack and Jerry MacMullen, "Ships of the Redwood Coast" (Stanford: Stanford University Press, 1970)

Merryman, J.H. "The United States Life-Saving Service—1880" (Golden, CO: Outbooks, 1981. Reprint of 1880 publication)

Methley, Noel T., "The Life-Boat and Its Story" (London: Sidgwick & Jackson, 1912)

Middleton, E.W., "Lifeboats of the World" (New York: Arco Pub., 1978)

Mobley, Joe A., "Ship Ashore: The U.S. Life-Savers of Coastal North Carolina" (Raleigh: North Carolina Division of Archives & History, 1994)

Nalty, Bernard C. and Truman Strobridge, "The U.S. Coast Guard, Midwife at the Birth of the Airplane" ("Aerospace Historian" Vol. 22, No. 3, Sept. 1975, 139-142) Wright brothers and the Life-Saving Service

Nichols, Joanna R., "The Life-Saving Service" (Frank Leslie's "Popular Monthly" April 1897)

Nichols-Kyle, Joanna R., "The U.S. Life-Saving Service" (c. 1900)

Noble, Dennis, "U.S. Life-Saving Service: Annotated Bibliography" (Washington: U.S. Coast Guard, 1976)

_____, "A Legacy: The United States Life-Saving Service," (Washington: U.S. Coast Guard, 1987)

_____, "That Others Might Live: The U.S. Life-Saving Service, 1878-1915" (Annapolis, MD: Naval Institute, 1994)

Noble, Dennis L. and T. Michael O'Brien, "That Others Might Live: The Saga of the U.S. Coast Guard" ("American History Illustrated Magazine," June 1977)

_____, "Sentinels of the Rocks" (Marquette, MI: Northern Michigan University Press, 1979) Lake Superior

O'Brien, T. Michael, "Guardians of the Eighth Sea: A History of the U.S. Coast Guard on the Great Lakes" (Washington: G.P.O., 1979)

O'Conner, William Douglas, "United States Life-Saving Service" Appleton's Annual Cyclopaedia, 1878

_____, "Heroes of the Storm" (Boston: Houghton, Mifflin, 1904) Life-Saving Service rescues by the USLSS Asst. Gen. Superintendent.

Oliver, Sandra, "The Life-Saving Service: Messroom Meals" in "Saltwater Foodways" (Mystic, CT: Mystic Seaport Museum, 1995)

Orleans Historical Society, "Rescue CG 36500" (Orleans, MA: Orleans Historical Society, 1985) 36-foot motor lifeboats

Osborne, Ernest and Victor West, "Men of Action" (Bandon, OR: Bandon Historical Society, 1981) Southern Oregon life-saving stations

Otis, James, "The Life Savers: A Story of the U.S. Life-Saving Service" (London: Sands & Co., 1899) Fiction

Perry, Glen, "Watchmen of the Sea" (New York: Charles Scribner's, 1938)

Pouliot, Richard A. and Julie J. Pouliot, "Shipwrecks of the Virginia Coast and the Men of the Life-Saving Service" (Centerville, MD: Tidewater Publishers, 1986)

Putnam, George, "Lighthouses & Lightships of the United States" (Boston: Houghton Mifflin, 1917)

Rand, Edward Augustus, "Atlantic Surfman" (Cincinnati: Jennngs and Graham, 1901)

Rattray, Jeannette Edwards, "Ship Ashore!" (NY: Coward-McCann, 1955) Long Island shipwrecks and rescues

Rolt-Wheeler, Francis, "The Boy with the U.S. Life-Savers" (Boston: Lothrop, Lee & Sheppard, 1915) Fiction

Ryder, Richard, "Old Harbor Station" (Norwich, CT: Ram Island Press, 1990) Detailed information on station supplies and equipment

Santos, David M., "Ties That Bind" (Commandants Bulletin," Feb. 1994, 18-19) Pea Island

Scheina, Robert L., "U.S. Coast Guard Cutters & Craft of World War II" (Annapolis: Naval Institute, 1982)

_____, "U.S. Coast Guard Cutters and Craft, 1946-1990" (Annapolis: Naval Institute, 1990)

Scully, Vincent J., Jr., "The Shingle Style and the Stick Style" (New Haven: Yale, 1971)

Shanks, Ralph, "The United States Life-Saving Service in California," (San Francisco: National Maritime Museum, "Sea Letter Magazine," No. 27, Spring 1977 and No. 31, Summer 1980. Two part article)

_____, "Lighthouses & Lifeboats on the Redwood Coast" (San Anselmo, CA: Costaño Books, 1978) Northern California life-saving stations

Shanks, Ralph and Lisa Woo Shanks, "Guardians of the Golden Gate: Lighthouses & Lifeboat Stations of San Francisco Bay" (Petaluma, CA: Costaño Books, 1990) Life-Saving Service in California

Shoemaker, C.F., "The Evolution of the Life-Saving System of the United States from 1837 to June 30, 1892" (ms. at U.S. Coast Guard Academy, New London, CT)

Smith, Darrell H., "The Office of Supervising Architect of the Treasury: Its History, Activities and Organization" (Baltimore: Institute for Government Research, Johns Hopkins Press, 1923)

Smith, Darrel H. and Fred W. Powell, "The Coast Guard: Its History, Activities & Organization" (Washington: Brookings Institute, 1929)

Smith, Joseph, "Gleanings from the Sea" (Andover, MA: Joseph W. Smith, 1887)

Stackpole, Edouard A., "Life Saving Nantucket" (Nantucket Island, MA: Stern-Majestic, 1972)

Stevenson, D. Alan, "The World's Lighthouses Before 1820" (London: Oxford, 1959)

Stick, David, "Graveyard of the Atlantic: Shipwrecks of the North Carolina Coast" (Chapel Hill, NC: University of North Carolina Press, 1987)

Stonehouse, Frederick, "Wreck Ashore: The United States Life-Saving Service on the Great Lakes" (Duluth: Lakes Superior Port Cities, Inc., 1994)

Surfman's Mutual Benefit Association, "Official Manual," 1905

Thoreau, Henry David, "Cape Cod" (Orleans, MA: Parnasus Imprints, 1984)

Tilly, John, "Out of Uniform: Civilians in the U.S. Coast Guard" ("Commandant's Bulletin" April 1994, 12-13 in supplement)

Tiffany, F., "Life of Dorothea Dix" (Boston & New York: Houghton, Mifflin, 1890)

U.S. Coast Guard, "Annual Reports," (Washington: G.P.O., 1915-1935)

_____, "Instructions for United States Coast Guard Stations" (Washington: G.P.O., 1934)

_____, "Register of Commissioned Warrent Officers and Cadets and Ships and Stations of the U.S. Coast Guard" (Washington: G.P.O., 1927-1941)

_____, "Register of the Officers, Vessels and Stations of the United States Coast Guard" (Washington: G.P.O., 1916-1940)

U.S. Coast Guard Auxiliary, "The U.S. Coast Guard: Its History, Vessels and Doctrine" (New York: U.S.C.G. Auxiliary, 1945)

U.S. Department of Commerce, "United States Coast Pilot" (Washington: G.P.O., various editions and years)

U.S. Life-Saving Service, "Annual Reports," (Washington: G.P.O., 1876-1914)

_____, "Beach Apparatus Drill" (Washington: G.P.O., 1899)

_____, "List of Persons Who Have Died By Reason of Injury or Disease contracted in the Line of Duty in the Life-Saving Service since Origin of the Present System" (Washington: G.P.O.: Treasury Department, 1914)

_____, "Register of the United States Life-Saving Service" (Washington: G.P.O., July 1, 1914)

_____, "Revised Regulations, Life-Saving Service" (Washington: G.P.O., 1884)

U.S. Navy, "Annual Reports" (Washington: G.P.O.,1918-1919)

U.S. Revenue Marine Bureau, "Annual Report" (Washington: G.P.O., 1872-1873)

U.S. Treasury Department, "Annual Report of the Secretary of the Treasury on the State of the Finances" (Washington: G.P.O., 1874-1876)

U.S. War Department, "Danger, Distress & Storm Signals for Signal Service Seacoast Stations" (Washington, G.P.O., 1883)

Waldron, Richard, "Maritime New Jersey: An Economic History of the Coast" (Trenton: New Jersey State Museum and New Jersey Historical Commission, 1983)

Whatley, Michael E., "Marconi Wireless on Cape Cod" (Cape Cod National Seashore, 1987)

Webber, Bernard C., "Chatham: The Lifeboatmen" (Orleans, MA: Lower Cape, 1985)

Wechter, Nell Wise, "The Mighty Midgetts of Chicamacomico" (Manteo, NC: Times Printing Co., 1974) North Carolina life-saving family

Whipple, Carlyle, "You Have to Go Out, But You Don't Have to Come Back!" ("USCG Commandant's Bulletin" Feb./March 1989, 21-23)

Whitnall, F.G., "Lionel Lukin: Inventor of the Life-boat" (U.K.: "Sea Breezes" Jan. 1966, 843-845)

_____, "Lionel Lukin—Builder of the First Life-boat" (Glasgow: "Nautical Magazine," Jan. 1966)

Wilkinson, William D., "The Standard 36-Foot Motor Lifeboat of the U.S. Life-Saving Service-1907" ("Nautical Research Journal," Summer 1960)

_____, "Surfboat Authority Sheds Light on Race Point Type" (Camden, ME: "National Fisherman," Nov. 1972)

_____, "American Coastal Lifeboat Development—An English Contribution" (England: "Lifeboat," Summer 1974)

_____, "Nineteenth Century Coastal Lifeboats in the collection of The Mariners Museum (Washington: National Trust for Historic Preservation, in "Wooden Shipbuilding & Small Craft Preservation," 1976)

Wolcott, Merlin D., "Great Lakes Lifesaving Service" ("Inland Sea: The Quarterly Journal of the Great Lakes Historical Society," vol. 18, 1962)

Wolff, Julius F., Jr. "The Coast Guard Comes to Lake Superior" ("Inland Sea," vol. 21, 1965)

Worcester, G.R.G., "Sail and Sweep in China" (London: Science Museum, Her Majesty's Printing Office, 1966)

York, Eugene V. "Wick", "The Architecture of the U.S. Life-Saving Service," (Mystic, CT: "The Log of the Mystic Seaport," vol. 34, no. 1, Spring 1982)

_____, "The Architecture of the United States Life-Saving Service," Masters thesis, Boston University, 1983

Index

ACKNOWLEDGMENTS

Many individuals and institutions made significant contributions to this book. Richard Boonisar, Life-Saving Service expert from Norwell, Massachusetts, Eoin Colin MacKenzie director of the Nautical Research Center of Petaluma, California and Dr. Robert Browning, U.S. Coast Guard Historian, all deserve special mention for repeated contributions. Mr. Boonisar and Mr. MacKenzie as well as Torrey Shanks and Beverly Kienitz read the manuscript and provided important suggestions. William Wilkinson, Director Emeritus of the Mariners Museum, read the chapter on boats and offered excellent suggestions. J. Revell Carr, director and president of Mystic Seaport Museum, graciously consented to write an introductory message for the book. Captain Gene Davis of Coast Guard Museum Northwest was particularly helpful over the years. Rodi York provided continued encouragement throughout the project. Two outstanding government agencies deserve highest marks for the best of public service, the U.S. Coast Guard and the National Park Service. Without their cooperation this book could not have been written.

Washington, D.C.: Besides Dr. Browning, two other members of the Coast Guard Historians Office were very helpful, Scott Price and Dr. Robert Scheina. Also unfailingly supportive were Rear Admiral Richard A. Bauman, USCG (Ret.); Candace Clifford of the National Park Service Maritime Initiative; as well as the Library of Congress; the National Archives and the Smithsonian Institution.

Alaska: Anchorage Historical and Fine Arts Museum.

California: Point Reyes National Seashore, esp. Dewey Livingston and Heidi Niehaus; Golden Gate National Recreational Area; National Maritime Museum; U.S. Coast Guard Civil Engineering Unit Oakland, esp. Ray McAllister; Capt. Cornelius Sullivan of the U.S. Life-Saving Service; Howard Underhill, Jr.; Robert J. Lee; University of California at Berkeley; Mike Jensen; and the faculty, staff and students of Davidson Middle School, San Rafael.

Connecticut: Mystic Seaport Museum; U.S. Coast Guard Academy Library, esp. Cindee Herrick, Betty Davis, and Paul Johnson.

Florida: Florida State Archives; Elliott Museum and Gilberts Bar House of Refuge, esp. Janet Hutchinson; St. Lucie County Historical Museum, esp. Dee Dee Roberts; Weona Cleveland, historian; Del Ray Beach Historical Society, esp. Virginia Schmidt.

Maine: Shore Village Museum, esp. Ken Black.

Maryland: Assateague Island National Seashore; Robert Stevens III.

Massachusetts: Cape Cod National Seashore, esp. Hope Morrill; Keith N. Morgan, Boston University; Massachusetts Humane Society, esp. Barbara Driscoll; Cohasset Historical Society, esp. David H. Wadsworth; Jim Claflin of Kendrick A. Claflin & Son Nautical Antiques; Bob & Ed Glick of Columbia Trading Company; Hull Lifesaving Museum, esp., Judith Van Hamm; Dukes County Historical Society; William Quinn, author and photographer; Nantucket Life-Saving Museum, esp. Maurice Gibbs; Nantucket Historical Society; Orleans Historical Society, Truro Historical Society, esp. Elizabeth "B.J." Allen.

Michigan: Pictured Rocks National Lakeshore, esp. Greg L. Bruff; Sleeping Bear Dunes National Lakeshore, esp. Bill Herd and Neil Bullington; Michigan State Archives, esp. John Curry; Lake Superior State University, esp. Tom Allan; Manistee County Historical Museum; Jesse Besser Museum; Ted C. and Kay Richardson.

New Jersey: Twin Lights State Historic Site, esp. Tom Laverty, George Moss of Moss Archives; Ocean City Historical Museum, esp. Sally Semple; Longport Historical Society, esp. Mike Cohn; Monmouth County Historical Association; Ocean County Cultural & Heritage Commission, esp. Pauline S. Miller.

New York: CWO4 Alvin E. Penny, USCG (Ret.); Long Island Maritime Museum, esp. Ruth Dougherty; Fire Island National Seashore; Gateway National Recreation Area; Van R. Field, historian; Queens Borough Public Library, Long Island Division.

North Carolina: Cape Hatteras National Seashore, esp. Mary Collier; North Carolina Department of Cultural Resources, esp. Stephen E. Massengill; Outer Banks History Center, esp. Win Dough; Joe A. Mobley, historian.

Oregon: National Motor Lifeboat School, esp. Bill Hamm; U.S. Coast Guard Group Astoria, esp. Capt. Rod Leland, Lt. Greg Blandford and Paul Bellona; Tim Flake; Bandon Historical Society; Lincoln County Historical Society; Columbia River Maritime Museum; Oregon Historical Society; Mike Hewitt of Port Orford Heads Wayside Park.

Ohio: USCG Cleveland, esp. F.T. Jennings

Rhode Island: U.S. Coast Guard Civil Engineer Unit Warwick, esp. Com. Jeff Florin; Robert Downie, Block Island historian.

Texas: Arthur Barr, USCG (Ret.).

Virginia: Mariners Museum, esp. William Wilkinson, Director Emeritus.

Washington: Coast Guard Museum Northwest; Dennis Noble, historian.

Wisconsin: Milwaukee Public Library, esp. Sandy Broder.

For production: McNaughton & Gunn, esp. Frank Gaynor; North Bay Photo of San Anselmo, CA, esp. Kathy Gray; The Lab, Santa Rosa, CA; Santa Rosa Blueprint; Rev. Ralph Shanks, Sr. and Viola Lacewell Shanks. The help of numerous other kind individuals and institutions is gratefully acknowledged.

ABOUT THE AUTHORS AND EDITOR

Ralph Shanks is a maritime historian, author and educator. Much of his research centers on the history of the Life-Saving Service, Coast Guard and Lighthouse Service. Among his books are his recent *Guardians of the Golden Gate: Lighthouses and Lifeboat Stations of San Francisco Bay, Lighthouses and Lifeboats on the Redwood Coast* and the *North American Indian Travel Guide*. His articles on the U.S. Life-Saving Service have been published in the *National Maritime Museum Sea Letter Magazine*. Mr. Shanks prepared the National Historic Landmark Nomination for the U.S. Coast Guard Cutter *FIR*, the last active American lighthouse tender. He has been a consultant and lecturer on life-saving and lighthouse interpretation, preservation and history for the National Park Service, U.S. Coast Guard, colleges, museums and organizations. He has a Masters degree in sociology from San Francisco State University and a BA from the University of California at Berkeley. For the past twenty-five years Mr. Shanks has been interviewing surfmen and lighthouse keepers, teaching and researching the history of the Coast Guard, Lighthouse Service and Life-Saving Service. Mr. Shanks grew up on the northern California coast around San Francisco Bay and Humboldt Bay among lighthouse keepers and surfmen. He is responsible for all except the architectural portions of this book.

Wick York grew up on the Connecticut coast and first became interested in the U.S. Life-Saving Service while working at Mystic Seaport Museum as an Architectural Restoration Specialist, where he was involved with the research and restoration of the Block Island (RI) Life-Saving Station. He holds a Master's degree in Historic Preservation from Boston University, and his research on the design of life-saving stations provided the basis for his thesis, the definitive typology of life-saving station architecture. His articles on the Life-Saving Service have appeared in *The Log of the Mystic Seaport* and *Island Journal* and he frequently lectures on the history and architecture of the Service. He has assisted the Maine Historic Preservation Commission on a historical survey of surviving life-saving stations on the Maine coast and authored a National Register Nomination of surviving lighthouses in Rhode Island. He is also a building restoration consultant who advises homeowners and museums on the preservation and restoration of their historic buildings. Among his projects has been the Old Stonington (CT) Lighthouse Museum. He is responsible for the architectural section of this book.

Lisa Woo Shanks is District Conservationist for the USDA Natural Resources Conservation Service, as well as an author and editor. She grew up on San Francisco Bay and began her career working for the National Park Service in San Francisco. She began by assisting with the planning of the Park Service's acquisition of Point Bonita Lighthouse in California and went on to work as a ranger on the National Park Service's historic ships in San Francisco. She has written technical articles for the vineyard industry and the University of Idaho's Women in Natural Resources magazine. She has edited four books including the present work. Lisa Shanks is married to author Ralph Shanks. She holds a degree in Natural Resource Planning and Interpretation from Humboldt State University.

Ralph Shanks, Lisa Woo Shanks and Wick York (left to right) at Cahoons Hollow Life-Saving Station, Cape Cod, Massachusetts. (Dewey Livingston)

An Invitation to Maritime Adventure

The drama of the U.S. Life-Saving Service launching in the surf. A Dobbins lifeboat is pulled into the surf on the boat carriage using two sturdy station horses. Golden Gate (Golden Gate Park) Life-Saving Station, Ocean Beach, San Francisco, California, circa 1908. (Shanks collection)

Share your Life-Saving Service adventures with others. Order additional copies of **U.S. Life-Saving Service** and share the rare thrill of experiencing the adventures of the valiant U.S. Life-Saving Service.
262 pages, 440 historic photographs, drawing and maps • Softcover edition: $21.95
Shipping please add $4.00. (California residents please add sales tax.)

Order...
U.S. Life-Saving Service   *from...***Costaño Books**
                                                                    P.O. Box 355
                                                                    Petaluma, CA 94953
                                                                    email: CostanoBooks@att.net